Studies in Radiation Effects in Solids
Volume 4

THE COMPACTED STATES OF VITREOUS SILICA

Studies in Radiation Effects in Solids

Editors: G. J. DIENES and LEWIS T. CHADDERTON

Other Volumes in Preparation

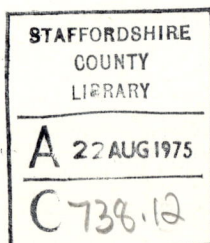

The Compacted States
of Vitreous Silica

William Primak

Argonne National Laboratory
Argonne, Illinois

GORDON AND BREACH SCIENCE PUBLISHERS

New York London Paris

Copyright © 1975 by

Gordon and Breach, Science Publishers, Inc.
One Park Avenue
New York, N.Y. 10016

Editorial office for the United Kingdom

Gordon and Breach, Science Publishers Ltd.
42 William IV Street
London W.C.2

Editorial office for France

Gordon & Breach
7–9 rue Emile Dubois
Paris 14ᵉ

Library of Congress catalog card number 66–24006. ISBN 0 677 033400 (*cloth*).
All rights reserved. No part of this book may be reproduced or utilized in any form
or by any means, electronic or mechanical, including photocopying, recording, or by
any information storage and retrieval system, without permission in writing from the
publishers. Printed in the German Democratic Republic by Offizin Andersen Nexö,
Leipzig.

Dedication

To MY TEACHER, Roland Ward, from whom I learned that true research is not rummaging for details along established pathways in the pastures of knowledge; rather, it is stepping into an unknown beyond the security of what we or others know.

Acknowledgement

This work was performed under the auspices of the U.S. Atomic Energy Commission.

Preface

DISCOVERY of the compacted states of vitreous silica must be classed among the accidental observations in science. The major observations were noted independently by at least three sets of investigators working in three different fields, all attempting other observations: Bridgman was trying to measure compressibility; Douglas and Isard were concerned about the quenching of high temperature configurations; Primak and Fuchs were studying radiation damage and expected an expansion from displaced atoms. The three observations were made in the same period, the early 1950's. Over the next decade, additional observations of compaction accumulated, and the compaction by shock waves and polishing were noted. The generality of the compacted state followed from another set of accidental observations, by Primak and his co-workers in the mid-1960's, of the release of compaction by ionization. This monograph began out of a commitment to compose a review article on radiation effects in silica at a time when the general nature of the compaction phenomena was becoming apparent. Gradually its scope narrowed into an inquiry into the compacted states of vitreous silica, serving both to stimulate our research and to organize our thoughts on this subject.

A literature search for a review article was performed by Roger Thompson in the Summer of 1965. This concluded the systematic search. Most of the references to the glass literature were collected then. The writing was begun in 1967, and was mostly concluded that year. Much additional reference material of direct concern to the argument was examined during the course of writing, and only a few additional items have been studied since. Completion of the manuscript was delayed because several very serious questions arose: first, about the effect of ionization; and, last, about the nature of the thermal spikes. These problems were solved through experimental work, most of which has now been published. The manuscript in its essentials was concluded in 1968, but the following year was required to place it into final form. Several interesting articles appeared in the interim, but their material was not incorporated in the interest of completing the manuscript. In February, 1970, at the final typing, the last section, X, was rewritten in the hope of arriving at a more satisfactory conclusion; but little more than a rearrangement of material and the citing of an example resulted—and the Epilogue. The series edited by Mackenzie[22a] was found long after the original text had been written. While in one sense this was unfortunate, for consulting the pertinent articles therein would have decreased the labor of preparing portions of this text appreciably; in another sense it was fortunate, because this writer examined the original literature himself and developed a fresh approach. It seemed desirable to insert references to these reviews despite the abruptness engendered by referring to them in a text built on other source materials.

Those finding his comments too critical may take comfort in noting that the author gave his own work no kinder treatment. While our observations, perforce, become part of the structure of science, our opinions rarely encompass more, more often less, than current knowledge. It would be presumptuous to hope that the opinions expressed in this monograph will prove less perishable. It is hoped that those finding them provocative will be stimulated to investigate the subject further. It is a source of regret to this author that he does not himself possess the means for establishing a more substantial foundation for his speculations and for answering some of his many remaining questions.

Unfortunate and unexpected delays have beset us in bringing this monograph to press. Typing was delayed for a year by a moving operation in which the author was involved; the manuscript reached the editor when he was occupied with other responsibilities; and the publisher received it when he was encountering difficulties with his compositors: each of these in turn caused a year's delay. This is the third time the author has reviewed his manuscript and altered its preface to establish the current context of this monograph.

We have become so accustomed to the awesome pace of science in recent years that it seems surprising so little can be added for these 5 years. The very significant investigations by Jack, Hetherington, and their collaborators, this author learned at a chance meeting with Professor Jack, resulted from concluded governmentally sponsored projects for the production of specific manufactured wares, hence were no longer active. The author's own investigations have been brought to a virtual standstill by decreased funding in a period of rampant inflation, but some results from a more affluent period are yet being prepared for publication, and the section on thermal spikes was revised at the last moment to accord with his latest work. The use of vitreous silica films in electronic microcircuitry has become a new source of interest and support for investigations of the silica structures and theoretical papers on the subject are now appearing. Heavy ion tracks caused by cosmic rays and other means have been developed in vitreous silica and in silicates by etching, and numerous papers on this subject have appeared. Bell and Dean have studied network dynamics of several models which they erected from balls and rods. Mozzi and Warren have published a very careful x-ray diffraction study of vitreous silica in which new techniques were utilized, and they considered how several models fitted the data. Neither of these studies consider the structure of real vitreous silica developed here: namely, that the 3-dimensional structure possesses numerous essential discontinuities, and is labile and motile; but some of their conclusions will probably possess permanent value. To avoid the extensive labor of revising the whole manuscript, some of these recent results are reviewed in appendices.

Contents

Prologue

THE CLASSICAL subdivision of chemistry has been into inorganic and organic; and, thus, of all the varied kinds of chemical bonding, that of carbon has attracted most attention. This is justified not only by its great personal interest and by its being basic to another of the sciences, but also by the technology based on it. Yet, consider: of this earth upon which we live, the bonding of silicon and oxygen is a far, far greater proportion. It, also, is involved in important technologies and in another of the sciences. However, it has received relatively little attention. Most of the interest in the silicon–oxygen combination has been in the fascinating crystallinity of the compounds in which it is found, but there has been little interest in the nature of this bond and its behavior. In vitreous silica, devoid of crystallinity, there is an opportunity to study the behavior and the nature of the silicon–oxygen combination without distractions.

1. Introduction

SCOPE AND DEFINITION OF TERMS

Existence of small differences in densities of vitreous silica specimens from different sources and even for different portions of a single specimen is well established in the older literature[2] and is confirmed by recent investigators.[8] It was an object of comment for Sosman[2] in his monumental monograph; but, at that time, he was at a loss for an explanation, whether to attribute it to differences in composition, constitution, state of strain, or thermal history. In the intervening years, a variety of treatments, among them mechanical, thermal, and radiation exposure, have been found to cause substantial increases in density. Some have termed the phases densified. Apparently, first Bridgman and Šimon,[9] and a little later, this author independently,[11] both having arrived at a similar concept of the structural changes which had ensued, referred to these phases as compacted. Weyl and Marboe[14] in a recent publication use densified and compacted alternatively. Sosman[16] in a recent monograph has distinguished silica M, suprapiezovitreous, α- and β-vitreous, and densified. This terminology based on origin is rejected here; it is customary to classify phases according to structure. All of these phases will be referred to as compacted, the most descriptive and euphonious of the terms suggested.

The vitreous silica is considered to consist of volume occupied by the ions, silicon and oxygen, and void space. The compaction is to be described principally by the change in void volume; the change in ionic volume (or polarization) makes only a small contribution. The compaction will be gauged by the negative dilatation, usually given in percent if it is large, or in parts per million if it is small. The following interconversions are readily demonstrated:

$$\delta \equiv \Delta V/V_0 = (\varrho_0/\varrho) - 1 = -(\Delta\varrho/\varrho_0)/[1 + (\Delta\varrho/\varrho_0)],$$

$$\Delta\varrho/\varrho_0 = (V_0/V) - 1 = -\delta/(1 + \delta),$$

where V is observed volume, V_0 original volume, ϱ observed density, ϱ_0 original density, δ dilatation, $\Delta V = V - V_0$, and $\Delta\varrho = \varrho - \varrho_0$. The difference of two dilatations is:

$$\delta_1 - \delta_2 = (\varrho_2 - \varrho_1)(\varrho_0/\varrho_1\varrho_2).$$

The term vitreous silica is used in this article to distinguish the glass from other amorphous phases of silica. The usage is justified by Sosman[3,17]; and it is used here in the sense he gives, to replace other usages such as fused quartz, silica glass, quartz glass, etc. The word phase is used rather loosely here, as is often customary in chemical parlance. In strict thermodynamic usage, phase implies a complete specification of the thermodynamic variables, including some measure of composition and constitution. Thus, what is referred to here is a phase manifold of similar composition and constitution. How the phase has arisen may be used as a modifier; e.g., pressure-compacted vitreous silica. The role of impurities in vitreous silica (and also in the crystalline phases) has been considered mainly in the literature of the absorption bands and in the effect on crystallization. It now appears that impurities profoundly affect many other properties. Impurities in vitreous silica may be of two general classes. Elements of high positive charge and low coordination number (e.g., Al, B, Ge, P) may substitute in the network. Ions of small charge and large coordination number (e.g., alkalis and alkaline earths) are found as non-network ions and will be referred to as non-network cations. Some ions (e.g., Al, Fe) may appear in either role. The role of other impurities has not been clarified, but it has been inferred that Cl can substitute for oxygen, and H may be a network interrupter. The nomenclature for the crystalline phases, quartz and cristobalite, will be used as follows: α- for the low temperature forms, and β- for the high temperature forms.

Weyl[26] uses the term compaction in a special sense: for the increase in density occurring during the annealing of a chilled glass which on quenching exhibited lower density and refractive index, and increased thermal expansion. As described below, quenched vitreous silica is more dense than annealed vitreous silica. The effect in the glasses considered by Weyl involves the non-network ions, and thus his usage refers to a different phenomenon from the one of interest here. Anderson[31] uses the terms compaction and densification to refer to the respective phenomena, irreversible and reversible volume changes.

RANGE OF THE LITERATURE

The literature on silica is a very diverse one, contributions having been made from natural history, experimental and theoretical science, and industry; by mineralogists, geologists, chemists, physicists, engineers; and, even, antiquarians interested in ancient artifacts. There is a long history of investigators having overlooked the research of others, and this writer makes no pretense to having undertaken a thoroughgoing search; even during the writing of this article he has continued to encounter significant items, and many others must have been overlooked.

For the older literature, the critical monograph by Sosman[1] is an excellent review. Morey[33] is a little newer, but less extensive. Sosman's recent monograph[15] does not have the stature of the earlier work because the volume of research has become so large, it can no longer be covered in a reasonable compass; and because he wrote during a transition period in our understanding of vitreous silica. Weyl and Marboe[13] is a valuable resource for a varied literature, but it is not a critical work, nor is it entirely consistent. There are a number of shorter review articles of related material. Weyl's[25] discussion of the transitions in glass is concerned largely with the mobile non-network ions and is peripheral to the behavior of relatively pure vitreous silica. Anderson and Dienes[34] sought an integrated view of the anomalous effects shown by vitreous silica, but were unable to derive them from the structure they considered, nor could they derive information about the structure from their consideration of the anomalies. Primak's[35] article treated a limited aspect of the radiation effects caused by corpuscular radiation. Lell, Kreidl, and Hensler[37] were concerned mainly with the local configurations in irradiated quartz and vitreous silica. The International Commission on Glass has organized several Congresses[38,39,40] whose proceedings have been published. These have been collections of technical papers rather than reviews; but, covering a wide range of subjects within a single volume with contributors from many countries, they have presented overviews of the current research. Some excellent review articles may be found in a series edited by J. D. Mackenzie[41].

The Russian literature has been largely inaccessible to investigators in the western world. Starting in 1958 and continuing through 1966, proceedings of a series of Russian conferences on glass have been translated into English. These volumes[42] introduce the English reader to a significant literature on fundamental and technological aspects of glass. The writer became familiar with this work only in the course of preparing this article. Consequently, the basic ideas given here, having developed without knowledge of the Russian work, must slight that work somewhat. What discussion is given of the Russian work is based upon translations of conference papers, some of which are quite extensive, some imaginative, others sketchy, rather than on a careful examination of original formal reports and papers.

In none of these sources have the compacted states of vitreous silica received more than casual discussion, nor has anyone discussed the significance of compaction in understanding the behavior of the Si–O network in vitreous silica or glass.

Dynamic Structural Effects Involved

A prominent part of the glass literature deals with the irregularities of the physical properties when studied as a function of temperature. It will be seen that these phenomena are closely related to the subject of this article. Among

1*

the explanations which have been given for the irregularities is that they are residues of inversions found in the crystalline phases of silica or of the silicates. Weyl attributed them largely to (1) mobility of non-network ions and (2) to cleavage and reconstruction of the Si–O network (hence akin to the reconstructive transformations) and (3) substitutional disordering.[27] The first is the most important in the behavior of the electrical properties, and little will be said of these phenomena here. The second is most evident in the mechanical properties. Since our interpretation will be different from his, it is important to consider his reasoning. Of the other types of crystalline disorder known at that time, he dismissed (1) rotational disorder as applying only to groups like NO_3^- and NH_4^+ and thus of little interest because the SiO_4 groups are (quoted), "firmly anchored"; and (2) the rapid inversions because they required: "... a symmetrical network and cooperative maneuvers between the structural units ..." and hence inapplicable to an amorphous substance. It will be shown here that the major characteristic of the rapid inversions is not to be considered their rapidity, their symmetry, or their cooperative nature; but, rather, that they occur without cleavage of the Si–O network in response to the thermal vibration of the oxygen ion; and that this kind of behavior of the oxygen ion is very prominent in the compaction phenomena. Cleavage of the network also appears to be very important— particularly in locking-in the effects.

ORGANIZATION

It was difficult to decide upon an order for presenting the subject. The viewpoint developed here arose from studying the radiation behavior of vitreous silica. To present the subject historically in this context would be too autobiographical, and it would be too difficult for the reader to follow the argument from this focal point to the diffuse ramifications to be considered here. It was not possible to base this article upon a substantial literature because the background material is so greatly confused there. It seemed best to first clarify the conflicting discussions found in the literature about the structure of vitreous silica even though, historically, it was the last aspect considered, and even though the real basis for the critique will be presented afterward.

It was equally difficult to decide upon an order for presenting the compaction data, for so much of it co-appeared in the literature done independently without cross-reference. Historically, the thermal compaction must have been performed first, but it was the last to have been so recognized. Second, was probably the radiation compaction, but since the radiation effects are here to be presented as a tool for studying the compaction, it seems best to present this work last, for reference will have to be made to prior compaction by other means. It thus seemed best to abandon historical order completely, leaving the reader to make his own reconstruction. The most definite case, that of pressure compaction, will be presented first, and then the various other cases of compaction. It will be noted that Section II and Section X treat quite the same problem: what vitreous silica is. No really suitable titles for these chapters came to mind. They treat what is more than structure and less than essence, less even than basic nature: something involving structure, constitution, behavior, and their relationships. Section II is based largely on our classical notions of structure and constitution, and serves as a prolegomenon. Section X emphasizes behavior of vitreous silica, and serves as an epilegomenon.

II. The Structure of Vitreous Silica

Intensities of x-ray diffraction patterns were not understood until the 1930's. Thus, early structure determinations were based largely upon symmetry considerations. These were sufficient to give the approximate location of the silicon positions in the silicon-oxygen network of many silicates. The probable locations of the oxygen atoms were then surmised, usually somewhat incorrectly, because the nature of the Si–O bond was not understood then. For our considerations here, these details of orientation of the Si–O tetrahedra are crucial. This information is available now, but because of its slow development and the tendency to quote older papers and reproduce their figures, the literature remains confused. The subject is therefore reviewed in detail here.

Early suggestions about a structure for vitreous solids of the class of the silicate glasses were of very small crystallites about the size of crystal unit cells or of frozen arrays of molecular units present in the liquid. This was the original crystallite theory. Zachariesen[43] criticized these structures as being inconsistent with physical properties of the solids and with structural principles established by Pauling[44] for the ionic crystals. He inferred, instead, the existence of a continuous irregular network of triangular (for coordination 3; e.g., about boron) or tetradehral (for coordination 4; e.g., about silicon) groupings of oxygens about the cation, the groupings sharing corners.

Warren[45,47,48] (with the assistance of various collaborators) undertook an extensive investigation of the x-ray diffraction of glass. Interpretation of intensities was just beginning, and the structure factors for x-ray scattering had not yet been established. He concluded[47] that a crystallite hypothesis did not accord with the glass structure shown by his diffraction patterns nor with the known physical properties of glasses, thus agreeing with Zachariesen. Warren added the further important evidence that the diffraction patterns show no evidence of crystallite growth during thermal treatment; and in devitrification, the diffraction rings of the crystalline phase do not appear as a sharpening of the diffuse rings in glass. Sharp rings appear immediately in a displaced position. We will return to the subject of crystallites twice again, first in commenting on the work of Porai–Koshits on the interpretation of the x-ray diffraction of complex silicate glasses (see pages 14–15), and second when discussing the work of Weissmann on neutron-irradiated vitreous silica (see pages 125–126).

In his first papers Warren[47,48] was content to show that the prominent feature in the x-ray diffraction pattern of vitreous silica was the first Si–O spacing, the one within the Si–O tetrahedron, 1.6 Å. He then assumed the Si–O–Si configuration to be nearly linear to calculate the first Si–Si distance 3.2 Å. From these values and an assumed atomic environment, he computed a diffraction pattern which he considered to be within experimental error of his observations. He then refined his techniques greatly by utilizing monochromatic x-ray radiation in evacuated cameras and by taking densitometer tracings of the photographic patterns. The data were inverted with the aid of a harmonic analyzing machine to obtain the radial electron density distribution.[49,50] Warren appears to have been keenly aware of the errors of measurement, the uncertainties in his procedure for assigning the scattering to the several atoms (this was yet in the course of being established, V.I.), other uncertainties in the computation, and the loss in resolution in the mathematical procedure. He states that areas under sections of the computed electron density curves may be in error by some 10%. His approach is well illustrated by the following quotation from the paper by Warren, Krutter, and Morningstar:[50] "The radial distribution curve for vitreous SiO_2 is shown in Fig. 6. The 1st peak occurs at 1.62 Å in good agreement with the average silicon-oxygen distance 1.60 Å found in various crystalline silicates..." (He then shows from the peak area that there are 4 oxygens about each silicon, hence they are tetrahedra and the oxygen-oxygen distance may be computed to be 2.65 Å.) "... The approximate position of the O–O peak at 2.65 Å proves the four oxygens are arranged tetrahedrally about the silicon." ... "Each silicon is tetrahedrally surrounded by 4 oxygens at a distance of about 1.62 Å and each oxygen is bonded between two silicons. Assuming that the two bonds to an oxygen are roughly diametrically opposite, the next few interatomic spacings are readily calculated ..." The position of the peak identified as Si–Si in the figure given in their article appears to be at a little less than 3.2 Å. However, it is clear that Warren did not believe at the time that the interpretation and computation were sufficiently secure to use the peak positions to compute a bond angle; he was more concerned with establishing the validity of his interpretation of the cause of the peaks. In his summary paper[45] he doesn't even mention the Si–Si distance. Others coming after him have considered the interpretation of the peaks to be reliable and have been far less conservative in employing these distances.[51] Some results are tabulated in Table 1. For these data, only Šimon computes the bond angle. His work possessed a number of modern refinements including reliable structure factors and digital computation. Zarzycki[52] considers the bond angle to be less than 180° but does not compute a value. The neutron scattering data are supposed to have fewer uncertainties because the scattering from the two atoms is more comparable, but at the time of these experiments (particularly Weber's), the techniques were in their infancy and neutron beam intensities available were too small for accurate work. Others have criticized this approach[53] and indeed the original electron density radial distribution curves require correction to conform to present-day theory.[54,56,57]

TABLE 1 Bond angle Si–O–Si from interatomic distances corresponding to first Si–O and Si–Si peaks

Investigator	Si–Si distance (Å)	Si–O distance (Å)	Si–O–Si bond angle (deg.)
Breen and Weber*	3.25	1.55	Impossible
Warren†	3.2	1.6	180 (assumed)
Milligan*	3.02	1.58	146
Šimon†			
unirradiated	3.03	1.61	140
irradiated	2.99	1.61	136
Zarzycki†	2.9	1.6	130

* Neutron diffraction.
† X-ray diffraction.

The problem in computing the Si–O–Si bond angle from the Si–O and Si–Si distances is that, because of the small slope of the sine function at these angles, a very small change in the Si–Si distance affects the angle greatly. Thus, if we are interested in identifying the peaks, whether we assume 140° or 180° affects the peak position in the radial electron density curves or in the scattered intensity only slightly; and, conversely, the slightest change in these distances affects the bond angle greatly. This may explain, in part, Warren's attitude in taking the bond angle to be 180° in his calculations; and it should be remembered, also, that the assumption of a 180° bond angle had been made in the determination of a number of silicate structures and a number of the crystalline phases of silica. The state of x-ray crystal structure analysis in this period, and Warren's position (as this author has interpreted it from an examination of his papers) has been carefully stated here because many authors have misconstrued his approach and his claims. In view of these difficulties in interpreting the diffraction patterns of vitreous silica, additional evidence is required to establish its structure. The technique and interpretation of the diffraction of x-rays by silicate glasses has been reviewed by Urnes.[57]

X-Ray Evidence for the Si–O–Si Bond Angle in Crystalline Phases

The problem of locating oxygens in silicate structures is a much older one for the crystalline phases of silica. Wyckoff[58] in 1925 attempted to determine the crystal structure of β-cristobalite from powder diffraction patterns. In all x-ray structure determinations, the dimensions of the unit cell and the number of atoms in it are determined independently of the structure. Thus the placement of groups within the unit cell in accordance with symmetry requirements of the diffraction patterns can be used to determine interatomic spacings within the unit cell. Wyckoff assumed the Si–O–Si bond angle in β-cristobalite to be 180°. On this basis the Si–O distances, 1.59 Å, are shorter than is usually found in the silicates. Barth[59,60] later showed there were complications in the diffraction pattern which Wyckoff had missed. A small alteration in the structure, which among other things decreased the bond angle and made the mean Si–O distance 1.63, gave a better fit to the powder diffraction patterns. Nieuwenkamp[61] succeeded in obtaining some crystals of cristobalite, presumably from a mineralogical source, which were large enough for rotation photographs. He proceeded to determine the structure of α-cristobalite (low). The space group proved different from the one suggested by Barth. The Si–O–Si angle calculated for the parameters obtained for the $P4_22_1$ space group gave the Si–O distance as 1.59 Å, O–O distances 2.63, 2.63, 2.59, 2.58 Å, and the Si–O–Si angle as 150°. Barth's suggested space group for the β-cristobalite (high) was not consistent with this determination of the α-cristobalite structure. Nieuwenkamp[62] took the same crystal and obtained rotation photographs above the inversion temperature, 270 °C. He obtained the space group Fd3m which implied a linear Si–O–Si configuration, but the bond distance Si–Si was 3.08 Å compared to 3.06 for the α-cristobalite, indicating a bond angle about the same as in that form. He concluded there was a rotation or a statistical disorder in β-cristobalite in which oxygens may occur in various radial orientations about a line joining two silicon atoms in the structure. The problem in working with cristobalite, and tridymite as well, is that they demonstrate polytypy and are easily twinned. The natural crystals are impure; and, in the case of cristobalite, the structure tends to be imperfect in a manner which was interpreted as caused by oxygen vacancies. It will be shown below that the impurities affect the crystal behavior profoundly. The calculations of structure were made before machine computation was developed, and the structures were never optimized for various Si–O distances and Si–O–Si bond angles. Thus, the details of the results (e.g., the particular different Si–O distances) cannot at this time be accepted without reservation as correct for the normal structure of the pure compound. However, it can be accepted as proven that the Si–O–Si bond angle in both cristobalites is nearer 140° than 180°.

Before intensities could be used effectively in x-ray crystal structure determinations, the direct determination of the α-quartz structure was not possible. Bragg and Gibbs[63] proceeded to determine the structure of β-quartz, a more symmetrical one. On the basis of the physical properties they concluded that the transformation to α-quartz did not involve a rearrangement of atoms; it only involved a small shift. Gibbs[65] calculated a shift which would give the symmetry class of α-quartz and presented this as a close approximation to its structure. He started with the assumption that in β-quartz the Si–O–Si angle was 180°; then for α-quartz got the result that for the shift: a 9° rotation of silicon atoms about the screw axis and the Si–O tetrahedra oriented to give the correct symmetry class, there was obtained an Si–O–Si bond angle 155° and an Si–O distance 1.55 Å, according to present knowledge, too small. Within a few years Fourier synthesis methods were developed. Wei[66], in Zachariesen's laboratory, applied them to α-quartz, and about the same time, Machatschki[67] in Europe. Brill, Hermann, and Peters[68] published another determination in 1942. In those days, the Fourier calculations were made by hand, a very laborious procedure usually requiring 6 months to a year for a single individual, subject to human error at many points. The confirmation these results provided for each other was therefore very necessary. Now, the α-quartz structure must be considered much more securely determined than the β-quartz structure. It is definitely determined that the Si–O bond distance in quartz is between 1.61 and 1.62 Å, and the Si–O–Si bond angle is between 142° and 144°. Brill, Hermann, and Peters were particularly concerned about the electron density distribution along this bond and to this end made a Fourier projection in its plane. They found that the electron density fell to only 2.25 el/Å^2 rather than to nil, as they would have expected for an ionic bond. For a covalent bond they expected a bond angle near 90°, for an ionic bond near 180°. Today we would expect the tetrahedral angle (about 109°) for the sp^3 bonds as exemplified[69] by H_2O (104°), OCl_2 (115°), $O(CH_3)_2$ (111°). Thus the Si–O–Si bond at ~140° is taken to be a case of intermediate binding. It is certain now that in none of the structures considered here is the normal Si–O–Si bond angle near 180°; it is near 140°.

Consider now the illustrations given in textbooks to explain the network structure of silicate glasses. They originate in the article by Zachariesen[43] and have been elaborated by some to indicate the location of the Si–O tetrahedra. Examples of these illustrations are reproduced in Fig. 1. They illustrate the coordination of the ions, the irregularity of the network, and its continuity—the major points made by Zachariesen; but they miss a major point of interest here: the Si–O–Si bond angle which cannot be shown in a planar figure, for nearly every adjacent tetrahedral configuration moves out of the plane.

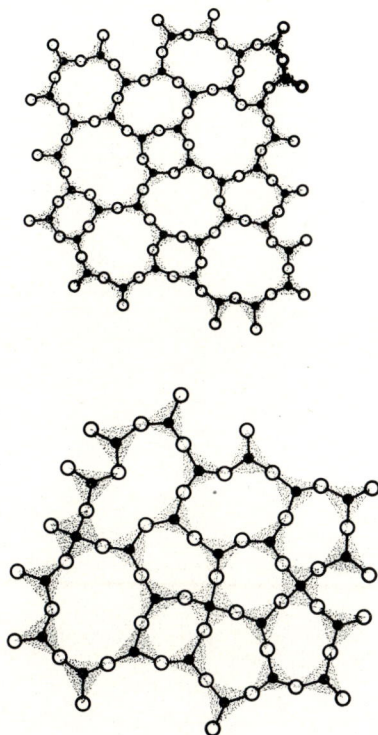

Figure 1. Examples of text-book illustrations of Zachariesen's concept of the vitreous structure.

IONIC RADII, SPACE FILLING FACTOR, POLARIZABILITY

The ionic radii for Si^{4+} and $O^=$ have been given the respective values 0.41 and 1.40 Å by both Goldschmidt and Pauling.[70] These values have been used indiscriminately by others for various calculations. However both Goldschmidt and Pauling recognized that for a tetrahedral configuration, a correction had to be applied to these radii. Pauling[71] discussed the AlO_4^{5-} case first:

In corundum, topaz, diaspore, and many other crystals with aluminum octa-hedra, the observed values for the Al–O distances lie close to 1.90 Å, the sum of the crystal radii of the ions. The values observed for tetrahedral coordination, in crystals as β-Al_2O_3, sillimanite, sodalite, and other aluminosilicates, lie between 1.66 and 1.76 Å. The sum of the radii corrected by the appropriate factor from the table is 1.78 Å, somewhat larger than the average of these experimental values. It seems likely that in AlO_4 tetrahedra the bonds have considerable covalent character, and that the interatomic distances are influenced by this. The same comment applies also to the Si–O distance for the SiO_4 tetrahedron, for which the observed value, 1.59 Å lies below the corrected ionic radius sum 1.69 Å.

This discussion is not entirely consistent with another given by Pauling[72] about the covalent nature of the binding.

Zwikker[73] gives a space filling factor for the ions in silica, 0.47, evidently utilizing an ionic radius near 1.4 Å for $O^=$; but in one of his graphs,[74] he draws a curve for the space filling factor for β-cristobalite structures near 0.3. This corresponds nearly to that for the experimental Si–O interatomic distance which gives an $O^=$ radius ~ 1.2 Å and a space filling factor 0.32. The ratio of the silicon to oxygen volume in silica (i.e., one silicon volume/ two oxygen volumes) on the basis of the respective radii 0.4 and 1.2 Å is 1/54. Therefore, for all practical purposes in discussing the dilatations, the volume occupied by silicon may be neglected; only the oxygen volume and the void volume are matters of concern.

The problem of the polarizability is a parallel one. Mueller[75] in his discussion of the stress birefringence of glasses quotes the values of the respective ionic refractions of Si^{4+} and $O^=$ as being 0.1 and 7 to derive the ratio 1/140 for silica. However, when he extrapolated the refractivities of a series of lead glasses to that of nil lead content (i.e., to the refractivity of oxygen), the value he obtained for the ionic refraction of oxygen was 3.9 cm^3/mole. This subject is discussed by Smyth:[77]

The effect of the central ion upon the oxygen octet is more clearly brought out by arranging the refractions of the latter as in Table VIII, in which the refraction of the oxygen octet is given after the symbol of the central ion binding it.

TABLE VIII   Refraction R_D of the oxygen octet bound by a central ion

C^{4+} 4.08	N^{5+} 3.66	S	
Si^{4+} 4.42	P^{5+} 4.05	S^{6+} 3.65	Cl^{7+} 3.32
Ti^{4+} 6.3			

It is evident that the tightness of binding increases with increase in the ionic charge and decreases with increase in the size of the ion. The refraction of the oxygen octet when bound to Ti^{4+}, 6.3, is close to the value for the O^{--} ion, 7, while the other values are not far from that of the octet linked to carbon, a linkage which is regarded as typically non-polar. It appears that we may have all degrees of binding here from the so-called polar to non-polar as in the case of the halides previously discussed.

Thus, the conclusions about the nature of the Si–O bond reached from considerations of the bond angle are supported by the values of the ionic radii and the index of refraction.

The ions are drawn to scale in Fig. 2.

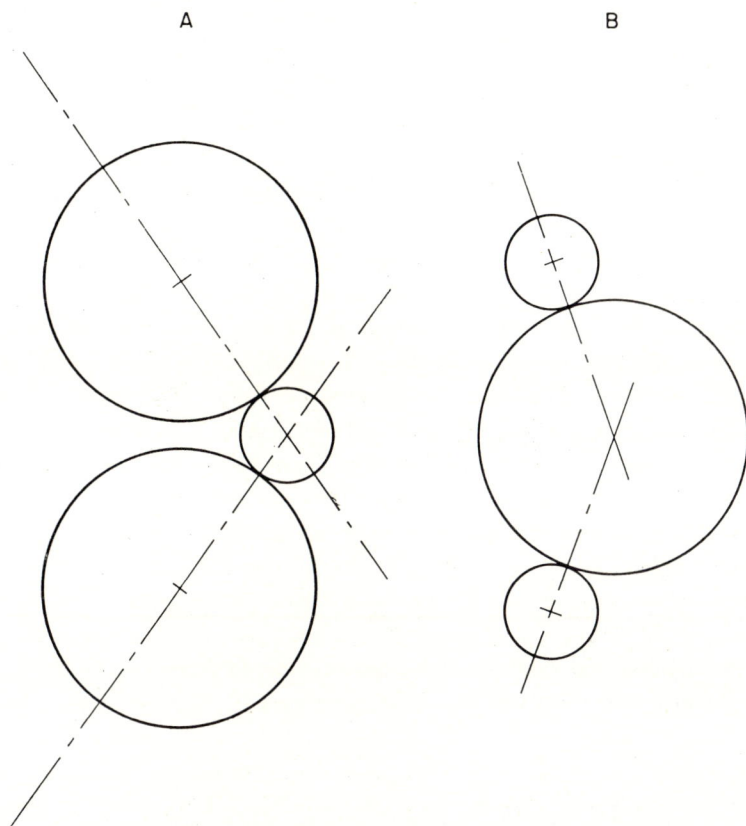

Figure 2.   (A) O–Si–O in the plane of the tetrahedral bond, and (B) Si–O–Si in the plane of the bond; drawn to the scale of the atomic radii.

MICROSCOPIC INHOMOGENEITY: CRYSTALLITE HYPOTHESIS

There has been an extended debate, largely carried on in the Russian literature, about the irregularity and continuity of the silica network, particularly in multicomponent glasses like the soda-silicate and the soda-borosilicate ones. The major points of the conflict are not of real interest when considering relatively pure vitreous silica, but the implications about motility in the silicate network are important here. The presentation available to us in translation[42] is highly polemical, caused (it is supposed) by the authoritative organization of Russian science and the important position held by Lebedov, once a supporter of the original crystallite hypothesis. We charitably suppose the subtleties of the English language were the cause of some of the American work being misrepresented; we hope the Russian work is more accurately presented here.

It is not necessary to review here the evidence presented for the original crystallite hypothesis for glass.[78] The x-ray diffraction aspects have been discussed above, and the irregularities in the thermal dependence of some of the physical properties (ascribed by some to residues of the α-β inversions of the silica structures appearing in the behavior of the silica network of the multicomponent silicate glasses) are now known to be caused largely by the behavior of the non-network ions. The present crystallite hypothesis appears to have originated in the work of Porai–Koshits[79]. Lukesh[80] pointed out that when the electron density radial distribution curve for vitreous silica is subtracted from the radial distribution curve for a sodium silicate glass, the Na–O and Na–Na peaks, hardly noticeable in the original curve for the sodium silicate glass, become very apparent in the differential curve. Lukesh was very cognizant of the difficulties of performing such a subtraction. In addition to the usual serious mathematical question involved in subtracting distribution curves, further problems arise here because the original curves contain large experimental errors, there are mathematical approximations in the Fourier inversion procedure used to obtain the curves, and there are changes in the Si–O network when a multicomponent glass is made from vitreous silica. If boron is present there is not only a change in the network, but the coordination number of the boron, a network ion, is also subject to change. Over the next decade, determinations of electron density radial distribution curves were refined somewhat.[56] Porai–Koshits[79] applied Lukesh's method to the borosilicate glasses and pointed out that the intensity and sharpness of the peaks in the differential curve was greater than would be expected for a homogeneous random distribution of sodium ions in a random irregular network of the kind hypothesized by Zachariesen[43]. The location of the peaks corresponded to those for sodium metasilicate. He concluded the glass was not homogeneous, and he estimated the radius of the inhomogeneities to be in the range 15–200 Å. Porai–Koshits was careful to state the regions are not crystalline; the use of the word crystallite thus has an unfortunate connotation, at least in English. The claim was that the glass is not truly homogeneous.

If the glass were inhomogeneous, it should show small angle scattering corresponding to the inhomogeneity. This was first found when the sodium borosilicate glasses were leached.[79] The product was porous and the small angle scattering corresponded to a pore size 15–17 Å radius. The electron density of the inhomogeneities is so nearly that of the matrix that the in-homogeneities could not be detected by small angle x-ray scattering in an original glass when the inhomogeneities were so small. However, with a borosilicate glass heated at 750 °C, which gave pores 50 Å radius on leaching, it was possible before leaching to observe the small angle scattering in a special camera, and the result corresponded to inhomogeneities of 55 Å radius.[55] Inhomogeneity of refractive index was found by Debye and Busche[81] by scattering of visible light from a borosilicate crown and also a flint optical glass. They calculated the radius of the inhomogeneities to be 270–300 Å. The refractive index fluctuations in the borosilicate crown glass were much larger than in the flint glass. Porai-Koshits quotes the work of Brosset[82] who found the appearance of a Cs–Ba distance in the radial distribution curve of a barium containing silicate glass to which cesium had been added, hardly to be expected for a homogeneous dispersion of ions in the network. Porai-Koshits[55] concluded that segregation is the typical behavior in multi-component glasses rather than the random statistical distribution suggested by Zachariesen[43].

GRANULARITY

The granularity of vitreous silica was considered by Robinson[83] to explain the behavior of the compressibility, the internal friction, and the appearance of electron microscope pictures. The last is considered here, the others later. A granular appearance was observed by Prebus and Michener[84] in glass fibers and powders observed directly in the electron microscope. Warshaw[85] observed them in carbon replicas of glasses. These investigations were criti-cized on the grounds that the glasses had been exposed to atmospheric action and might have been subject to surface alteration. Zarzycki and Mezard[86] therefore pulled fresh fibres in the electron microscope in an argon atmos-phere. They also observed the granularity. This technique could not be used for vitreous silica, and for it they resorted to the examination of the edge of a fractured fragment, for which they also reported granularity. Seward, Uhl-mann, Turnbull, and Pierce[87] reinvestigated the subject. They examined fractured and mechanically polished specimens, and also carbon replicas. They found granularity in glasses, as did the previous investigators, regions ranging from 20–200 Å. In vitreous silica granularity was observed when specimens were coated with carbon, but no granularity to a resolution of 10 Å was seen in the absence of carbon film. Therefore, the observations of granularity were attributed to a non-uniform carbon deposit. The electron microscope data can now be taken as confirming the results of x-ray diffrac-tion and light scattering studies.

Network Motility (1)

Belov[89], in a crystal chemistry approach to glasses, suggested that in a glass, the Si–O network is not the rigid structure but weaves itself about as needed among the other structures. This view is disproved by the well established mobility of the cations in glass. Because of their mobility, it would seem the cations would be trapped at sites where normal coordination can occur and normal bond distances are most favorably met. The introduction of alkali or alkaline earth involves not only the introduction of a non-network cation, but also the rupture of the Si–O network by the additional oxygen ions. The kind of network adjustments which become possible as a consequence will be referred to as network motility. Thus the segregation indicates (1) some regions in the random structure provide a more favorable environment for the cations, and (2) a motility in the network can result in a more favorable arrangement of the network in the vicinity of a cation; but this is hardly the weaving as described in the translation of Belov's article.

Borate Anomaly

By the borate anomaly is meant that the molar additivity relations for refractive index and density do not hold for the addition of alkali to a borosilicate glass of a composition low in non-network cations. Warren[46] showed this was caused by a progressive change of the coordination number of boron atoms from 3 to 4 in the early stages of addition of oxides to boro-silicate glass. Vogel[90] pointed out that in the absence of stabilizers such as alumina, there is a segregation of alkali in the vicinity of boron which is associated with the borate anomaly. The inhomogeneity effect is very prominent in borosilicate glasses. It is of great technological importance; negatively, because it can lead to failure in the production of Pyrex type glasses; positively, because it is the basis for making Vycor type glasses. The Russian writers[42] indicate the segregation is a stage in the production of vitroceramics. Winter[91] explored the segregation phenomenon by examining the Rayleigh scattering of visible light. For vitreous silica, the scattering was normal and obeyed the $1/\lambda^4$ law, indicating it was thermal. The addition of alkalis or lead caused a 10 to 15-fold increase, and the addition of B_2O_3 a 100-fold increase, in light scattering. After heating near the region of devitrification, there occurred a 50 to 100-fold increase in scattering without the appearance of crystals, indicating a 10-fold increase in the volume of the scattering inhomogeneities. Again, it appears that the inhomogeneity is primarily an effect caused by the mobility of the cations; but, this writer infers there is a further effect, a limited motility of the network.

RAPID INVERSIONS AND NETWORK MOTILITY

The rapid inversions in the silica system played an important role in the determination of the crystal structure of quartz and cristobalite, as described above. The inversion in quartz was the first to be discovered, by Le Chatelier in 1889; and since then, there have been many investigations of the behavior of varoius physical properties as a consequence of, and during, the inversion. After reviewing these, Bragg and Gibbs[64] conclude, "... at which the atoms take up a new arrangement almost as suddenly, it may be, as a lock turns over at the last. But the atomic movements are not large; certainly not large enough to cause a marked change in the structure of the crystal." Gibbs describes the movement (as stated above); and while the quantitative values must be altered slightly to accord with later work (most textbooks still quote the original results without qualification), his qualitative description is still the one held. There is a movement of silicon atoms from just inside the unit cell of the α-quartz to the face of the unit cell to form β-quartz, and the Si–O tetrahedra are all twisted slightly. Since there is no precise determination of the β-quartz structure in which the oxygen positions are located, there is no experimental verification; but it is generally considered by x-ray crystallographers (contrary to the statements of some reviewers) that the Si–O–Si angle is not altered appreciably in the inversion. In consequence, the axial ratio must change, the unit cell increase in volume, the density decrease, and the inversion temperature must increase with pressure. This seems to be the case for all the fast inversions in the silica system.

Although the fast inversions in the silica system have captured the imagination of many investigators and are described in detail by several authors[1,19,92], few have ventured an explanation for their occurrence. The three explanations which this writer has seen are obviously incorrect. Barth[60] and also Niewenkamp[61] have suggested free rotation may be taking place in the β-cristobalite. Such motion in the covalently bonded silica structures is hard to imagine because the Si–O tetrahedra would not be free to rotate independently, and a correlated motion would be characteristic not of these temperatures, but rather of very low temperatures; independent vibration of the atoms is the major phenomenon at these temperatures. Buerger[93] writes of the silica framework crystals,

Of the three major, stable, crystalline forms of silica, the low temperature form, quartz is a relatively closely packed structure, while the higher temperature forms, tridymite and cristobalite, are very open structures. Both open structures evidently owe their existences to the necessity of providing space for thermal agitations. With falling temperature, these structures must collapse (high-low inversions); if a solvent is present, these forms may dissolve and reprecipitate as the more closely packed structure, quartz (sluggish inversions).

...the open structures may not only be held open by thermal agitations, but also by the presence of foreign ions filling the voids, the foreign ions thus buttressing the structure and preventing the repacking to quartz at low temperatures.

Buerger is referring here to the stability of a crystal like nepheline (NaAlSiO$_4$) which takes a form similar to cristobalite. Accommodation of the thermal vibration is a reasonable explanation for crystalline inversion, but our examination of the inversions will show quartz is to be regarded not as a closely packed, but as an open structure. In the case of quartz, introduction of non-network ions tends to stabilize the high temperature form, hence the major effect must be an alteration of the network; the quantity of non-network ions cannot be sufficient to cause an effect by packing the interstices. The role of non-network ions may be more significant in compounds of the kind discussed by Buerger and in the heavier multicomponent glasses.

We are handicapped in attempting to explain the dynamics of the α–β-transition by a lack of accurate crystal structure data. As explained above, the oxygen positions in β-quartz have never been determined accurately. In the cases of tridymite and cristobalite, good pure crystals are not available. An explanation must therefore be based in part on speculation as supported by the behavior of the physical properties. Quartz for which there is most data available (see pages 9–11) will be the model. As seen in Fig. 3, the void space about the oxygen ions is very unsymmetrical. The easiest direction for thermal motion should be into the void space about the Si–O helices, and an elastic constant for such motion should be smaller than for other directions, e.g., along the helix. Since the void space outward from the helices is greater than toward their axes, the potential curve for this vibration must be very unsymmetrical and the amplitude of motion outward must be greater than the amplitude inward. This kind of motion causes a twisting of a segment of the helix and causes the neighboring silicons to approach each other. The transition to the β-form leads to a more symmetrical motion and presumably a smaller torque on the helix. Now, if all the Si–O distances are maintained, and the Si–O–Si bond angle is not altered, why is not the more symmetrical β-form stable at room temperature? Since the Si–O bond distance could, presumably, adjust itself to any reasonable configuration merely by altering the unit cell dimensions, it is concluded that the Si–O–Si bond angle is the critical item, although it is not quite clear just how it should change because of the complex interaction of the covalent and ionic forces. Tentatively, it is suggested that as the temperature of the α-form rises, the increased amplitude of motion of the oxygen tends to cause a decrease in mean Si–O–Si bond angle. The transition to the β-form results in an increase in Si–O–Si bond angle beyond the most desirable one. A further increase in temperature re-

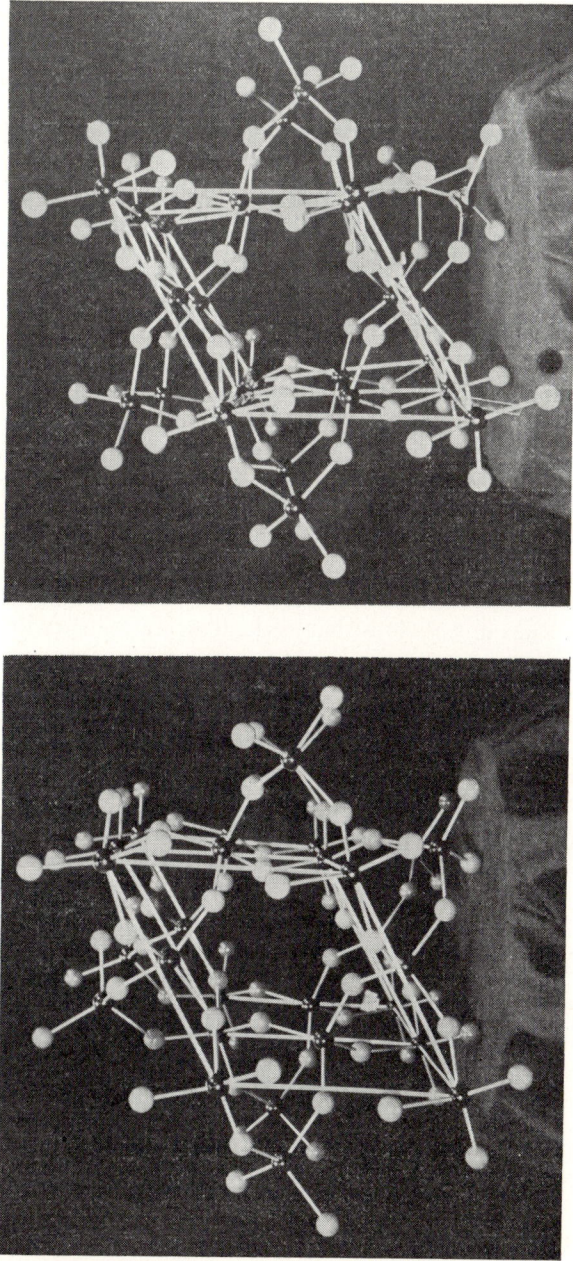

(A)

(B)

Figure 3. Structure model of quartz showing two unit cells along the optic axis, and a few additional adjacent Si–O tetrahedra, to permit a visualization of the helical structure. The dark balls are silicon, the light ones are oxygen. (A) α-quartz: note that the Si–O tetrahedra near the centers of the unit cell faces are not in the planes of the faces (best seen on the left face); and (B) β-quartz: note that Si–O tetrahedra are in the planes of the unit cell faces parallel to the optic axis.

sults in a more nearly satisfactory Si–O–Si bond angle, and thus the thermal expansion in the β-form is very small.

THE REFRACTIVITY

The refractivity of vitreous silica was considered by Primak and Post[94], and their treatment is of interest here. Mueller[76] pointed out that in considering the polarizability of silica, the contribution of the silicon may be neglected because the volume occupied by the silicon atoms is but a small fraction of the volume occupied by the oxygen ions. Thus, the calculation of the specific refractivity gives a number proportional to the oxygen ionic volume/g. The temperature dependence is shown in Fig. 4, and it is seen that the specific refractivity increases in a very regular manner, in contrast to the manner in which the specific volume changes. Thus the Si–O distance increases in a very regular manner with temperature. By comparing this with the manner in which the unit cell expands (or, what is the same thing, the axial expansions) it can be inferred how the structure is altering. In the α-form and in the transition, the expansion is greater perpendicular to the optic axis than parallel to it; and for the β-form it is slightly negative and slightly more negative perpendicular to the optic axis. Thus it is obvious that as the temperature rises the Si–O tetrahedra twist in such a manner as to decrease the helical angle. This would increase the Si–O–Si bond angle and thus compensate in part for the decrease occasioned by the unsymmetrical increased amplitude of motion of the oxygen. The net effect is a slightly decreased bond angle. In passing to the β-form, the bond angle increases beyond the most favorable one; and, thus, increased amplitude of thermal motion results in restoration of a more satisfactory bond angle with slight contraction.

These changes, the twisting of the Si–O tetrahedra, the decrease in the helical angle of the spiral Si–O network, and the decrease in Si–O–Si angle, affect the aeolotropic properties perpendicular to the helical axis (also the optic axis) but have little effect on those parallel to it. Thus, corresponding to the decrease in bond angle with rising temperature in the α-form, Young's modulus decreases perpendicular to the optic axis and is less than the value parallel to the optic axis. In the transition to the β-form, Young's modulus perpendicular to the optic axis rises and becomes greater than that parallel to the optic axis, and both increase with temperature.

VARIABILITY OF THE INVERSIONS

Sosman, in his first monograph, comments on the constancy of the temperature of the $\alpha - \beta$-quartz transition[4] but wondered about the range of values reported although it was small.[5] The work of Tuttle,[95] and Keith and Tuttle[96] provided an explanation for the variability. Of over 200 specimens from natural sources, inversion temperatures of 95 % of the specimens were between 572.2 and 574.1°C, but specimens were found for which it was as low as 536°C and as high as 577°C. Hydrothermal quartz made from a glass of composition 7% GeO_2, 93% SiO_2 in water at 15,000 PSI gave quartz showing a higher temperature of inversion. Hydrothermal quartz made from a glass of composition $Li_2O \cdot Al_2O_3 \cdot 12SiO_2$ gave a lower than normal inversion temperature. A product of that composition, sintered at 1300°, inverted at still lower temperature. For the impure quartz, a high temperature x-ray camera was used to determine the α–β-quartz transition, as the differential thermal analysis peak became indistinct. In these samples the transition was spread over a range of temperature. Natural quartz crystals are frequently zoned with different impurity concentrations which can be made evident by irradiation. Keith and Tuttle examined one sample, naturally zoned citrine and clear, and they found similar zoning for the inversion temperature. This was a very dramatic demonstration of the influence of impurity on the α–β-quartz transition, but since the composition was not reported, the quantitative effect is unknown. Primak, Fuchs, and Day[97] reported the peak in the differential thermal analysis curves associated with the α–β-quartz transition disappeared when quartz was exposed in a nuclear reactor sufficiently. Mayer[98] reported measurements for smaller exposures and found the peak was shifted to lower temperatures by several degrees and was decreased in area. Later work with a high temperature camera indicated the transition occurred over a greater temperature range.[99] This observation accords with Keith and Tuttle's[96] experience with impurities introduced into the quartz. Zhdanov, et al.[100] also write about the effect of "neutron" irradiation on the transition.

Since volume increases in the α–β-quartz transition, it is to be expected that the transition temperature will rise with pressure. The effect of pressure was measured by Gibson[101] and by Yoder.[102] It increases by about 0.025°/atmosphere, being over 800°C at 10^4 atmospheres.

Sosman[20,21] lists a number of principle characteristics of the α–β-inversions in the silica phases. Two receive comment here: first, that the inversion does not proceed topochemically from a nucleus, but rather occurs simultaneously through a portion of the crystal large enough to be easily measurable; and, second, that there is a true temperature hysteresis. In his older monograph he describes, in detail, direct observations of the transition by optical means and comments on the disorderly way it has been observed to proceed through the crystal. The aeolotropic volume changes cause large local stresses which may result in twinning or breakage. The sudden change in heat capacity makes temperature control difficult. These two factors may account for some of the hysteresis, but the much larger hysteresis observed for cristobalite indicates other effects. Perhaps disorder and non-uniform composition are the other major contributors to the disorderly progress of the transition.

The behavior of the tridymite and cristobalite forms a link to the consideration of vitreous silica. Fast inversions in both these substances occur not far above room temperature. The temperature range for these inversions is greater than for the temperature range of inversion in the majority of quartz samples.[22,23,103] The effect is most marked in cristobalite where the inversion in a specimen may occur gradually over a 50 °C temperature range with a hysteresis of 16–42 °C. Part of this may be caused by variations in purity. However, Hill and Roy[104] found that heating the cristobalite, particularly above 1470 °C, caused a rise in the inversion temperature. Thus, imperfection in the cristobalite lattice caused a depression of the inversion temperature much as has been found for quartz. Disorder appears to be the usual occurrence in cristobalite.

THERMAL VARIATION OF CRYSTAL STRUCTURE

Quartz and tridymite are anisotropic substances with aeolotropic coefficients of thermal expansion. It is possible that in such a substance relative atomic positions in the unit cell will be maintained as the temperature changes, but then interatomic distances must alter correspondingly. It has been shown here for quartz that because of the covalent binding, the asymmetrical spacial distribution of void space, and the non-colinearity of oxygen and silicon atoms, the relative positions of oxygen in the unit cell do change with temperature. It seems likely (to this writer) that in α-quartz the relative positions of the silicons not at the corners of the unit cell also change, moving closer to the unit cell face, but to prove this would require a detailed investigation. Wahl, Grim, and Graf[105] have studied the diffraction lines as a function of temperature but have not interpreted their data in this manner. The existence and similarity of the fast inversions in tridymite and cristobalite are taken to indicate that in these polymorphs also, the relative positions of atoms in the unit cells alter with temperature. Thus, properly, their crystal structures are functions of temperature, and the phase manifolds are also crystal structure manifolds. At the thermal boundaries of the phase manifolds, the bond strain has become so great that the structure is unstable with respect to another, and inversion occurs. The effect has been described in terms of the behavior of the Si–O–Si bond angle, but other strain may also be introduced. Some investigators[61] have concluded that the oxygens are not equivalent in the structures, and thus the Si–O bonds may be strained; but whether this may be the result of inexact experimental data and incomplete calculation is yet to be ascertained. Some investigators[96] have noted changes in line intensities in x-ray diffraction patterns of quartz specimens before the major property changes (like heat absorption) occurred in the α–β-inversion. Some of this may result from local inversion at lower temperature, of regions containing impurity or disorder, as has been shown for quartz containing aluminum or which had been exposed in a nuclear reactor. However, even pure perfect quartz should show changes in line intensities in the x-ray diffraction pattern near the inversion temperature because of the large aeolotropy of the thermal expansion coefficients in this region of temperature and the concomitant progressive alteration in crystal structure, but no investigation of the subject has been reported.

NETWORK MOTILITY (II)

Factors affecting the temperature of fast inversion appear to be the openness of the network, its asymmetry, the continuity of the network, and the strain in the network. Thus, tridymite and cristobalite with more void space show inversions at a temperature several hundred degrees lower than does quartz. Cristobalite with a more symmetrical structure does not show an inversion at as low a temperature as does tridymite. Introduction of aluminum ions weakens the quartz network, presumably permitting larger amplitude thermal motion, and inversion occurs at a lower temperature. It was explained above that the change from α- to the β-form resulted in an increase in Si–O–Si bond angle. The Ge–O–Ge bond angle is reported[52] to be 180°. It may therefore be anticipated that introduction of Ge into quartz will introduce a strain into the network which tends to increase the bond angles, thus countering the effect of increasing temperature on the α-form (decreases the bond angle) and, accordingly, stabilizes to the α-form to higher temperatures.

The existence of the fast inversions is taken here as a demonstration of the motility of the Si–O network. In tridymite and cristobalite, the inversions occur nearly at room temperature. In cristobalite, presumably because of imperfection, over a 50° temperature range; and in quartz, by the introduction of impurity of imperfection can be made to occur over about a 200° temperature range. In quartz and cristobalite, the inversions can be local, depending on local composition. It is reasonable, therefore, to inquire whether in vitreous silica, in which all manner of configurations are present locally, local inversions may be occurring continuously over this or any other span of temperature. Resort to the indirect evidence of the behavior of the physical properties during the inversions of the crystalline phases was had because details of interest here have not yet been developed directly by diffraction methods; it is to be anticipated that such investigations will be made. In the case of vitreous silica, conventional diffraction techniques cannot give the needed detail of structure, and other techniques which might possibly give direct information (such as atomic microscopy of various kinds) have been singularly ineffective with insulators. Thus, the only evidence which can be considered is the indirect evidence of the physical properties.

ANOMALIES IN VITREOUS SILICA

The physical properties of vitreous silica have aroused a great deal of interest because their behavior is anomalous. Among the best known of these anomalies[106] are:

1. small or negative coefficients of expansion over the whole span of temperature,
2. elastic moduli increase with temperature,
3. elastic moduli decrease with pressure, and compressibility increases with pressure, and
4. refractive index increases with temperature.

In addition, there are related effects:—a low frequency dielectric and acoustical loss and a large contribution to the heat capacity at low temperature. Attempts[34] have been made to explain the effects phenomenologically and also atomically; others have been content to point out that there are also other substances which show such anomalies.

An extensive discussion of these anomalies was given by Anderson and Dienes[34] following individual work by these authors[11,107,108] on particular ones. Their approach was essentially phenomenological through the thermodynamic relations. One of their several summaries was, "From a phenomenological point of view, four of the anomalies—temperature dependence of the elastic moduli, variation of refractive index with temperature, of compressibility with pressure, and of thermal expansion with temperature—are equivalent. In these cases thermodynamic self-consistency is satisfied." Their results may be interpreted as indicating that if the cause of the small coefficient of thermal expansion were understood, the whole problem would be solved. It will be indicated below that it may be incorrect (as Dienes[108] did, and Anderson and Dienes[34] also) to combine pressure and temperature partial derivatives of the volume of vitreous silica in the manner used in gas thermodynamics, because the thermodynamic state is not uniquely specified by the volume. In addition, there were difficulties in evaluating some of the thermodynamic quantities. Thus, some may feel other conclusions might have been reached had the behavior of vitreous silica been unknown. However, their conclusions are taken here as being essentially correct despite these difficulties of detail which may require modification. Their conservative conclusion, "However, these anomalies yield no direct evidence on the structure of vitreous silica.", and, "However, it appears that the controversy on the structure of vitreous silica must be settled on the basis of direct measurements of the structure itself: the physical properties of vitreous silica are not particularly helpful in deciding the issue.", and the difficulties encountered by others (described below) in attempting to deal with these properties, it will be seen, arose from careless reading of the papers on the network structure, so prevalent in the glass literature, that the long critical discussion given here was considered imperative.

The phenomenological view taken by Primak and Post[94] and by Primak[12] was introduced above in the discussion of the volume changes in quartz. They pointed out that although vitreous silica shows a small negative thermal expansion coefficient near room temperature, the refractivity increases in a perfectly normal manner at about the rate seen in multicomponent glasses and in the crystalline phases of silica. This is shown in Fig. 4. They concluded that the volume occupied by the oxygen increased in a perfectly normal manner in vitreous silica (as explained above the volume of silicon may be disregarded), but that the expansion took place into the void space of the solid. The inquiry made now is whether displacements in mean relative atomic positions occur in the process; and if they occur, how extensive they are.

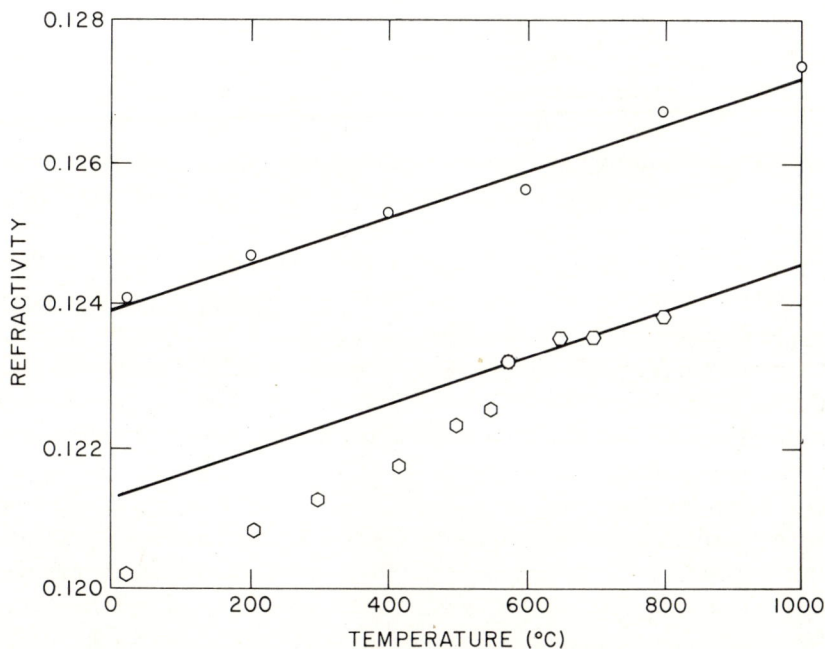

Figure 4.   Refractivity of silica: circles, vitreous silica; vertical hexagons, α-quartz; horizontal hexagons, β-quartz.

THERMAL BEHAVIOR

The evidence presented above indicates that pure vitreous silica possesses a random glass structure like that conceived by Zachariesen.[43] The preferred Si–O–Si bond angle, about 143°, cannot be maintained in such a random glass structure; and therefore a microscopic state of balanced stress, the Si–O tetrahedra twisted, some bond angles deformed positively, others negatively, has to be considered. With an increase in temperature, the increase in oxygen ionic volume must be accommodated. It was seen above that in α-quartz this is done in part by twisting of the Si–O tetrahedra, a motion which was possible because they could twist coherently. Because such a motion is not possible, in general, in vitreous silica, the stress balance alters and the oxygen moves into the void volume, decreasing the Si–O–Si bond angle. The reason for excluding local inversion here as anything more than a rare and unimportant incidental phenomenon, is that the large volume changes in the compaction phenomena, their annealing and radiation behavior, are to be explained through such processes; and the host of phenomena associated with them are absent here.

The concept of local inversion is similar to one of the alternatives considered by Babcock, Barber, and Fajans[106] to explain the anomalies in the physical properties of vitreous silica. Of their two alternatives: that throughout, the phase angles and distances change more or less continuously; or that two well defined ionic arrangements coexist within the glass, changing continuously in relative amounts with temperature, they preferred the latter which we reject because we reserve it to explain other phenomena. They made their choice because of the behavior of the 1115 Å peak in the infra-red, related to the Si–O–Si linkage. It will be seen that several other authors also have focussed their interest on this linkage, even as has been done here, with other emphasis.

The above description was qualified as applying to the ordinary range of temperatures. A specification of the temperature range can be obtained from the behavior of the elastic constants. If the modulus of rigidity is measured statically or with low frequency techniques, the apparent result obtained[6] is that it increases with temperature to a maximum at about 880°C; then it falls rapidly, approaching zero at about 1010°C. However, if it is measured by high frequency audio or ultrasonic techniques, it continues to rise through this whole range of temperatures.[109,110] Thus it is apparent that the decrease in Si–O–Si bond angle and the increase in microscopic stress continues, but that a macroscopic stress relaxation takes place. It will be seen that a common way for motility to occur in the vitreous silica network is by occasional rupture of a network bond. This unbalances the microscopic stress and frees a segment of the network, permitting it to twist. Such behavior must occur on irradiation at ordinary temperature. It should be sought in the thermal behavior at high temperature by magnetic resonance and optical absorption experiments; but since such studies are not known to this writer, the possibility of local inversion at high temperature without bond rupture, although they seem unlikely, are not excluded at this time.

The more rapid and drastic changes observed above 1000 °C are interpreted here as indirect evidence of a contribution from bond rupture in the network. Kats[111] describes changes in fluorescence (which he associates with a germanium center) resulting from heating, as involving an ordering about a Ge in the temperature range 1100–1400 °C, and a disordering above 1400 °C. Devitrification to cristobalite becomes significant above 1400 °C, indicating bond rupture is active. The hypothesis presented here is that below 1400 °C bond rupture is just occasional; particularly, it can occur in association with impurities in the network; and most of the flow is by progressive local inversion, a twisting of the Si–O tetrahedra with respect to each other. Even at 1400 °C, bond rupture cannot be a very rapid process and must be reversible because the transformation to cristobalite is a slow one, requiring days to months for massive vitreous silica.

The permanent changes in density (in this section referred to as *altered*) produced at high temperature are described in detail below (see page 61). What is of interest here, is that when the altered vitreous silica is annealed slowly, the original density is obtained. It is therefore concluded that broken bonds are re-established and that the structure reverts to one of balanced stress statistically equivalent to (evidence presented below indicates that it is not identical with) the original. The significance of this conclusion is that all structures for vitreous silica (and by inference, for silicate glasses) derived from consideration of the molecular constitution of the melt are eliminated. The view expressed by Turnbull and Cohen[112] (though largely with the intention of applying it to other cases), "... That there is no essential structural difference between a liquid and a glass; both may be considered thermodynamically as a single (amorphous) phase.", does not apply to the silicate glasses and particularly, not to vitreous silica. Here, both chemical alteration (i.e., changes in bonding) and structural alteration (changes in configuration) occur during the cooling of the melt; here, solidification is not just a physical process.

EFFECT OF PRESSURE

The effect of pressure on vitreous silica is to decrease the polarizability of the oxygen ion.[113] Not only is the solid compressed, but the ions are also. This is not an effect unique to vitreous silica, it is the usual occurrence.[94,75]

The peculiarity of vitreous silica, as described above, is that the elastic moduli decrease and the compressibility increases on compression. At some higher pressure, perhaps 20–40 Mega g/cm² the compressibility begins to decrease with further increase in pressure, but as will be described below, this is not a simple effect.

The high pressure data which are quoted are all due to Bridgman.[114,115,116] In his work, the compressibility was determined by a static method: by differencing the experimental data, the relative volume as a function of pressure. The differences are small. Succeeding sets of data were obtained with different and improved apparatus as Bridgman developed and extended his high pressure techniques to higher pressures. However, concerning the different absolute values he obtained, he says,[116] "This difference is not necessarily all instrumental, because there is reason to think that quartz glass is not a perfectly well defined substance." The nature of the non-constancy of commercial grades of vitreous silica is discussed below. Bridgman states about his material,[115] "... quartz glass was from laboratory stock, selected to be free from internal striations." This is not sufficient to characterize the material, and the effect of kind of vitreous silica has yet to be investigated. Bridgman did investigate a number of multi-component glasses; and, from their behavior, it seems unlikely that the much smaller differences to be expected for different grades and purity of vitreous silica will account for the variations since his results were probably obtained on vitreous silica from the same source. In one paper he describes the procedure he used,[116] "Each substance involves two applications of maximum pressure, a preliminary 'seasoning' application and the second stepwise application, up and down in steps of approximately 2,000 kg/cm², giving 43 readings in all." Since the different apparatuses had different pressure ranges and extended to pressures at which permanent changes are produced in vitreous silica, it seems reasonable to suppose that the data he gives are not for ordinary vitreous silica at all. This feature of his results will be discussed more fully in the section on pressure-compacted vitreous silica (see Section III page 44 et seq.). What is of interest here is that the compaction, which must have occurred prior to his measurements, affected the data so little, as indicated by the similarity of results from the different apparatuses operating in different respective pressure ranges. This is confirmed by the data of several other investigators who worked at lower pressures. The data given in Table 2 are taken from a paper by Reitzel, Šimon, and Walker.[117] For this reason, it seems reasonable in this section to disregard the effect of compaction, although future investigators should reconsider the matter.

Although the range of pressures over which the compressibility increases extends to 20–40 Mega g/cm², the total change in the compressibility is as if

TABLE 2 Linear compressibility of vitreous silica[a, b]
$$-(\Delta V/V) = AP + BP^2$$

Source	$10^7 A$	$10^{12} B$
Bridgman[c]	26.33	18.8
Adams and Williamson[d]	26.36	19.3
Birch and Law[e]	25.57	31.8
Birch and Dow[f]	26.31	20.8
Reitzel, Šimon, and Walker[g]	26.31	20.8

[a] From 22 to 259°C A and B decrease linearly with temperature.

[b] Coefficients A and B decrease with pressure; by -0.27% at 3000 kg/cm^2.

[c] Ref. 118.

[d] Ref. 119.

[e] Ref. 120.

[f] Ref. 121.

[g] Ref. 117.

it were linear from 0 to 13,000 kg/cm^2. Unfortunately, polarizability data is available only for the lower part of this pressure range. It would be very useful to have polarizability or refractivity data to much higher pressures. The approximate relations are that the decrease in volume extrapolated to 13,000 kg/cm^2 on a linear basis is some 3.9 % while the decrease in polarizability is some 2 %. That, is about half of the volume change is caused by compression of the oxygen ion. Because of the unsymmetrical bonding, the oxygen ion must be deformed unsymmetrically. Some interesting information about the structural change may be inferred immediately from geometrical considerations. Since the decrease in external volume is twice the decrease in oxygen volume, the oxygen ion must be forced into the void space. As pointed out above, in vitreous silica this would require a small decrease in Si–O–Si bond angle. The oblate deformation of the oxygen ion would require that the Si–O distances decrease somewhat. Here, as in the case of the thermal behavior, there arises the question about the extent and contribution of twisting of the Si–O tetrahedra to the structural change. No quantitative estimates are available, and again an attempt is made to answer this question from qualitative arguments and a consideration of the experimental observations. Starting from the original state of balanced stress resulting from some Si–O–Si bond angles being too small and others too large, those which are too large would be easily compressed, and those which are too small would be more difficult to compress. Thus the compression would not be uniform, and the Si–O tetrahedra would tend to twist until a new state of balanced stress was achieved. Again, here as in the thermal case, this is viewed as being, in general, the kind of small twisting which occurs within the range of the α-phase of quartz rather than the kind of major change represented by the α–β-inversions; and again for the same reason—that the process of local inversion must be reserved to explain the pressure compaction phenomena, its annealing and radiation behavior. The major distinction in the pressure behavior as compared to the thermal behavior is that in the former, the ionic oxygen volume is decreased; while in the latter, it is increased. In the former, the twisting relaxation accompanies, therefore, a decreased Si–O bond length; in the latter an increased bond length. In this picture, it is no longer necessary to postulate a Morse potential curve which is shallow at short distances (the reverse of the usual form) as would be necessary were the twisting relaxation disregarded. The picture now becomes the following:

A.   Contributions to hardening: –

   (1) Decrease in under-size Si–O–Si bond angles.
   (2) Increased Si–Si repulsion because of decreased mean Si–Si distances.

B.   Contributions to softening: –

   (1) Decrease in over-size Si–O–Si bond angles.
   (2) Increased Si–O attraction because of decreased Si–O distances.
   (3) Relaxation of increased bond angle stress by twisting of Si–O tetrahedra.
   (4) Normal Si–O–Si bond angle decreased because of increased covalent binding associated with oxygen ion deformation and decreased Si–O distances.

It is seen that items (1) and (2) under each heading counteract each other in part, and that (3) and (4) in that order must be the major factors in the softening under pressure. There have been no attempts to evaluate items 1, 3, and 4. The attempt to evaluate item 2, it will be seen, was faulty (see page 31).

It should be noted that the softening begins to saturate at a negative dilatation of about 3% and is saturated at about 4%. The value 3% will appear as a critical one in several aspects of the dilatations of vitreous silica. In the curious formalism developed by Primak,[124] the void space in vitreous silica is regarded as occurring in cells surrounded on the average by about 14 oxygen ions. The critical value thus corresponds to a mean collapse of an ionic oxygen volume in alternate cells. This formalism will be discussed more fully for the subjects to which it was applied originally. From the viewpoint considered here, it appears that relaxation through twisting is inhibited beyond a negative dilatation of 3%. Under conditions in which the oxygen ionic volume is not compressed (as in the radiation case) the value seems a little smaller than 3%; where it is compressed (as in the case of compression), a little larger than 3%. It is concluded that from the kinetic point of view, this is a value at which oxygen motions begin to interfere with each other; and, consequently, the twisting relaxation of adjacent segments of the network interfere with each other. From an atomic viewpoint, O–O repulsion is becoming evident. An alternative suggestion, that the state of the network in ordinary vitreous silica is quenched from 750°C, where the ionic volume is about 2% greater than at room temperature, leaving the material in a state of negative microscopic stress which is relieved by compression has been considered by another writer,[28,29] but is rejected here, because, as will be shown below (see Section IV page 61), the effect which has been observed in such a quenching of vitreous silica has been a compaction; i.e., in the present sense, a state of positive microscopic stress.

The contrast made just above between the thermal and the compressional behavior of vitreous silica is the justification for the statement made earlier, that the volume does not uniquely specify the state of the material. Therefore, care must be used in combining thermodynamic quantities involving derivatives with respect to volume.

ELECTROSTATIC CALCULATIONS – NETWORK DYNAMICS

A number of authors have attempted to explain some of the peculiar properties of vitreous silica by the behavior of the Si–O–Si linkage; in particular, to explain the low temperature heat capacity, the low temperature dielectric loss and acoustical loss, the negative thermal expansion at low temperature, and the infra-red peak at about 9.09 μ. The flaw in these proposals was that the configuration was taken to be linear, and the difficulties encountered serve as further confirmation (hardly needed!) of its non-linearity. Even though the quantitative calculations were hardly successful, some of the conclusions are of interest; and further work on the subject should be pursued. Smyth and collaborators[125,126,127] performed a series of calculations in which pairwise electrostatic energy associated with Si–O and Si–Si attractions were considered for the linear Si–O–Si configuration. Their general conclusions about the heat capacity[126] would appear to be valid today. Because of the disorder, the heat capacity is not to be treated as a Debye function, but rather as a sum of Einstein functions. They chose Einstein terms for 3 silicon vibrations, 4 transverse oxygen vibrations, and two longitudinal oxygen vibrations. They found that at low temperatures only the transverse oxygen vibrations proved important. The calculation would have to be repeated today to take into account the proper configuration of this oxygen if it is desired to incorporate physically realistic constants. To explain the increase of compressibility[125] with pressure, they calculated the electrostatic energy of Si–O and Si–Si attractions and repulsions. The softening was explained by the buckling of a linear Si–O–Si configuration and the major difficulty encountered was that the calculated compressibility changed too steeply and non-linearly as compared to the experimental behavior, as might be expected for such a model. If the calculation were repeated with Si–O–Si bond angles dispersed about 143° and account taken of the fact that some were strained positively and some negatively from the preferred angle, the effect would surely be found to be negligible; another explanation was given above (see pages 28–29). Smyth[127] also considered the effect of the buckling of a linear configuration on the thermal expansion. He pointed out that if there is a transverse mode whose frequency decreases as the structure shrinks, a contraction takes place. He assigned this to buckling of the linear Si–O–Si configuration. It is seen that his effect does not occur in vitreous silica because the configuration is not linear a-priori. It is difficult to formulate a realistic qualitative argument for the behavior of the frequency of the transverse modes. The decrease in refractivity with decreasing temperature may be taken to indicate a reduced moment of inertia for the oxygen ion; but, because of the changes in configuration with temperature, the behavior of the force constants is not apparent. A comparison of the thermal expansions of α- and β-quartz, substances with uniform structures which are fairly well known, indicates that the expansion is largely controlled by the balance of electrostatic and covalent binding and the twisting relaxation of the Si–O tetrahedra. It therefore seems best to abandon Smyth's approach until a satisfactory calculation is available. The appearance of an important transverse dissipation in a particular temperature range may be associated with the limitation of other modes of motion. A twisting mode of the Si–O tetrahedra should be considered. This is a transverse oxygen vibration mode for which some spacial coherence may develop at lower temperatures.

It was pointed out by Robinson[83] that an increase in compressibility with pressure is observed in organic polymer systems where it has been associated with a micellar structure. He saw evidence for a micellar structure in published electron microscopy of glasses. As described above, the present evidence is that the kind of micellar structure considered by Robinson, micelles of the magnitude of the crystallites discussed by the Russian writers, do not exist in vitreous silica. In further work with Warshavsky[128] he pointed out that the behavior of the internal friction of vitreous silica corresponds to that of a granular medium. Earlier writers[106,30,107] have thought it desirable for different reasons to invoke a 2 phase concept to explain the behavior of the elastic or other properties of vitreous silica. From the discussion given just above, some of the behavior of the vitreous silica may result from strain in the network, part of which is strained positively (stretched), part negatively (compressed). However, these units may be too small to show the kind of behavior discussed by Warshavsky and Robinson. Another possible source for behavior of the sort they consider might be the effect of impurities. As will be shown below, impurities disturb the integrity of the network at distances corresponding to the size of crystallites. The impurities would not be expected to affect the compressibility in the same manner as they would the internal friction; and since there is the possibility of altering their concentration, the subject should be amenable to experimental investigation.

REAL VITREOUS SILICA

In all of the above considerations, vitreous silica has been treated as being an Si–O network in balanced equilibrium. Such a material does not exist. Most specimens are quite inhomogeneous macroscopically; and by standards customarily employed in physical research in which structural defects are studied, such as color centers in crystals and carrier concentrations in semiconductors, most commercially available vitreous silica samples are so grossly impure that they may well be considered as dilute multi-component glasses. However, there are other aspects of purity which are uniquely part of the vitreous silica structure problem. The importance of the impurities has now received general recognition from investigators of radiation-induced color centers,[37] but has received little consideration from most other workers. The best exposition of the compositional nature and relationships of real vitreous silicas is in the writings of Jack and Hetherington and their co-authors.
[129–139]

INHOMOGENEITY

Macroscopic inhomogeneity of vitreous silica was first observed about a century ago. The early observations are summarized by Sosman.[7] The inhomogeneity is readily observed in a suitable polarimeter as a birefringent patchwork. The same patterns are also observed in a schlieren apparatus.[140] Thus the inhomogeneities are both birefringent and of different refractive index. Primak[141] gives a summary of inhomogeneity in birefringence for a number of commercial samples, mostly obtained about a decade ago. A patchwork of color appears on irradiation of some specimens. Dunn, Hetherington, and Jack[137] studied respective samples of vitreous silica made by usual commercial methods from quartz reduced to powder by two different techniques, (1) crushing after prior shattering by rapid transport through the α–β-transition, and (2) mechanical crushing without prior thermal treatment. The first technique yields acicular shards while the second gives an "equi-axed" granular powder. The refractive index patchworks found in the respective samples of vitreous silica corresponded to the powders from which they were prepared. The shards tended to align. The high temperature electrolytic transport through the vitreous silica made from the shards possessed aeolotropy corresponding to the c-axis channels of the original quartz and was two orders of magnitude greater than for the vitreous silica made from the granular powder. Thus, they proved conclusively that, at least for vitreous silica made in this manner, inhomogeneity can be, at least in part, residual structure from the quartz starting material and represents incomplete vitrification.

Photographs published by Primak, Fuchs, and Day[97] show one of the sources of the radiation-induced patchwork. The radiation-induced coloration in two irradiated quartz plates was zoned, but quite uniform within the zones, corresponding, presumably, to zoning of impurity content. Irradiated vitreous silica plates possessed patterns reminiscent of vari-colored book edges of yesteryear, indicative of non-uniform mixing or puddling.

The schlieren observed patchwork indicates variations in refractive index, and it may be presumed that the density varies correspondingly. The birefringent patchwork may, in part, be evidence of an actual residual anisotropy. However, individual small birefringent zones in this patchwork, for the most part, appear much the same when examined from different directions;[142] hence, it appears likely that much of it is strain birefringence and therefore indicative of differences in thermal coefficient of expansion over the temperature range to the annealing temperature (a little over $1000\,°C$). The radiation-induced patchwork is, of course, caused by the inhomogeneity of impurity content, largely that associated with the Al content, although coloration may be modified by the compensating ion present. The inhomogeneity arises from the inhomogeneity of the powdered quartz raw material, and hence a similarity in the patchworks may be anticipated, but no careful correlation is known to this writer.

VARIATION OF DENSITY

Early observations of variation in density are considered by Sosman,[2] but not with regard to the particular material studied; rather with regard to the constancy of the property. Primak and Edwards[8] gave densities for a number of their specimens, and additional values are available from the work of Primak and Kampwirth.[143] These are given in Table 3. In general, it appears that products made by fusing quartz have a higher density than those made from the hydrolysis of silicon compounds.

TABLE 3   Density of commercial vitreous silicas

	Density[a] (g/cm^3)	Density range[b] (g/cm^3)
GE 101	2.2031	2.20383–2.20386
GE 103	2.2032	
Optosil	2.2031	
Herasil	2.2021	
Homosil	2.2018	
Suprasil	2.2000	2.20023–2.20033
Corning High Purity	2.2006	
Corning Schlieren		2.20083–2.20093
Corning 7943 (OH free)		2.20266
Unknown[c]	2.2035	
Unknown[c]	2.2035	
Unknown[c]	2.2032	

[a] Ref. 8.
[b] Ref. 143.
[c] Probably Amersil Commercial or GE 101.

MANUFACTURE AND COMPOSITION

The manufacture of vitreous silica is described by Jack and Hetherington[129], and they also give the properties of the material. A classification of the commercially available grades taken from Hetherington, Jack, and Ramsay[136] is reproduced in Table 4. Analysis for purity presents special problems for the purer grades because the concentration may be less than the sensitivity of simple direct methods of trace analysis, like spectrum analysis; and even for the less pure grades, because the material is not in a form suitable for analysis. Hetherington and Bell[132] have provided us with comparative results of analyses for metallic impurities as obtained in several different laboratories (Table 5), and they give a critical discussion of the problems of analysis. These results demonstrate that solution concentration of impurity for spectral analysis, even with careful use of blank samples, may be unreliable. Direct methods like neutron activation are considered to be better. Weeks and Lell,[145] and Primak and Kampwirth[146] mention partial analyses made in relation to some of the work considered in detail in later sections. The OH content proves very significant in affecting properties of vitreous silica and will be discussed further below. It is usually taken from the near infra-red absorption bands.[147] Hetherington[130] states that in Type IV vitreous silicas, Cl may be present in quantities of several hundred ppm. Hetherington, Jack, and Kennedy[138] state that Spectrosil WF (a Type IV product) contains appreciable amounts of chlorine as determined by direct chemical analysis. In different batches, and even within a single piece, the chlorine concentration

TABLE 4 Classification[136] of commercially available vitreous silicas

Type	Source	Melting	Metallic impurity[b] (ppm)	OH, etc.[a]	Cl	Examples
I	Quartz crystal powder	Electric furnace	Like quartz mainly Al 30–100 Na 4	Nil	Nil	I.R. Vitreosil Infrasil, Pursil
II	Quartz crystal powder	Flame	Less than type I	0.015–0.04 wt.%	Nil	O.G. and O.H. Vitreosil, Herasil, Homosil, Ultrasil
III	Vapor phase hydrolysis of pure silicon compounds e.g., $SiCl_4$	Flame	Nil	0.1 wt.%	If from $SiCl_4$ ~50 ppm	Corning 7940, Spectrosil, Suprasil
IV	Oxidizing pure silicon compounds	Water free flame or electric furnace	Nil	Nil	Several hundred ppm	Corning 7943 Spectrosil WF

[a] All vitreous silica which contains hydroxyl exhibits strong absorption at 2.73 μ by the Si–OH stretching vibration and weaker bands at 2.6, 2.22, and 1.38 μ, among others, identified as overtones or combinations involving Si–O vibrations.

[b] Increasing metallic impurities shift the ultra-violet "cut-off" at ~0.18 μ to longer wavelengths. Thus, types III and IV have the best ultra-violet transmissions.

[c] All vitreous silicas made from quartz crystal by either electric fusion or flame fusion exhibit absorption at 0.24 μ, and associated with this are fluorescence emission bands at 0.28 and 0.39 μ; the latter is visibly excited by a 0.254 μ mercury source. Both this fluorescence and the 0.24 μ absorption are removed by an oxidising heat-treatment. In fused quartz type I containing no hydroxyl, removal is very slow and is governed by diffusion of oxygen through the solid. For fused quartz containing hydroxyl, oxidation is much faster and occurs by the reaction

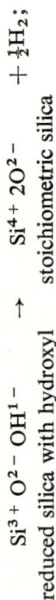

$$Si^{3+} O^{2-} OH^{1-} \rightarrow Si^{4+} 2O^{2-} + \tfrac{1}{2}H_2;$$

reduced silica with hydroxyl → stoichiometric silica

thus, its rate is governed by diffusion and removal of hydrogen. Garino-Canina showed that the 0.240 μ absorption and the 0.39 μ fluorescence were also removed by electrolysis at 1080°C under a potential gradient of ~1000 V/cm. Absorption and fluorescence occur simultaneously and require the silica to be in a chemically reduced state. There is some doubt about the nature of the centres. They re-occur when types I and II vitreous silicas, fully oxidised by heat-treatment or electrolysis, are reduced by heating in hydrogen. Types III and IV do not show fluorescence or 0.24 μ absorption when manufactured, and they are not introduced by hydrogen treatment. The presence of metallic impurities seems essential; germanium and aluminium have been suggested.

   ᵈ Types I and II vitreous silicas when subjected to x-ray, γ-ray, or nuclear pile irradiation are coloured brown-violet and show three absorption bands at about 0.55, 0.30, and at a lower wavelength given variously as 0.221, 0.220, 0.223, and 0.215 μ. Type II materials, because of metallic impurity or greater hydroxyl content, or both, show less optical absorption than similarly irradiated type I silicas. In types III and IV synthetic vitreous silicas the 0.55 and 0.30 μ bands are absent, but they show a 0.215 μ absorption. Lell ascribed coloration to the simultaneous presence of aluminium and alkali impurities. Type IV vitreous silica, shows a much higher 0.215 μ absorption. The 0.215 μ absorption in type IV synthetic silica is reduced progressively as hydroxyl is introduced.

TABLE 5 Chemical analysis of vitreous silicas

	I.R. Vitreosil (ppm)	OG and OH Vitreosil (ppm)	Spectrosil (ppm)	Spectrosil WF (ppm)
Al	50–70	10	<0.02	
Sb	0.23	0.07	<0.0001	
As	–	–	<0.0002	
B	<0.5	<0.5	<0.01	
Ca	0.4	0.35	<0.1	
Cu	0.01	<0.0003	<0.0002	
Ga	–	–	<0.004	
Fe	0.74	0.51	<0.1	
Mn	0.026	0.0017	<0.001	
P	0.01	0.005	<0.001	
K	–	–	0.005	
Na	4.0	0.06	0.04	
Li			<0.1	
Cl				500.0
OH	3.0	400.0	1250.0	
Total metal[a]			<1 ppm	

[a] H_2SO_4–HF residue.

was found to vary widely. In a particular specimen which they used for vis-cosity measurements, they state that it was 0.05 wt. % Cl, with some uncer-tainty. It will be shown below that the Cl acts as a network interrupter simi-lar to OH, and therefore it must be bonded to Si. It is to be noted that the sum of other impurities is not adequate to compensate charge for the Al, assuming the Al to be all network substitutional. Some of this may be caused by inadequate sensitivity in the Li analysis. However, it does not appear pos-sible to account for all the compensation required in this manner. It has there-fore been suggested that some of the compensation is by H^+. The behavior of H^+ may help account for some of the "oxidation" results (see pages 31, 40, 42).

The method of manufacture influences the homogeneity. Inhomogeneity because of incomplete vitrification when the source of the silica is quartz is discussed above. Inhomogeneity caused by variation in OH is discussed below. The methods of fusion, flame or electric furnace, greatly influences the amount of OH in the product, it being much greater for flame fusion if hydrogen or hydrocarbon is present. Flame fusion often causes a decrease of volatile impurities like alkalis, but this does not necessarily give a more per-fect structure, because the alkali may be compensating a trivalent network ion; the product from which the alkali is volatilized may then be an oxidized glass (multivalent impurity oxidized to its higher valency) or the compensation altered to H$^+$. The respective source of silica, whether quartz or oxidation of purified volatile silicon compounds, influences the purity and structure. The product of the former will contain a somewhat variable amount of metallic impurities (of which substitutional Al is best known because of its radiation behavior); of the latter, may contain large quantities of OH and some Cl but may be among the purest of substances with regard to metallic impurity.

WATER AND HYDROGEN DIFFUSION

The studies by Hetherington, *et al.*, on OH in vitreous silica are most suggestive about effects of network interrupting impurities in vitreous silica. Their work was confined to the behavior of Vitreosil and Spectrosil, products of The Thermal Syndicate, Ltd., in whose laboratories the investigations were made. Hetherington and Jack[134] found that at temperatures $\sim 1000°C$, water could diffuse both into and out of vitreous silica. The concentration was followed by measuring the near I.R. absorption bands and by direct weighing, and the results showed OH groups were introduced into the structure. The reaction was diffusion controlled and the "solubility" of water varied with the square root of the water vapor pressure. The results were close to those reported earlier by Moulson and Roberts[148] who gave different diffusion constants for entry, 7.2×10^{-10} cm^3/sec, and for removal, 2.9×10^{-10} cm^3/sec, from infra-red absorption measurements for OH whereas Stephenson and Jack[333] by direct weighing obtained 3.4×10^{-10} cm^3/sec, all results for 1000°C. Both I.R. Vitreosil and Spectrosil gave the same solubility, indicating the reaction is an Si–O network effect. It is accounted for by the following network interrupting reaction:—

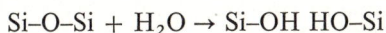

$$\text{Si–O–Si} + \text{H}_2\text{O} \rightarrow \text{Si–OH HO–Si}$$

Hetherington and Jack[134] found the OH caused a small but measurable change in properties. The change was comparable to that caused by thermal compaction (see Section V, page 61), and hence it was necessary to give all the specimens a similar suitable heat treatment prior to measurement. Introduction of OH caused a reduction in density,* velocity of sound, refractive index, and activation energy for viscous flow.[138] It accounted for most of the

---

* Density data given by Hetherington and Jack[134] are ~ 0.003 g/cm^3 less than data given by Primak and Edwards[8] for similar grades but of different manufacture. It is suspected that these differences result from different weight standards rather than differences in the vitreous silicas. Data by Primak and Edwards have been carefully referred to a set of weights calibrated by the U.S. National Bureau of Standards and are based on the density of water given in the International Critical Tables. Hetherington and Jack do not give details of their density determinations.

density variation noted above, 0.003 g/cm³. Change in the OH content of the vitreous silica is sufficiently rapid that it will occur during normal processing of vitreous silica. Thus if a prism is heated (e.g., annealed) in an atmosphere whose water content does not correspond to that in which the vitreous silica was made, variations in refractive index will be introduced into the prism. These are in the 10^{-5} range. The whole variation in refractive index from an I.R. vitreous silica (negligible 2.45 μ absorption) to a high OH vitreous silica (e.g., Spectrosil) is about 1.4×10^{-4}. When the vitreous silica is made from quartz grains in an atmosphere in water disequilibrium, a granularity is introduced by the OH concentration gradients in each small particle as it fuses, and this is easily seen in a schlieren examination. Hetherington and Jack[134] account for the inhomogeneity in some commercial products in this manner. The density variation caused by OH is $\sim 3 \times 10^{-3}$. It may be expected that the thermal expansion is also affected (although it has not been reported, to this writer's knowledge), and this would cause granular strain birefringence on cooling. It should not be assumed that the OH gradient accounts for all of the inhomogeneity in vitreous silica made from quartz particles, because gradients of other impurities which are partially volatilized in the flame fusion should also cause effects. The most volatile species are the alkalis and thus Al compensation is altered. This would cause a granularity of the radiation induced coloration.

Bell, Hetherington, and Jack[135] studied the introduction of H_2 into vitreous silica at 800 and 1000°C. They found the process to be governed by diffusion and that OH was introduced. The diffusion coefficient was about 4 orders of magnitude greater than that for the water reaction. The OH solubility depended on the square root of H_2 pressure. The outward diffusion was studied in various atmospheres for OG Vitreosil (~ 10 ppm Al) and found to be about the same as the inward diffusion in I.R. Vitreosil (~ 60 ppm Al) indicating the same species was diffusing. Thus the reaction appeared to be reversible. It accounted for previous reports of diffusion of H_2 in vitreous silica and of solubility of hydrogen in vitreous silica. Other reports of solubility of hydrogen in vitreous silica give considerably different values.

A confusing aspect of the investigation by Bell, Hetherington, and Jack[135] of the diffusion of hydrogen into vitreous silica is that it was performed with I.R. Vitreosil, a material which contains about 3.4×10^{18} Al atoms/cm³. They attributed the effect to the breaking of the Si–O–Si linkage, but the Al–O–Si linkage should be more vulnerable. The maximum solubility found was nearly the same from 700 to 1000°C and corresponded to 1.39×10^{18} H atoms/cm³. The reaction then becomes

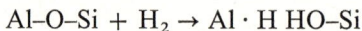

$$Al-O-Si + H_2 \rightarrow Al \cdot H \; HO-Si$$

which gives the proper square root dependence. This reaction requires 2H for each aluminum center and thus corresponds to affecting about 20% of the aluminum centers; they therefore are not equally vulnerable. It corresponds to a change in the compensating ion, and this would account for part of the difference in vulnerability. However, variable vulnerability is a fundamental characteristic of vitreous silica and is discussed below (see pages 101, 146).

Bubbles are found occasionally in vitreous silica of type III manufacture. Bell, Hetherington, and Jack[135] state the bubbles in Spectrosil, such a product, are shown to be pure hydrogen by mass spectrometry and are at several atmospheres pressure in the plastic range where they are formed. If the above speculations about the solubility of hydrogen in the aluminum-containing products are correct, the behavior of hydrogen in Spectrosil would be a different one. The divergent results reported by various investigators for the solubility of hydrogen in vitreous silica are reasonable if network impurity and charge compensation are involved in the phenomena. Another effect of the same magnitude associated with impurity is found in the radiation behavior of impure vitreous silicas[146] and is described below (see page 94).

VISCOSITY

The study of the viscosity of vitreous silica by Hetherington, Jack, and Kennedy[138] is of interest because it shows the role of Cl in the silica structure. They found that the OH content caused a decrease in the activation energy for viscous flow. Spectrosil WF (WF means water free and is a Type IV product) is a product free of OH but possesses Cl in about the same concentration as the OH in OG Vitroesil. These two products possessed the same activation energy for viscous flow. Their results are given in Table 6. Thus the Cl seems to perform the same function as OH in being a network interrupter. They found that introduction of Ti, Cr, or B into Spectrosil (a Type III product) caused a decrease in the pre-exponential factor while the activation energy for viscous flow was not altered noticeably. The time required to

TABLE 6   Equilibrium viscosity ($\eta = \eta_0 \exp E/RT$) of vitreous silicas
at temperatures 900–1400°C[a]

Material	Hydroxyl content (wt.%)	η_0 (poise)	E (kcal/mole)
I.R. Vitreosil	0.0003	3.1×10^{-13}	170
O.G. Vitreosil	0.027	2.3×10^{-11}	154
	0.04	1.9×10^{-8}	131
Spectrosil	0.12	1.9×10^{-7}	122

[a] From Hetherington, Jack, and Kennedy.[138]

reach constancy of the viscosity at a given temperature was greater than the stabilizing times for density reported by Douglas and Isard[149] for the time to reach a constant density (see Section IV, page 61). Hetherington et al.[138] speculate whether the stabilizing time depends on the property under examination. However, the material used by Douglas and Isard was not a well defined one and could have been much more impure. They stated their specimens were hooks drawn from clear fused quartz rod (which would indicate an undefined flame treatment subsequent to manufacture), and the source, character, and purity of the original stock was not stated. The differences may therefore be one of material. Further, Douglas and Isard were unaware of the water equilibrium, and a changing OH concentration may have been superimposed on other behavior noted by them.

OXIDATION

Hetherington and Jack[139] have studied the so called "oxidation" of vitreous silica. The oxidation of glasses is a complex phenomenon usually involving compensating ions and the valence state of transition metal impurities. These are nearly absent in the commercial relatively pure vitreous silicas, where the phenomena appear to be associated with H and OH. Hetherington and Jack found that in the OH containing vitreous silica, OG Vitreosil, the diffusion constants associated with the oxidation as studied by measuring the $0.24\,\mu$ absorption band corresponded to the H diffusion obtained by measuring the absorption of the $2.7\,\mu$ band, and they therefore wrote the reaction:

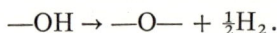

$$-\text{OH} \rightarrow -\text{O}- + \tfrac{1}{2}\text{H}_2.$$

In the OH free vitreous silica, I. R. Vitreosil, the diffusion constants corresponded to that of oxygen, very much smaller. It was followed by the blue-violet fluorescence under 2537 Å U.V. irradiation. They associated the effect with the reaction:

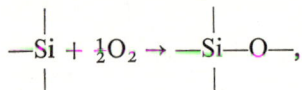

$$-\overset{|}{\underset{|}{\text{Si}}} + \tfrac{1}{2}\text{O}_2 \rightarrow -\overset{|}{\underset{|}{\text{Si}}}-\text{O}-,$$

an oxidation of silicon. It should be noted that both vitreous silicas studied contained Al and that the quantity of change corresponded reasonably well to the Al content. The phenomena should be reconsidered, and whether the Al ion and its compensation plays a role should be determined. The Al–O bond is much more labile than the Si–O bond and could much more readily partake in reaction.

SEGMENTATION

If Tables 5 and 7 are compared, it is seen that in actual specimens of vitreous silica, the network is frequently interrupted either by breaking an Si–O–Si

TABLE 7   Relative impurity spacing

	Concentration (ppm)	Atomic Spacing[a]
Al	70	1/18
Al	10	1/36
Na	4	1/45
OH	3	1/45
OH	400	1/8.9
OH	1250	1/6.1
Cl	500	1/10.6

[a] Mean relative linear spacing based on a cubic lattice.

link or by the substitution of a metallic ion for Si. For the purest vitreous silica, the average segment length corresponding to a uniform impurity distribution for atoms distributed on a cubic lattice is but 13 Si–O tetrahedra long. It would be but slightly longer for a random structure. In Spectrosil it is only 6 Si–O tetrahedra long. These are among the purer grades of vitreous silica. For less pure vitreous silica, corresponding mean network segment lengths are only 3–4 tetrahedra long. Such a material is hardly the continuous network which has been discussed above at great length. It begins to approach models employed by the Russian crystal chemists.[88]

STATUS

The role of impurities and incomplete vitrification and the effects which arise from them have been largely neglected. In addition to the effects noted above, Primak and Kampwirth[146] noted an effect on the radiation-induced dilatation which is discussed in detail below (see page 94). Small increases in OH content have been shown to have a profound effect on the devitrification of vitreous silica at moderately high pressures.[151,154,155] It would be of interest to study the effect of impurity on thermal expansion, on internal friction,* on the rate of stress relaxation; on the rates of thermal and pressure compaction; and to correlate inhomogeneity in density, refractive index, and stress birefringence.

---

* Such a study was published some months after this was written.[156]

III. Pressure Compacted Vitreous Silica

HISTORICAL INTRODUCTION

In the course of his investigations on high pressure, Bridgman measured the relative volume of vitreous silica as a function of pressure on several occasions. Agreement between these determinations was much poorer than the presumed experimental accuracy, and he concluded there was some inconstancy in the material.[116] In 1952, in a paper[157] on electrical resistance at pressures up to 100 Mega g/cm^2, he described an attempt to use soda lime glass in this work,

During the preliminary work the possibility of using glass as a pressure transmitting solid was extensively investigated and for the first time measurably large plastic flow with permanent increase of density was observed in glass at room temperature. A disc of commercial lime glass 0.25 inch in diameter and 0.006 inch thick was compressed between two flat carboloy blocks to a mean stress of 100,000 kg/cm^2. Under this pressure there was a permanent decrease of thickness of 22 per cent, and a permanent increase of density from 2.497 to 2.617, that is, by 4.8 per cent. The glass, although copiously cracked, was not reduced to powder but was broken into clear blocks of the order of a millimeter or somewhat less on a side. Professor E.P.Larsen was so kind as to make an optical examination and found marked double refraction, with an increase of mean index for Na light from 1.515 to 1.527. Prolonging the time of loading does not perceptibly increase the permanent alteration, so that the behavior is *not* that of a viscous liquid. That is, under these conditions glass work hardens.

At about this time, Arthur D.Little, Inc., attempted to secure his services as a consultant on a glass project for an industrial sponsor. He consented only with great reluctance, for he was deeply engrossed in his own investigations. Out of this casual relationship arose an investigation of great historical significance to our subject. Šimon recalls the relationship warmly,[158]

This work was an outgrowth of research project initiated at A.D.Little, Inc. in 1951 by Dr. H.O.McMahon to investigate the effect of high pressure on molten glass. The work was performed under industrial sponsorship and its results (which turned out to be rather inconclusive) were recorded only in an internal report supplied to the client sometime in 1952. Prof. Bridgman was consulting to us during this period, largely in the matter of techniques and apparatus design. In the course of this work Bridgman told us of his experience with cold compaction of glass he observed with his anvil apparatus earlier.[157] ...Since McMahon and myself were at that time already in the midst of various studies on the nature of

44

the vitreous state we became keenly interested in the phenomenon related to us by Bridgman and decided to study it in more detail. We obtained support of the Owens-Illinois Glass Co. for continuation of the work, and I proceeded with the project in our laboratories while McMahon became involved in other projects of more urgent nature. Prof. Bridgman followed the work with interest, and we had several conferences regarding the progress of work during that period; however, he was too busy with his own research and left me quite free to do as I saw fit. My own interests at that time were in X-ray diffraction and IR spectroscopy and consequently I was eager to combine these methods with the high pressure technique to learn something new about the structure of glass. The result of this work was the paper published jointly with Bridgman.[9]...

This was enlightened industrial sponsorship granting freedom of research. To our knowledge, no practical applications arose at the time. We wonder whether the sponsor appreciated how much he was contributing to the development of our knowledge about the structure of glass!

Except for a single determination, Bridgman and Šimon's data were obtained at room temperature. A single compression at 150°C and 170 Kiloatmospheres gave a greater compaction than observed at room temperature, indicating a rise in temperature facilitated compaction. This was confirmed by Cohen and Roy who extended the compaction data to 600°C. It became obvious that pressure compaction had been observed by Douglas and Isard[149] before it was observed by Bridgman in an investigation in which they referred to it as volume relaxation. They reported, for a specimen which had been heated initially for 40 hr at 1075°C, a 0.2% density increase for a uniaxial load of 348 kg/cm² at 1075°C. They considered this the equivalent of a triaxial (hydrostatic) stress of 116 kg/cm²; but, as will be seen below, it is difficult to determine the stress in such experiments because it is difficult to determine the confinement. Their assumption that shearing stresses have no effect on volume has become a subject of controversy and will be discussed below (see page 56). They found that the density increase occurred over a 5 hr period; and when the load was removed, relaxation required about the same time. They were not certain that they had reached an equilibrium density under stress because they were forced to discontinue application of stress when lateral deformation became as great as could be tolerated in their apparatus. The kinetics of the compaction is a subject of disagreement among investigators, and for this reason the data obtained by Douglas and Isard are reproduced here in Fig. 5. It is unfortunate that they did not describe their material, because their work was in a range in which impurity effects might be observed. The various problems raised here about their investigation plague the whole subject, and none of them are settled yet. Other aspects of their investigation will be discussed below in Section III on Thermal Compaction (see page 61), for the thermal effects were their main concern.

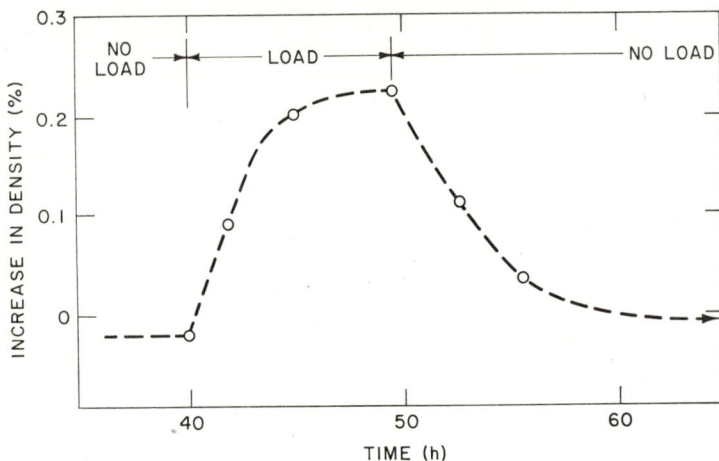

Figure 5.   Effect of 3.41×10^8 dyn/cm^2 uniaxial load on the density of vitreous silica maintained at 1075°C. (From Douglas and Isard[149].)

Loading in the Uniaxial Press

Bridgman and Šimon[9] used ground and polished discs 0.15–0.25 mm (6–10 mils) thick, 5–8 mm diameter. The discs were placed between flat carboloy surfaces which were loaded uniaxially. The pressures reported by them are mean stress on the area of the glass disc. The recovered material was fragmented, and they reported the density of fragments taken from the central areas of the fragmented discs. It is known now that such a density cannot be taken as caused by a pressure equal to the mean stress because the loading is not uniform. Christiansen, Kistler, and Gogarty[159] attempted to obtain the distribution of stress in such a press on the assumption that the density of the compacted vitreous silica can be used as a piezometer. Mackenzie[160] has criticized this assumption on the grounds that shear plays an important role in the compaction, but this matter is far from settled and is discussed further below (see page 56). Christiansen, Kistler, and Gogarty's data, given in their Fig. 7, does not seem to agree with their assumed relationship. At high pressures it appears as if the anvils are being supported by part of the sample between them. These investigators placed their specimens within a pipestone confining toroid and used lead as a pressure transmitting medium. It will be recalled that Bridgman and Šimon did not use confinement other than specimen friction itself. In one experiment in which Bridgman later attempted the use of a pipestone confining ring[161] and lead as a pressure transmitting medium, he obtained no compaction. Primak and Kampwirth[162] tried confining toroids of several metals: annealed nickel, aluminum, platinum, and silver; and pressure transmitting media of aluminum, lead, indium, and silver;

and they altered the ratio of transmitting medium to volume of vitreous silica. They tried polished and roughened anvil faces. They compared results for assemblies left under pressure for brief periods (minutes) with some left under pressure for many hours. All these affected the compactions attained. The behavior of such a mixed body depends upon the reversible volume changes, the hardening, and the gradual plastic flow. Thus, when the pressure transmitting medium is lead (which has a greater compressibility than vitreous silica), a nickel retaining ring may support most of the load. Primak and Kampwirth obtained their best results with silver retaining rings and a mixture of silver and lead for packing of the cell, presumably by matching the compressibility of the vitreous silica with the mixture, lead (more compressible) and silver (less compressible). When pipestone is used, it crushes, at which time the transmitted load changes. The vitreous silica may fragment in two stages. It may fragment first when the pressure is raised; and marked compaction may occur at this time, presumably because of changing loading. Second, fragmentation may also occur during release of loading; and Christiansen, Kistler, and Gogarty[159] attributed this to the changing stress distribution resulting from the different deformations in the specimen and anvil assemblies. Their work clearly shows how deformation of the anvils results in greater deformation and work hardening of the peripheral area of the discs, which then can support the load. This effect would appear even in unconfined discs like those used by Bridgman and Šimon.[9] Since Bridgman and Šimon reported the density of the central region for the mean anvil stress on the specimen, their compaction must correspond to lower local pressures (and they pointed this out, but the fact appears to have been disregarded by many of those who subsequently reviewed or criticized their work) and are lower than those reported by most subsequent investigators. It would be valuable to obtain further data for the several glasses they used, because they were the only ones to study a group of glasses which might indicate the effects of altering the Si–O network. They showed that in their opposed anvil press, the amount of lateral flow differed for the several glasses studied. Thus, it is likely that there was a different stress distribution for each glass even though, for the ones to be discussed here, they claimed the density change corresponded to the change in thickness.

It is difficult to perform experiments on the kinetics of compaction in Bridgman's uniaxial press because the flow phenomena in the anvils, discs, confining rings, and pressure transmitting medium results in stress distributions which change with time; and, indeed, this is a problem which plagues all work at very high pressures in some degree. Bridgman and Šimon[9] found greater compactions at a mean stress rate 45 kbar/sec than at 2 kbar/sec, their usual rate of compression. They considered it might have been caused by an adiabatic increase in temperature; this reviewer would attribute a greater effect to a different stress distribution in the rapid compression.

The Work of Bridgman and Šimon

As pointed out above, the compactions reported by Bridgman and Šimon do not correspond to pressures given in their graphs. The differences in the behavior of their several glasses and of silica at two temperatures correspond to a combination of two factors- an actual difference in compaction for a given pressure, and a difference in pressure distribution resulting from differences in lateral flow. Thus a glass which compacted more readily (less work hardening) might show a greater compaction because it compacted more readily; but, in addition, a greater pressure might be achieved in the central area of the disc because of a more uniform pressure distribution; and the compaction would correspond to a higher pressure. Thus their experiments should give the qualitative effect correctly, though exaggerated quantitatively. They found little central compaction for vitreous silica below a mean stress of 100 kbar. Compaction (per cent volume change) rose gradually at first, and then steeply, to reach a value near 6% at a mean stress of 200 kbar, although fragments (presumably peripheral) with compactions as high as 15% were observed (17.5% density increase). For Vycor, a glass containing $\sim 3\%$ boron and $\sim 1\%$ other oxides, central compaction was observed at a mean stress of 80 kbar. For sodium silicate glasses: at 10% Na_2O, central compaction began at a mean stress 25 kbar, rising to 7.7% by a mean stress of 125 kbar. For larger Na_2O concentration (23 and 31% were investigated), compaction was not noted until somewhat higher mean stress; and compaction achieved was much less: e.g., at 31% Na_2O, 1% at a mean stress of 150 kbar, and the lateral flow is stated as very great. It is thus evident that initially, breaking up the network makes compaction more easily achieved. With increased cation content, the recovered glass was of much lower compaction. Because complications may be intruding here, discussion is deferred (see page 60). A single experiment at 150°C gave 6% compaction at 170 kbar, considerably greater than their data for room temperature, indicating increased compaction at higher temperature. The compression assembly was massive, and the time required to raise and lower the temperature must have been considerable compared to the time required to raise and lower the pressure. There is no statement about how their 150°C experiment was performed, and it will be seen, the details are important.

Bridgman had noted previously[157] that crown glass became anisotropic on compression as shown by its refractive indexes. Bridgman and Šimon[9] found a distinct uniaxial anisotropy in the x-ray diffraction patterns, still those of vitreous materials. It would be desirable to have a comparison for the behavior of the several glasses because special effects have been observed for multicomponent glasses, but they did not give any. They gave a detailed description only for Vycor glass. They state the decrease in average interatomic spacing takes place predominantly along the direction of applied pressure. However, the work of Cohen and Roy[153] would indicate the source of the birefringence and the x-ray effect may not be the same, and this is discussed below (see page 52). For a specimen of their Vycor glass, Bridgman and Šimon found a thickness reduction of 7.6% for a compaction of 6.4%. The lateral expansion (flow) is not stated. The x-ray evidence, it is stated, does not indicate a shortened Si–O bond length; more likely a change in Si–O–Si bond angle. More detailed x-ray diffraction information was later obtained by Šimon[163,164] when he investigated the radiation compaction found on pile exposure and compared it with the pressure compaction. He confirmed the virtual constancy of the Si–O distance and the decrease in Si–Si distance. Infra-red absorption data were not given in the original paper but were given subsequently.[166] Measurements in the infra-red must be corrected for change in index of refraction,[165,167] and this entails measurements at oblique incidence, difficult for a fragmented specimen. Although these determinations could not be made as precisely as they were for the pile-exposed vitreous silica later, the results were sufficient to confirm a change in the Si–O–Si configuration as indicated in the 9.09 μ band. Bridgman and Šimon[9] found no appreciable self-annealing (i.e., annealing at room temperature) of compaction in vitreous silica (it was observed in compacted vitreous B_2O_3). A specimen of vitreous silica compacted 14.9% after heating for 1 hr at 430°C showed a compaction of 7.3%.

CORRECT PRESSURES

There have been several attempts besides that of Christiansen, Kistler, and Gogarty's[159] to obtain realistic determinations of the pressure associated with the compaction. Earlier, as mentioned above, Bridgman himself[161] attempted the use of pipestone confinement with lead transmitting medium (the technique adopted by Christiansen, Kistler, and Gogarty). Unfortunately the glass studied was a soda lime glass, and its behavior is not sufficiently well known. In the high pressure range, Cohen and Roy[168,170] used powder techniques perfected by Dachille and Roy,[171] and Mackenzie[160,172,173] studied the effect in a belt type press. In the lower pressure region, Cohen and Roy[174] used hydrostatic gas pressure, and Mackenzie[160] used oil pressure. The powder technique used by Cohen and Roy[168] had been used by Dachille and Roy[171] for phase transition work; and this work was so abundant, their pressures must be among the best established for this pressure range. Cohen and Roy[150,168,170] measured the refractive index and used it to gauge the compaction. The density was difficult to measure because of the small grain size;[174] it was later accomplished by using density liquids in the centrifuge. They give a curve of refractive index *vs.* density.[177] They also[174,152] give the molar refractivity for one determination, and the result agrees with those of Mackenzie[160] who published results for both density and refractive index measurements.

BOROSILICATE EFFECT

Before confirmation that the refractive index could be used to gauge compaction of vitreous silica, Weir and Spinner[178] criticized Cohen and Roy's[168] work on the basis of results obtained by Weir, Spinner, Malitsen, and Rodney,[179] following earlier work by Anderson,[30] on the behavior of borosilicate crown glass at 9 kbar. They found a refractive index change which recovered in 12 hr. Changes in density were too small to be determined accurately, but appeared to be much lower than expected for such a refractive index change, indicating an anomalously large change in refractivity. No effect was found in vitreous silica. Since the glass contained 8% Na_2O and 12% K_2O in addition to 12% B_2O_3, whether to correlate the effect with the alkali addition or the boron or both, is problematical at this time, for both resulted in softening and both gave evidence of transient behavior in Bridgman and Šimon's study. However, the existence of the borate anomaly in glasses makes the boron a likely candidate for contributing a peculiar refractive index effect. Since no evidence for the effect has been reported in vitreous silica, we leave this subject with the comment that it deserves further investigation.

TRANSFORMATION

Dachille and Roy[171] found rather rapid transformation to quartz or coesite at pressures 25–40 kbar and temperatures $\sim 500°C$. Cohen and Roy[151] found that the rapid transformation was caused by traces of moisture in the powders. If the powder was carefully dried, transformation hardly occurred even at the limit of their apparatus, 80 kbar at 700°C. The subject has been investigated further by Uhlmann, Hays, and Turnbull[154] who confirmed these findings and found that shear did not accelerate the transformation. Mackenzie[160] found that transformation occurred in 2 min at either 85 kbar, 600°C or 60 kbar, 750°C. The material used was G. E. laboratory quartz rod, hand-drawn in a flame to 2 mm diameter, cut to 2 mm length, and wrapped in 1 mil platinum foil. It would appear that moisture or mineralizer content was greater in Mackenzie's than in Cohen and Roy's[151] vitreous silica.

EFFECT OF NON-HYDROSTATIC STRESS

If the volume changes reported by Bridgman[114-116] are reasonably correct [non-uniform stress distributions and prior compaction discussed above (see page 44), if anything, should have resulted in low values], the volume decrease $(-\Delta V/V)$ at pressure is over 20% by 100 kbar; i.e., a density increase $(\Delta \varrho/\varrho)$ of over 25%. The density has become 2.75 g/cm³, a value which should be compared to quartz 2.65 and coesite 3.01. This density is greater than for random packing of tetrahedral configurations, as determined by Cohen and Roy,[176] with the normal Si–O distance 1.62 Å, but it has been pointed out above (see pages 27, 29) that under compression the normal Si–O atmospheric distance is not maintained; it is decreased as shown by the change in polarizability. At what kind of volume changes does compaction ensue? The original data of Bridgman and Šimon,[9] it was pointed out above, cannot be used for this purpose. The compaction obtained by Cohen and Roy[168] for powders begins at a nominal value of 20 kbar at room temperature, much lower than found by Christiansen, Kistler, and Gogarty,[159] but both sets of data seem alike by about 80 kbar. Mackenzie[160] could not attain measurable compaction using cylinders 2 mm diameter × 2 mm long at room temperature with silver chloride as a pressure transmitting medium in a belt press limited to 80 kbar, and his data are for temperatures 200 to 575°C. Cohen and Roy's[168] compactions for 40 kbar, given as a function of temperature, are very much higher than his. He states the specimens were recovered whole and with few cracks, and that there was little variation in density between the whole piece and after powdering. Similar results were obtained using either isopentane or silicone oil as the pressure transmitting medium. On the other hand, when alumina powder was used to transmit pressure, much higher compactions were attained, and the density was not uniform. Mackenzie[160] concluded that shear was an important component in causing the large compaction observed by Cohen and Roy. In his experiment using silver chloride, an attempt was made to measure rate of compaction, but this was done only for periods from a few minutes to one hour duration. A small increase in compaction was seen, but Mackenzie was not certain that temperature and pressure remained sufficiently constant; and it should be noted that $1\frac{1}{2}$ decades of time is hardly long enough to study a reaction which may show a logarithmic dependence on time. Although external shear would be high in Cohen and Roy's work, high local pressures would also be established during loading the powder. In Mackenzie's alumina packed cell, stress would not be uniform, hence there would be high local pressure. In the uniformly loaded cell, the press may be supported by reversible hardening of the specimen. Thus it is not yet established what may be the contribution of local high pressure and high pressures resulting from im-

4*

pulsive forces developing on fracture, both arising from non-uniform loading and from macroscopic shear stresses; and what may be the contribution of microscopic shear as concluded by Mackenzie. All that can be concluded now is that conditions which result in non-uniform loading, fracture, or shear can result in large, non-uniform compactions at lower mean stress on the cell. The experiments have been conducted for only times of the order of magnitude of minutes or a few hours, hence the question of whether shear increases the compaction or accelerates it is not firmly settled either; experiments of the duration of several months should be performed.

PERIPHERAL HARDENING

The role of hardening in the compaction is not clear at the present time. Specimens compacted by Wentorf at room temperature for Keiffer[122] were fairly large cylinders about 5 mm diam by 5 mm high. Compaction was found to have occurred largely in a peripheral zone.[181] Later, similar cylinders were compressed at 40 kbar and 400°C by Hoekstra in a tetrahedral press for Primak and Kampwirth. Again, compaction was found largely in a peripheral zone.[181] Thus, temperature was not the critical feature in the surface compaction. However, the specimens were much larger than those used by other investigators. They were also of a purer and more homogeneous grade of vitreous silica.

BIREFRINGENCE

The question of the nature of the birefringence of vitreous silica compacted in the uniaxial press was resolved by Cohen and Roy[153] by the simple expedient of crushing the birefringent grains. They found that the birefringence vanished. It is concluded that the birefringence was anomalous rather than intrinsic and was associated with non-uniformity of compaction rather than with the formation of a uniaxial solid.

EFFECT OF HEATING AFTER PRESSURE RELEASE

Szymanski and his co-workers[182] found that vitreous silica which was compacted at room temperature annealed between 200 and 700°C and followed kinetics similar to that investigated earlier by Primak and Szymanski[183] for the annealing of the radiation compacted vitreous silica, except that the frequency factor and activation energies were lower. Mackenzie[172] found similar behavior for vitreous silica compacted at higher temperature and quenched at pressure. Some annealing occurred at temperatures as low as 200°C even though this was much below the temperature of compaction (500°C).

However, the data which are reported are insufficient to establish a relationship between the temperature of compaction and the annealing.

Cohen and Roy who released pressure and then cooled their samples did not observe annealing below the compaction temperature. From the data, themselves, it is not clear whether Mackenzie induced additional compaction which annealed at low temperature, or whether Cohen and Roy annealed compaction on pressure release. However, from our understanding of the process, it would seem that Mackenzie's interpretation that the latter was the case must be nearly if not absolutely correct; that little additional compaction is introduced on cooling. Since greater compactions are found at higher temperatures, it may be concluded that no additional compaction would be introduced on quenching; and this may be the case in a truly hydrostatic environment, but it may not be the case in practice because load may be redistributed on quenching. However, this last effect should usually be a small one.

Devitrification on Annealing

Mackenzie's specimens became cloudy after heating for several hundred hours at 500° or at 700°C and gave cristobalite x-ray diffraction patterns.[172] His was an impure vitreous silica, and the surface contamination is not stated. However, this was a very low temperature for devitrification at atmospheric pressure. The devitrification of pressure compacted vitreous should be studied further.

High Temperature Compaction

Mackenzie[173] found that vitreous silica compacted at 1600 or 2000°C at 15 kbar did not show annealing below 700°C. He attributed this to compaction in the non-rigid state. However, it is not known how non-rigid vitreous silica is at that pressure. Mackenzie assumed the glass transition temperature to be 1200°C for vitreous silica; and in the absence of experimental data, he estimated the increase with pressure from relations established for other glasses as 40°/kbar or equivalent to that associated with about 600° temperature change. However, vitreous silica may be anomalous here as it is in some other regards. Nor can we depend on the pressure having been maintained on the vitreous silica during the whole of quenching, even though load was maintained on the cell. Extrapolation of Cohen and Roy's data[168] from 600°C through the data reported by Mackenzie at the high temperature gives the curve shown in Fig. 6 which is not unreasonable, but some intermediate points would be very desirable.

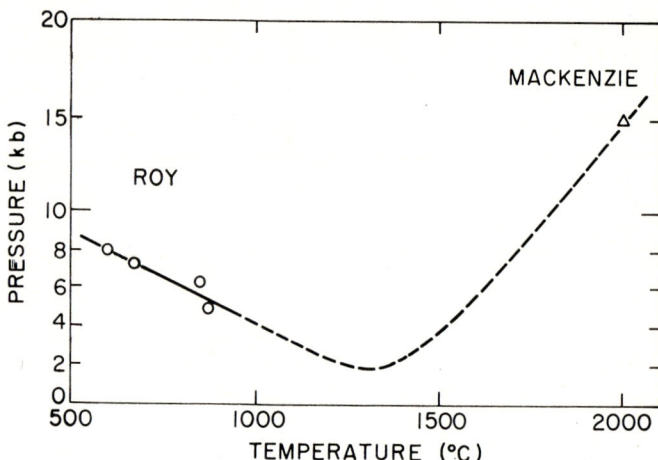

Figure 6.   The static pressure required to cause a 2.7–2.9% compaction of vitreous silica as calculated from data given by Cohen and Roy[168] and Mackenzie.[173]

KINETICS OF COMPACTION

The fact that at the same pressure, greater compaction is attained in a given length of time at higher temperature implies kinetics: i.e., rate phenomena. Cohen and Roy sought evidence for such phenomena. They reported first[169] that they found no evidence of further change after $\frac{1}{2}$ to 1 min loading. Later they reported[175] data which gives some evidence of change with time, but the data are inadequate to provide evidence for the nature of the kinetics. It is reasonable to assume that the kinetics of compaction are similar to the kinetics of annealing compaction; i.e., it occurs on a nearly logarithmic time scale. Since the loading time, even for simple presses, is of the order of magnitude of minutes, valid kinetic experiments would necessarily be of long duration; they must be conducted over decades of time. One of Cohen and Roy's experiments was at 40 kbar and 25°C, with adequate time intervals, 15 sec, 22 hr, and 5 days; but the quantity measured, refractive index to ±0.006, was too imprecise for such an experiment. Further data reported for 30 kbar and 600°C for 15 sec, 2 min, 6 min, and 50 min, covers too short an interval; and although progressive change was reported, from 1.475 to 1.482, this is within the precision of the determinations. Mackenzie's criticism[172] that Cohen and Roy's compaction had partially annealed does not apply to these observations because the specimens were quenched before release of loading. While the specimens could be brought to temperature before loading, and loading could be performed in a relatively short time without sample destruction at the higher temperatures, the mass of the anvils places a limit on the time of quenching. Mackenzie[60] considers the problem of adiabatic heating in rapid loading. These factors place limits on the shortest possible time of observation. With the uniaxial press, problems arise also for long time observations because the load distribution alters with time in such a way that at some point in the loading a maximum pressure is attained on the specimen, and then it decreases as further flow occurs. Mackenzie[160] reports data showing compaction altering with time for short periods, but he was uncertain about constancy of pressure and temperature. The problem of friction and extrusion exists for belt presses also. There is thus a question whether suitable data can be obtained in presently available equipment. From Mackenzie's data it would appear that to obtain satisfactory kinetic data over the range of temperatures 200–500°C and pressures 40–80 kbar, temperature would have to be controlled to 1 °C and specimen pressure to $\frac{1}{4}$ kbar.

HYPOTHESIS ABOUT COMPACTION

What may be the nature of the transformation which occurs during compaction? Vitreous silica was presented above (see pages 26, 27) as a strained network in which stress was balanced. If a homogeneous compression were to occur, the balance would not alter. However, it was shown above (see pages 26, 29, 30) that this does not occur. During the compression, the Si–O tetrahedra twist with respect to each other and thus alter their relative configurations; and, consequently, the distribution of stress in the network is altered. Because of the disorder, induced strain is not locally isotropic; it is isotropic only when taken over many strands in the network. Thus, if the external stress is not isotropic, the induced strain in the network would be anisotropic to establish the new balance of stress. It was shown above (see page 43) that much of the induced strain in the network appears to be completely reversible; the bonds unbend and the tetrahedra untwist on releasing external stress. However, if the stress is great enough, or if the temperature is raised, a higher density persists. There have been no attempts to formulate a realistic atomic hypothesis for the transformation. From the behavior of the Si–O network described above, the following possibilities are considered:

(1) A small portion of the material, several neighboring segments of the network, are deformed by the Si–O bonds bending and the tetrahedra twisting with respect to each other to a point where an alternative configuration which is less badly strained under pressure results. This would be like a local inversion. Such a transformation would be very rapid once the required static conditions were met. The product need not readily invert on release of pressure since, even in the much more regular cristobalite, there is a large thermal hysteresis, 50°C or greater; the hysteresis could be very much

greater for a small region in vitreous silica where a new balance of stress would tend to support the new configuration.

(2)   Bond cleavage occurs and permits a segment of the network to alter its configuration. Since the segment of the network is still tied into a three dimensional configuration, the process is not very different from (1) except in the vicinity of the cleaved bond, and a smaller portion of the network may be involved. It was pointed out above (see page 43) that the continuous segments of the network are quite short because of abundant interruption by impurities. These would be prime locations for bond cleavage. Such processes would be thermally activated.

Bridgman and Šimon's[9] hypothesis of an infolding of a portion of the intact network is rejected for the reasons given above (see page 51); namely, that there is virtually a complete collapse of the largest void space by 80–100 kbar; yet at room temperature, in a relatively hydrostatic application of stress, there is virtually complete reversibility of the compression. The important point about the compaction is that the amount of compaction attained is always less than the volume decrease under pressure. It was shown above (see page 29) that a portion of the volume decrease on compression is caused by compression of the ions themselves; but, the reversible decrease in volume on compression, some 30%, requires that practically all the infolding possible has already occurred. Something else is required to give the irreversible component: the compaction which remains when external stress is released. This must be some gross movement of Si–O tetrahedra to attain a new configuration of balanced stress in the network.

Now consider the possibility (1) above. The change in the inversion may be of the order of magnitude of 10°/kbar; hence, at the pressures of interest, it may be in the hundreds of degrees. The compaction involves formation of a more dense phase; i.e., the low temperature form. Yet in the compaction, raising the temperature causes an increase in compaction. Thus it does not appear that spontaneous inversion can be the primary process in the compaction. The primary process would seem to be the possibility (2) involving bond cleavage. Then, following bond cleavage, the configuration of a small segment or of several adjacent segments may alter. Some of the latter events may be reminiscent of an inversion, but the primary process is considered to be the movement about a ruptured bond in the network.

EFFECT OF FLOW

Differential flow in a 3-dimensional network requires bond cleavage. Thus, it may be possible to facilitate mechanically, compaction requiring a higher temperature when secured by thermal means alone. In colloquial parlance, differential flow is sometimes referred to as shear. It is clear that the contribution of such a process to the compaction would not be through the stresses involved but, rather, by the bond cleavage during differential flow. Mackenzie[160] did not clearly describe what process he had in mind when he suggested shear may be an important factor in compaction.

STRUCTURAL DISORDERING

It has been assumed by some that the increased density of the compacted state of vitreous silica implies greater structural order. The direct evidence of x-ray diffraction is that the dispersion of bond distances is increased, which *a priori* would indicate greater disorder. However, the experimental result is from the work of Bridgman and Šimon,[9] and the evidence from the birefringence which they reported is that their material was quite inhomogeneously compacted. Thus, on closer examination, the question arises, whether the observed greater dispersion was representative of a true local condition or whether it was caused by macroscopic inhomogeneity, a mixture of variously compacted vitreous silica having been exposed to the x-ray beam. Thus additional x-ray work, preferably on material separated according to density, would be desirable. However, homogeneous compaction has been achieved by irradiation, and a greater dispersion of bond distances than in vitreous silica was found there. This evidence will be presented below (see page 90). It is safe to say that the network in the compacted vitreous silica is more disordered than in vitreous silica from a structural point of view. However, the oxygen atoms must be more uniformly spaced in the compacted material. This matter will be discussed further in connection with the thermal, shock, and radiation compaction (see pages 124, 155).

SURFACE COMPACTION

The mechanism of the surface compaction observed in large specimens is yet a matter of conjecture. It is completely illogical that the compacted periphery should occupy a greater volume, thereby supporting the interior and preventing it from becoming compacted. It was pointed out above that the reversible volume change far exceeds the compaction. It now seems reasonable to suggest that the load is largely supported by the reversible volume change and that compaction is facilitated peripherally by macroscopic flow. The mechanism of flow may be non-uniform contact with the granular pressure-transmitting medium. On this basis, the flow and surface compaction would be associated with high local stresses accompanying non-uniform surface loading.

ANNEALING OF COMPACTION

The compacted state is not stable at room temperature. From the kinetics determined by Szymanski and his co-workers[182] and the calculations made by Keiffer,[122] that the frequency factor is low, perhaps 10^5–10^6/sec, the observation of annealing below 200°C can be accounted for by room temperature annealing of several weeks or more according to the theory of processes distributed in activation energy.[184] Low temperature (200°C or less) annealing was found by Mackenzie even for specimens compacted at 500°C; but, as mentioned above, the interpretation is not clear; and now, also for the additional reason, that during the compressions, heatings were for so short a time that the specimens can hardly be considered to have stabilized at the elevated temperature. Thus, the quantitative relations between annealing and the conditions of compaction remain to be established. However, some of the qualitative observations will prove useful in considering the radiation compaction.

There is evidence for more than one class of processes in the thermal annealing. The low temperature thermal annealing appears to occur with a low frequency factor and would thus seem to be associated with the rearrangement of segments of the network. It appears from the work of Szymanski et al.,[182] that all of the room temperature compaction anneals in this manner. When compaction is performed at higher temperature, a portion of the compaction anneals in the 700–1000°C range, but the kinetics have not been investigated. If we assume the kinetics is similar to that found for the radiation compaction which anneals in this temperature range,[185] the processes would be of high frequency factor, probably controlled by a bond cleavage mechanism, the temperature being high enough to permit movement of network segments as soon as they are freed. This would imply that bonds cleaved during compaction re-form in the compacted configuration, a reasonable event on the basis of the hypothesis proposed here; because impurity bonds, the ones which it was suggested were mainly involved (see page 56), would have more electrostatic character than Si–O bonds, and their cleavage represents little more than forming an excited state. Support for the hypothesis appears in the radiation behavior of compacted vitreous silica (see page 96), and evidence for the nature of the alteration in the balance of stress during compaction appears also (see page 146). Further discussion of these topics is deferred to the discussion of the radiation behavior.

When the compacted vitreous silica is annealed, the density attained is closely that of ordinary vitreous silica. For each of the modes of compaction, the question will arise whether the annealed material is the same as the original. While we may conceive conditions under which it may be, particularly if the compaction were slight; in general, the annealed material would not be structurally identical. This would be clear had some gross change like devitrification occurred; but even in the absence of such gross change, any small amount of flow during compaction would preclude restoration of the identical original structure. It is interesting that a statistically equivalent state is reached;—that an equilibrium state of stress, though surely arrived at in ways different in structural detail, gives the same density. Direct observation of change in structural detail for compaction followed by annealing has not been reported for pressure-compacted vitreous silica. It is suggested that such evidence might be obtained by studying alterations in original inhomogeneity by optical or electrical measurements when specimens are compacted and annealed.

PRIMAK'S FORMALISM

To make order of magnitude estimates of the number of events associated with compaction, Primak, Edwards, Szymanski, and Keiffer[124] used the ionic oxygen volume as a unit of compaction. This is based on the concept of the collapse of Si–O tetrahedra into the void space of the network, an idea similar to that suggested by Bridgman and Šimon.[9] Although the mechanism for the change is quite different, as pointed out here, and involves a much more comfortable alteration in the network, the structural changes are not very different than they would be had an infolding taken place. The formalism of Primak, et al., would thus give the order of magnitude estimates they sought. Since there may be ~15 oxygens, on the average, surrounding a void space, a region which will be referred to as a cell, an 18% compaction corresponds to ~2 ionic oxygen volumes/cell. This does not correspond to the maximum packing of oxygen: even in quartz there remains a void space ~2 ionic oxygen volumes cell. However, the packing achieved is not very different from that of random packing of tetrahedra.[176] The subject is referred to only in passing here, because in pressure compaction and in the annealing of the product, individual events are not counted. The formalism will be discussed further when considering the radiation effects (see page 94). There, counting of individual events does have significance.

WORK TO BE DONE

From this summary, it would seem that the most valuable work which could be done on the compaction now, would be to explore the role of the impurities in the Si–O network. In this connection, it should be noted that all of the work heretofore has been with very impure materials. The qualitative effect of large quantities of impurity was indicated by Bridgman and Šimon's work.[9] When the impurity concentration was increased (i.e., the network segments were shortened), compaction at first became easier; but then, at higher impurity concentration, the compaction observed was small. It is suggested here, that in addition to the effect of loading the void space, there is the effect of the segments of Si–O tetrahedra becoming so short that their motility becomes too great to retain a compacted configuration on release of pressure; i.e., spontaneous annealing is very great at room temperature. Quantitative kinetic studies of the compaction would be of interest, but the experimental difficulties seem too great at present. Systematic annealing studies of the kind which were made for the radiation-compacted vitreous silica[183,185] could be made quite easily and would be very valuable.

IV. Thermal Compaction of Vitreous Silica

INTRODUCTION

The literature on the thermal compaction of vitreous silica is brief, consisting of a single detailed investigation, Douglas and Isard's.[149] Related work is that by Brückner[186] who studied thermal expansion of quenched vitreous silica. Fraser[187,188]* reported some results verbally at the 1966 Ultrasonics Symposium in Cleveland. The term, quenched vitreous silica, will be used to describe the material obtained by cooling rapidly from high temperature.

Douglas and Isard's investigation of the thermal behavior of vitreous silica stemmed from their interest in the transformation temperature of glasses. It was pointed out above that the transformation behavior of the multicomponent glasses is largely associated with the non-network cations (see page 2). The phenomena in vitreous silica must be of quite different origin. The interpretation given here will accord with our present hypothesis rather than with suggestions made in the articles from which the data are taken. It should be remembered that these writers were not familiar with the concept of a thermal compaction.

THERMAL COMPACTION PROCEDURE AND RESULTS

Douglas and Isard studied clear vitreous silica rods. For density studies, specimens were drawn in a flame to pear shapes ending in small hooks. It is assumed that their work was with a laboratory grade material made from natural quartz, hence of Class I above (see pages 35, 36). They determined density at room temperature after heating for various times. The times reported for reaching "equilibrium" density at various temperatures were: 903°C, > 500 hr, probably ~ 10,000 hr; 993°, 600 hr; 1080°, 40 hr; 1300°, a few sec. Accordingly, at temperatures below 1400°C, air cooling was adequate, but at 1400 and 1500°C they resorted to dropping specimens into cold water. Above 1500°C they were unable to quench sufficiently rapidly. Above 1300°C surface devitrification was noted, and it was either scraped away or dissolved with hydrofluoric acid. Their results are given in Fig. 7. Several of

---

* The important results by Fraser[156] appeared after this monograph had been written.

Fraser's[188,189] results are also included in this figure. It was pointed out above that Hetherington, Jack, and Kennedy[138] found longer times were required to establish a constant rate of viscous flow (see pages 41–42). This is further discussed in Section X (see page 156).

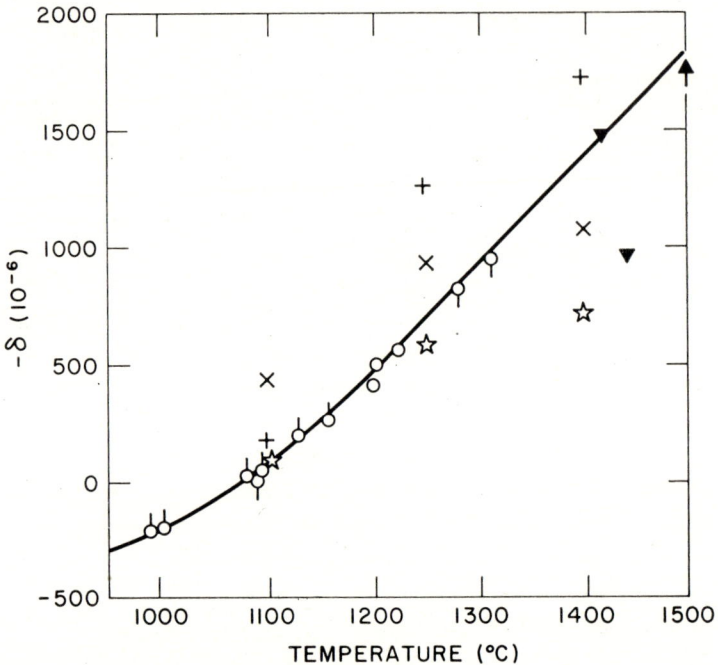

Figure 7.   Thermal compaction of vitreous silica according to Douglas and Isard[149] (circles, cooled; inverted triangles or nablas, air quenched; triangle or delta, water quenched) and Fraser[188,189] (stars, Corning 7940; x's, low OH Suprasil; crosses, Vitreosil).

THERMAL EXPANSION

The differences between the thermal expansion (not the coefficient of) of quenched long vitreous silica rods and vitreous silica heat treated at 990°C were determined with the aid of an optical lever arrangement. The mean thermal expansion for all of the quenched specimens was greater. The difference was quite constant up to 200°C and then increased linearly, indicating an increased coefficient of expansion. That this change is noted at 200°C is reminiscent of the annealing behavior of pressure compacted vitreous silica, a matter which is discussed further below (see page 135). Douglas and Isard did not give absolute values for the expansion of annealed vitreous silica. The changes caused by quenching are large compared to the thermal expansion data. For the quenching temperatures 1100, 1200, 1290, 1300, and 1480°C, the respective changes in the mean coefficient of linear expansion between 400°C and 800°C were 0.075, 0.13, 0.17, 0.16, and 0.25, all $\times 10^{-6}$, compared to the value 0.55×10^{-6} Sosman[1] gives for the mean coefficient of expansion.

Anomalous Volume Relaxation

Although the work of Douglas and Isard was very careful, and it is hard to understand how they could have fallen into such a trap, it appears from the work of Brückner,[186] that some annealing of compaction may take place between 200 and 400°C, an effect he called an "anomalous volume relaxation". Thus some of the excess expansion reported by Douglas and Isard may have stemmed from this; it is discussed further below (see page 65).

Effect of Impurity

Fraser[187-189] showed the thermal compaction to be quite different for different grades of vitreous silica. The compaction which he got, increased for the order: Low OH-Suprasil, Corning 7940, and IR Vitreosil; but it is not known whether this represents a steady state or a rate effect. It is certain that at least some of the material used by Brückner (one specimen was reported as being Homosil) was different from the material used by Douglas and Isard.

Low Temperature Thermal Expansion

The magnitude of change in expansion reported by Brückner was about the same as that reported by Douglas and Isard. However, in addition to changes in the room temperature and the high temperature thermal expansion, he also found changes in the low temperature thermal expansion—the anomalous expansion at $-100°C$ [by anomalous behavior here is meant a negative thermal expansion; (see pages 24 *et seq.*)—the anomalous low temperature thermal expansion was greater (i.e., its negative value decreased in magnitude). Thus, the minimum of the anomalous low temperature thermal expansion occurs at a higher temperature for the thermally compacted vitreous silica. This decrease in anomalous behavior appears to be typical of compaction, and it will be discussed in greater detail for the radiation compaction for which more detailed studies have been made (see page 127).

Density at Temperature

Douglas and Isard used their thermal expansion data to calculate the density of the vitreous silica at temperature. It is clear that if their thermal expansion included an element of annealing, the density calculated at temperature would be low, though how low, it is difficult to guess. The following are examples of the magnitude of the effect of quenching. Upon quenching from 1000–1150°C, the compaction is nil; and the density at temperature is about 0.13 % lower than for unquenched material at room temperature. For quenching from 1480°C, compaction is 0.14 %; and density at temperature is 0.073 % lower than for unquenched material at room temperature. Thus, according to them, the density at temperature is less than at room temperature although it is greater the higher the temperature; i.e., the "equilibrium" density shows a high temperature minimum.

The existence of a kinetics of thermal compaction is well proven by the experiments of Douglas and Isard. There is no reason to believe that this kinetics will be different from that found in other investigations of vitreous silica; i.e., the time scale should be logarithmic. Since their data is given only in small graphs, it is difficult to test this hypothesis. Only one set of data, that at 993°C covers a reasonably long period of time, some 3 decades. When this data is replotted against *log* time, it is found to be quite linear as shown in Fig. 8. Thus, the approach to an equilibrium state would be difficult to follow by studying the behavior of a single specimen. However, Douglas and Isard performed experiments with specimens subjected to prior heat treatments both above and below the final temperature studied and found that both sets approached the same density. At 1080°C about 40 hr were required.

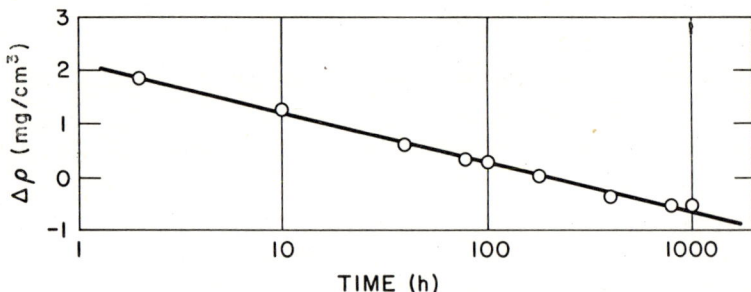

Figure 8. Change in the density of Douglas and Isard's vitreous silica when it was heated at 993°C. Data taken from their[149] Fig. 1(d) replotted on a logarithmic scale.

MECHANISM

Thermal compaction begins at a temperature where static rigidity is falling but dynamic rigidity is still rising, and indicates that bond cleavage and reconstitution are active. The kind of rearrangement which occurs during compaction, as noted above in discussing the pressure compaction (see page 51), one which results in a greater dispersion of bond angles and distances for other than the first Si–O ones, is indicative of the dynamics of the processes leading to thermal compaction. The increased amplitude of thermal oscillation is preferentially accommodated in the void space of the structure, a mechanism which must be similar to that described above for the α–β-inversions, and there results a partially compensating twisting reorientation of Si–O tetrahedra. As pointed out above for the pressure compaction (see page 55), such a reorientation in vitreous silica may be difficult without bond cleavage because of the random network. If such a twisting reorientation of Si–O tetrahedra did not occur, no compaction could be quenched in. When the temperature is raised above 1400°C, as evidenced by the onset of rapid devitrification, the network must be greatly fragmented, and mobility must soon become too great to permit the state to be quenched. As shown by Douglas and Isard, at high temperature, the vitreous silica has a lower density than it does at room temperature; but the density is higher than it would be had compaction not occurred. It is when the compacted state cools that the density becomes greater than the density of uncompacted material at room temperature. While this appears to be a correct qualitative description of the relative density of the compacted and annealed material, the quantitative description by Douglas and Isard may be in error if volume relaxation effects did occur during their thermal expansion measurements.

STATUS

The mechanism for the thermal compaction which has been proposed here, indicates impurities may play a very important role in thermal compaction, affecting both the kinetic behavior and the final state of compaction attained. Currently, it is the most important area of investigation for the thermal compaction.

The high temperature thermal compaction data are also annealing data. The work of Douglas and Isard shows how sluggish change had become when temperature was reduced to 900°C. It thus seems unlikely that change should be observed at much lower temperatures. From this, the "anomalous volume relaxation" of Brückner at 200°C seems surprising and may be other than an annealing of thermal compaction. Perhaps an element of pressure compaction, an impurity effect, or a devitrification was involved; these points should be examined.

It has been definitely established that the thermal expansion of vitreous silica is increased by thermal compaction. The high temperature behavior is the least known; but all of the data are for specimens which are poorly defined. In view of the demonstrated effects of impurity, it would be desirable to have new data which cover the whole range of temperatures for a variety of well-defined specimens.

V. Polishing Compaction and Related Phenomena

INTRODUCTION

In this section there are assembled several curious observations which may involve compaction phenomena. They are items which this writer happened upon over the years. No search was attempted because it would have been most difficult to conduct a search for such miscellaneous observations, most of which would have been interpreted in other ways.

THE POLISHING PROCESS

The mechanism of the grinding and polishing of substances is a highly controversial subject. Some of the confusion has arisen from attempts to generalize behavior found for one material to others, while the data indicate a most diverse behavior. Not only are the individual techniques developed to establish smooth surfaces on different materials different; but, also, the property changes found to accompany the polishing vary greatly. Thus, in some substances, particularly soft metals, microcrystalline layers form;[190] with salts and oxides, some will form amorphous layers, others remain crystalline;[192] in magnesium oxide there develops a layer of increased refractive index[194] which appears to be amorphous by electron diffraction;[195] in metals there is evidence of surface flow.[196] There has been an attempt to correlate this behavior to hardness, for many substances with a hardness 5 (Moh's scale) or below have been observed to lose their Kikuchi line patterns (electron diffraction) on polishing. However, spinel (hardness 8) appears to lose its surface crystallinity, while others, like quartz (hardness 7) and corundum (hardness 9) appear to retain it.

Because of its commercial importance, there have been extensive investigations of the process of polishing glass.[190,196] In ordinary operations in which water slurries are used, it has been found that chemical additives can slow down or speed up polishing, indicating solution or hydrolytic processes are involved. On the other hand, polishing can be accomplished with non-aqueous slurries. Thus, the distinction suggested by Rayleigh[199] and others that the only difference between the lapping process and the polishing process is that in the former the particles of the slurry are free to roll, is not valid. Rabinowicz has pointed out that load is an important factor.[200] The diverse operations actually performed by the optician in his work have rarely been taken into account. One optician will use only very little polishing material on his tool (the pitch or wax upon which the polishing is done), while another will use a great deal. One will take the work off a wet tool, another will let it run dry before removing the work. Some investigators have studied scratches assiduously, but there is no indication of procedures taken to eliminate the major source of these: contamination, often caused by fragments (particularly crumbling at the edges) of the plate which is being polished; hence a secondary rather than a fundamental part of the process. Rabinowicz[200] has studied the relationship of the polishing of a metal to the burnishing process and concluded that in both burnishing and polishing below a critical stress, a removal of material on a molecular scale occurs; but that above a critical stress, the compressional wave caused by a particle of polishing compound is followed by a tensional wave which develops stresses greater than the breaking strength, and a particle of the material breaks away from the surface.

Thus, the processes involved in the grinding or lapping operations and the polishing operations performed on glass involve gouging, scratching, indenting, tensile waves, chemical attack, and molecular removal. Also, evidence of high temperature effects, plastic flow, and melting have been assembled.[191] What exactly occurs in the optical preparation of vitreous silica surfaces is yet to be determined. The polishing is not just a smearing or a plastic flow, for there is a removal of material. While there may be a chemical action, it need not be one of dissolution. Even atmospheric exposure causes a tremendous decrease in the breaking strength of glass.[198,201] Such an alteration of the surface by the polishing medium could facilitate the mechanical action in the polishing process.

SURFACE STRUCTURE

The usual modern tools of structure analysis have not proven useful in studying the polishing of glass or of vitreous silica. The electron microscope pictures of polished surfaces appear little different from those of fracture surfaces.[87]

Etching studies of glass have shown that the pattern of scratches which is obliterated in polishing reappears on etching.[191] Thus, either, scratching the glass causes a change in the etching behavior; or else, the material formed by polishing is different over the grooves that it is over the hillocks. Since these results were obtained for multicomponent glasses, the possibility of chemical differences exists. Since the effects of details in the polishing procedure were not investigated in these studies, many questions remain. This reviewer has not seen similar studies for vitreous silica.

SURFACE REFRACTIVE INDEX

There have been several determinations of the refractive index of glass surfaces. A recent one by Yokota, Kinosita, and Sakata[203] is of special interest here because measurements on optical glass, vitreous silica (grade unspecified), and Vycor are included. The refractive index was calculated from ellipsometric data. For vitreous silica they found the refractive index to be 0.003 to 0.006 greater for a surface layer, its thickness 0.04–0.06 μ, than for the interior, and for Vycor 0.003 to 0.004 greater for the surface; and they attributed the increased refractive index to a surface compaction under polishing stress. They said their results for vitreous silica agreed with those reported by Rayleigh. For several optical glasses they found a reduced refractive index which they attributed to leaching of cations. Their results on the optical glasses were in accord with previous results given by Sissingh and Groosmuller[204] and by Vasicek.[205]

The amount of compaction which would be associated with such a refractive index change would be $\sim 0.7\%$, an appreciable amount and should be visible by other means. Primak[206] found no evidence for such a layer by the dispersed depolarization phenomenon,[207] but the layer may have been too thin to be observed in this manner. A surface transmission experiment[208] may be of interest. Neither was any evidence seen in the polarimeter (birefringence in the body of the material caused by surface stress). However, stress relaxation may occur during polishing, and this would destroy strain birefringence in the body of the plate. However, since Primak's observations were not made for the purpose of detecting a surface compaction, they do not have the force had that been the case.

THE TWYMAN EFFECT

The Twyman Effect is the warping of a plate when one side is polished.[197] To observe it, both sides are first lapped. Then, if one side is polished and figured, the figure will change when the other side is polished. An alternative demonstration is to reverse the operation. Both sides are first polished. Then, if one side is figured, the figure will change if the other side is lapped. The effect has usually been explained as the lapping operation destroying the surface tension. The effect has been observed for both multicomponent glasses and vitreous silica, hence it is not primarily a chemical effect. However, the effect could occur were the polishing operation to compact the surface and were the lapping operation to remove the compacted layer. There are no calculations to determine the plausibility of such an explanation.

SURFACE STRAIN

Lapping with coarse powder and diamond sawing (using saws made of metal with diamond embedded in the edges) increase the birefringence of vitreous silica specimens.[141] It appears possible to remove some of this birefringence by polishing or by etching. Thus the state of stress has developed because of a condition of the surface. If a compaction has occurred, the surface should be in a state of tension. This has not yet been determined. Because the surface layer affected is so thin compared to the body of the material, the surface would be stretched to the dimensions of the underlying material, and thus its density change in this condition would be much less than what it would be, were it detached from the body of the material. However, if its dimensions are known, its dilatation, were it removed from the body of the material, can be calculated.[209] For the case cited by Primak,[141] of a $\frac{5}{8}$ in. slab of vitreous silica which had been very gently sawn and developed an additional 1 mμ of birefringence, if this were caused by compacting 3 μ thick layers on the surfaces, the mean compaction in these layers, were they separated from the body of the material, would be 0.15%; or if they were of the thickness given by Yokota, et al., 0.05 μ, the compaction would be 9%.

STATUS

Whereas in the other cases of compaction, the major present interest is in establishing details of the compaction, here it is yet necessary to establish the existence of a compaction. If the compaction were shown to exist; and, in addition, the annealing and radiation behavior of the compaction could be established, it would be possible to answer some of the important questions about the polishing process for this material: the contributions of flow, heating, and stress.

VI.   Shock Wave Compaction of Vitreous Silica

HISTORICAL INTRODUCTION

The first study of the shock wave compaction of vitreous silica appears to be that by Wackerle[210] and it remains the most extensive. The data published by De Carli and Jamieson[211] on the observation of an amorphous product of density 2.22 g/cm³, higher than that of vitreous silica, resulting from shock compression of quartz might be taken as a prior observation of compacted vitreous silica formed by shock compression, but Wackerle's work indicates further investigation would be needed to confirm their last digit.

Wackerle's study arose from an interest in employing the piezoelectric effect in quartz to measure shock wave pressures,[212] but the scope of his investigation grew far beyond this. Much of the remaining work stemmed from geophysical or geological interests. One was an attempt to study the behavior of minerals at pressures and temperatures corresponding to mantle conditions deep in the earth and other large bodies. The nature of the phases and their behavior is of interest in interpreting seismic phenomena, and the phase changes are of consequence in understanding vulcanism and crustal movements. Another area of interest was the study of meteoritic impact, a subject not only of geological interest, but also of interest in current space exploration.

THE SHOCK WAVE EXPERIMENT

The shock wave experiments are performed by machining explosive to the desired configuration (usually a cylinder for lower pressures, or a suitable lens structure for higher pressures), fastening it to the front face of a driving plate, and fastening the specimen to the back face of the driving plate. A plane parallel wave is desired to permit the calculations to be made. The specimens must be short to avoid having rarifactions generated at the walls overtake the shock front and interfere with it. Optical means, usually high speed photography, are used to follow the progress of the shock wave. Also, the velocity of the driving plate or the velocity of the free specimen surface is determined. The experiment may be performed above a water barrel if fragments of the specimen are desired for further examination. The configuration used by Fowles[213,214] is shown in Fig. 9.

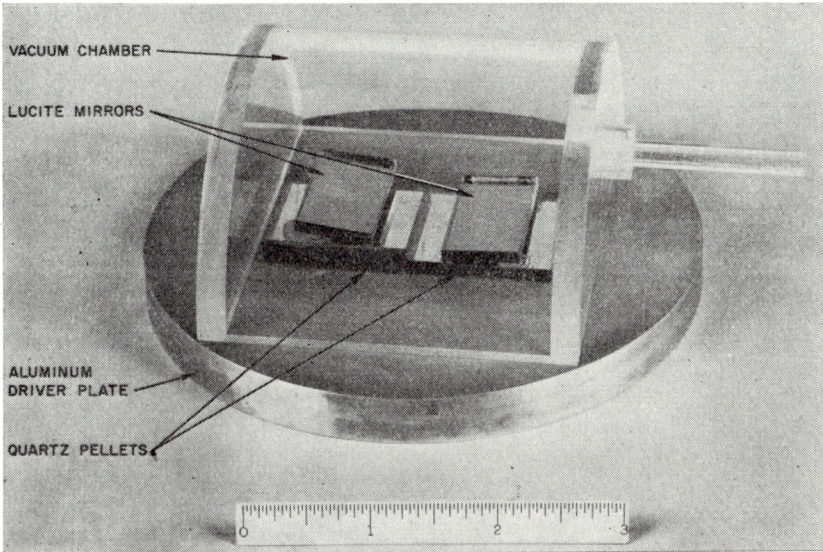

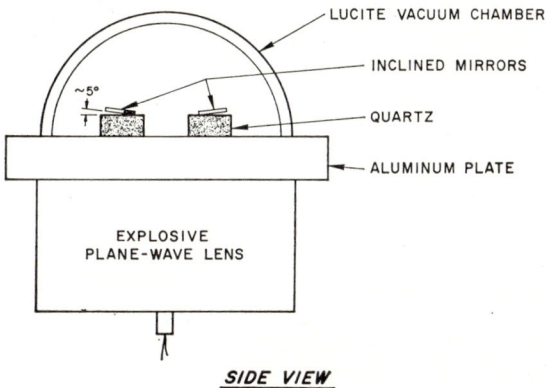

Figure 9. A typical experimental assembly for a shock wave experiment. (From G.R.Fowles[213], Poulter Laboratories, Stanford Research Institute.)

The quantities used to characterize a phase are pressure, volume, and temperature. None can be measured in the shock wave experiments. What can be measured are the wave velocities and the free-surface velocities. The pressure-volume relations involve mass transport. The equations which hold are the Rankine-Hugoniot relations, and the P–V behavior (usually reciprocal volume or density is used) is referred to as the Hugoniot.[213,215] The Hugoniot is steeper than the adiabat (or isentropic behavior) which, in turn, is steeper than the isothermal behavior. To calculate the pressure from the

Rankine-Hugoniot relations, it is necessary to know the particle velocities; but again, these cannot be measured. Two alternatives have been used: to make the calculation by matching impedances of the driving plate and the specimen (which involves assumptions about their elastic behavior) or to use the isentropic approximation (reasonably good for lower pressures where the Hugoniot and adiabat are close to each other) that the particle velocity is half the free surface velocity. In this manner, the pressure is calculated. The volume is determined by following the path of the Hugoniot.

Each shock experiment gives a point on the Hugoniot, and thus a series of shock experiments of different intensities are required to determine the Hugoniot. A cusp in the Hugoniot indicates a departure from elastic behavior, and then calculation of the Hugoniot requires *ad hoc* assumptions which leave this portion of the Hugoniot open to interpretation. If the equation of state were known, the temperature could be calculated. Grüneisen's Law or a modification of it is frequently employed, but since the constants can only be estimated, the temperatures are uncertain, although suggestive. Two temperatures may be calculated: one for the maximum intensity of the shock wave, and the other for the adiabatic temperature after passage of the shock wave. In addition, the recovery products may be examined for quenched states.

It is seen that the phase data obtained from the shock experiment are quite uncertain compared to the data obtained in static experiments. Further, temperatures cannot usually be controlled independently of pressure, for they are determined by the properties of the material. Although they may be altered somewhat by altering the material mechanically or by admixing other materials, this has not usually been attempted. The advantage of the shock method is that higher pressures and temperatures have been attained through its use than have been achieved in static experiments. In the laboratory, control of the duration of the shock wave is limited by the procedure and dimensions of the experiments; the shock produced on meteoritic impact appears to be of longer duration. In the limited control of conditions, in the transient nature of the phenomena, and in the inexactness of the data obtained, the shock experiments are thus intermediate; for in the radiation compactions, in the sequence of events following an individual scattering, conditions are less under control, less certain, and the times much shorter.

RESULTS OF THE SHOCK EXPERIMENTS

De Carli and Jamieson[211] reported an amorphous product of about the density of vitreous silica was recovered from shocked quartz. Wackerle[210] studied the effects of shock waves of different intensities on vitreous silica and on quartz of X, Y, and Z orientations. The Hugoniots are shown in Fig. 10. Contemporary work by Fowles[213,214,216] confirmed the work of Wackerle.

Ahrens and co-workers[217] studied the effect of shock waves on Coconino sandstone, largely a quartz material, in which Meteor Crater (Arizona) occurs. These results also confirmed Wackerle's observations.

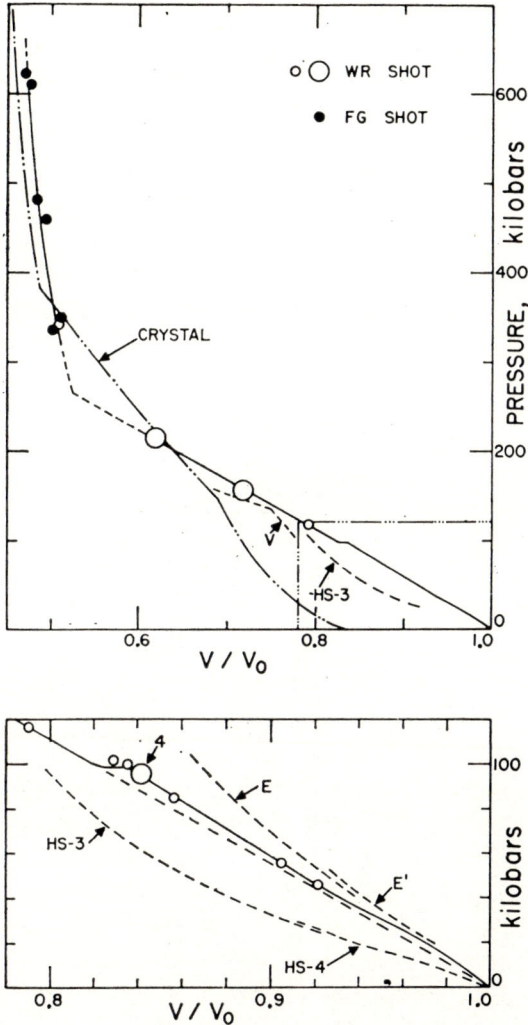

Figure 10. Pressure as a function of relative volume Hugoniot for vitreous silica. The hydrostatic curves, HS-3 and HS-4, are from the literature; and the predicted elastic curve, E, is by transposition of that data. Viard's data is shown by the curve segment labelled "V". The open circles represent data obtained with the wire reflection technique, and the solid dots are for flash-gap shots. (b) is an enlargement of the low pressure region of (a). The large data point labelled "4" represents 4 data points, the double size points are for two data points. (From Wackerle[210]).

Vitreous silica and quartz both show cusps in their Hugoniots at about 100 kbar, terminating a region of elastic behavior. The cusp, in the case of vitreous silica, was first observed by Viard, according to Wackerle. From here to about 380 kbar is a region confused by the appearance of a second wave and its interaction with a rarifaction, and additional assumptions are required to calculate the Hugoniot. It is evident from the Hugoniot in this region, lying below the extension of the Hugoniot from lower pressure, that the shock compressibility has increased. Wackerle refers to this region as one of collapse. Above about 380 kbar the compressibility decreases sharply; and, again, a single shock wave is seen. Wackerle states that it "demonstrates some manner of shock-induced transformation occurs in the material".

Wackerle determined the recovery products from several of his shocks, and the results are given in Table 8. These results indicate that the product from the high pressure region above 380 kbar is vitreous silica; from the intermediate pressure region (100–380 kbar) quartz is obtained from quartz starting material, compacted vitreous silica from the vitreous silica; and in the elastic region, the starting materials. However, it would be of interest to examine carefully material from other parts of the Hugoniot, particularly

TABLE 8　Calculated temperatures and densities resulting from various shock pressures in crystalline quartz and vitreous silica (from Wackerle[210])

Pressure (kbar)	Crystalline quartz					Fused quartz		
	T_H (°C)	T_A (°C)	$T_{H'}$ (°C)	$T_{A'}$ (°C)	$\varrho_H{}^d$ (g/cm³)	T_H (°C)	T_A (°C)	$\varrho_H{}^d$ (g/cm³)
50	36	18	36	18	2.92	1	0	2.40
100	117	81	117	81	3.08	2	0	2.69
144[a]	203	153	203	153	3.18	...	...	...
150	206	156	206	156	3.21	3	0	3.02
200	238	168	238	168	3.43	4	0	3.44
250	282	190	282	190	3.69	5	0	4.02
262[b]	...	...	...	...	...	5	0	4.18
300	336	214	336	214	3.98	495	470	4.27
350	398	248	398	248	4.29	1185	1155	4.36
383[c]	454	282	454	282	4.53	...	...	...
400	640	465	640	610	4.55	1895	1860	4.43
450	1125	780	1115	1080	4.62	2560	2610	4.49
500	1630	1160	1610	1580	4.68	3390	3310	4.55
600	2650	1920	2640	2580	4.77	4890	4790	4.64
700	3665	2670	3655	3580	4.85	...	...	...

[a] Pressure of first break in crystalline quartz equilibrium Hugoniot.
[b] Pressure of break in fused quartz Hugoniot.
[c] Pressure of second break in crystalline quartz Hugoniot.
[d] Evaluated on equilibrium Hugoniots.

near the boundaries of these regions, to look for additional products, the high pressure phases of silica described below, and determine the density of recovered vitreous silica to check the results of De Carli and Jamieson.

The temperatures attained during and just after passage of the shock wave were calculated assuming adiabatic conditions and the Gürneisen Law,

$$\gamma = V\left[(\partial P/\partial E)_V\right] \cong \alpha v_B^2/C_p$$

the last from values at atmospheric pressure. This gave $\gamma = 0.653$ for quartz and 0.036 for vitreous silica. It will be realized these constants must alter greatly on compression, and thus the temperatures he calculates are probably too high and the temperature distribution altered somewhat. However, as is mentioned below, the flow of energy from the heated region is controlled largely by the thermal constants of the surrounding medium rather than the constants within the heated zone, thus causing less of an effect than might be surmised from the altered values of the constants (see pages 128, 150). Wackerle's results are given in Table 8.

HIGH PRESSURE PHASES FROM BLAST CRATERS

Chao, Shoemaker, and Madsen[218] found coesite[219,24] in the impact meta-morphosed Coconino sandstone collected at Meteor Crater, Arizona. Two years later, after Stishov and Papova[220] reported a new high pressure form of silica, Chao, Fahey, Littler, and Milton[221] reported finding this high pressure form in the material collected from Meteor Crater and named it stishovite. The impact metamorphosed Coconino sandstone is a quartz-coesite-amorphous silica (lechatelierite)-stishovite assemblage, mainly quartz, a little coesite and letchatelierite, and much less ($<1\%$) stishovite. Chao, Fahey, and Littler[222] studied material from the Wabar Crater (near Al Hadida, Arabia) and found coesite among hand picked fractured quartz grains. In this crater there is a large amount of black glass (Wabar glass) partly vesicular, partly dense, with inclusions of fractured white sandstone, and about 1% coesite. Lechatelierite is also reported present. The study of the Wabar material was made prior to the discovery of stishovite, and hence no report on stishovite was made. There are no reports of compacted glass in these specimens, but there is no indication of its having been sought.[223]

HIGH PRESSURE CRYSTALLINE PHASES

The phase, coesite, was discovered by Coes;[219,24] and it is readily prepared between 400 and 1700°C with suitable pressure between 25 and 40 kbar. Stishovite was discovered by Stishov and Papova[220] at pressures in excess of 100 kbar and temperature between 1200 and 1400°C. It has been prepared at temperatures as low as 550°C at a pressure of 120 kbar and between 800 and 1250°C at pressures between 80 and 100 kbar. The coesite-stishovite phase boundary has been investigated by Stishov[224] who gives $p = 97500 \pm 5000 + 20.33T$ (bars) and by Ostrovskii[225] who gives $p = 85 + 0.0364T$ (kbar). Other work on the transformation is that by Bell.[226] Stishov and Papova[220] identified the phase by refractive index and density and gave the x-ray diffraction pattern. It was identified as P4/mnm isotypic with rutile by Preisinger[227] and by Chao, et al.[221] Preisinger states the oxygen octahedron is regular with the Si–O distance 1.778 Å; $a = 4.179$, $c = 2.6649$ Å; and the oxygen parameter 0.301. Relative intensities of higher order reflections reported by Chao et al.[221] for stishovite isolated from Meteor Crater are lower than relative intensities reported by Stishov and Papova.[220] Whether the cause was a difference in instrumentation or specimen preparation, or whether the natural material is not as well ordered a crystal structure, is unknown. Sclar, Carrison and Cocks[228] found that the crystal habit of stishovite prepared at 120 kbar was bipyrimidal when prepared below 600 °C, granular when prepared between 600 and 900 °C, and acicular when prepared above 900 °C.

TRANSFORMATION OF THE HIGH PRESSURE PHASES

Stishov and Papova[220] reported that after a long heating at 900 °C stishovite had transformed to cristobalite. Dachille, Zeto, and Roy[229] found that coesite persisted indefinitely at temperatures below 1000 °C, but that stishovite transformed into a vitreous phase within minutes at temperatures above 500–600 °C. Between 1100 and 1350 °C, coesite transformed to quartz, and the quartz then transformed to cristobalite. Skinner and Fahey[230] made an elaborate study of the transformation of stishovite which was separated from the impact metamorphosed Coconino sandstone from Meteor Crater by leaching with aqueous $HF–HNO_3$. The rate of dissolution of the phases of silica is very different, decreasing in the order, vitreous silica, quartz, coesite, stishovite. Fahey[231] describes a procedure for obtaining a nearly pure concentrate (containing about 1.3 wt. % zircon impurity) with about 50% recovery, from the finely powdered starting material. Skinner and Fahey[230] found that the stishovite transformed to vitreous silica on heating. They determined the fraction transformed as a function of time at a number of temperatures by measuring the refractive index of the powder. The kinetics observed in isothermal annealing was nearly with the *log t*, but the authors do not appear to have appreciated the significance of this dependence. Evidence of transformation was seen at a temperature as low as 300 °C; and although completion of the transformation could be observed at 600 °C, it could be studied at temperatures as high as 800 °C. Their data is reproduced in Fig. 11 and shows the typical characteristics of a distribution in activation energy.[184] The writer estimated the frequency factor using the data at 451 °C

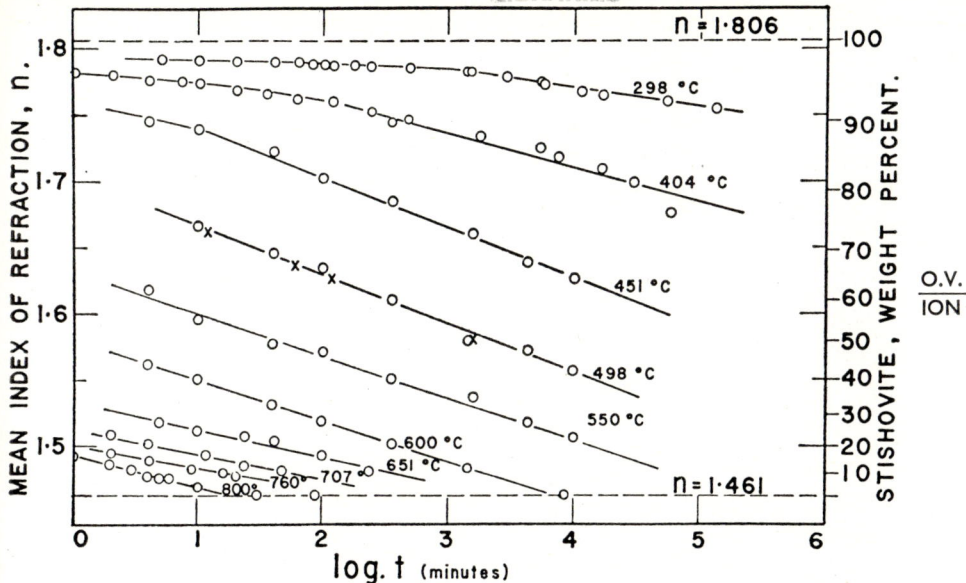

Figure 11. Mean index of refraction n for stishovite and vitreous silica mixtures as a function of the logarithm of the heating time t at different temperatures. The mean refractive index decreases from 1.806, the value for stishovite, to 1.461, the value for vitreous silica. Runs marked "X" were contained in platinum envelopes. (From Skinner and Fahey[230].)

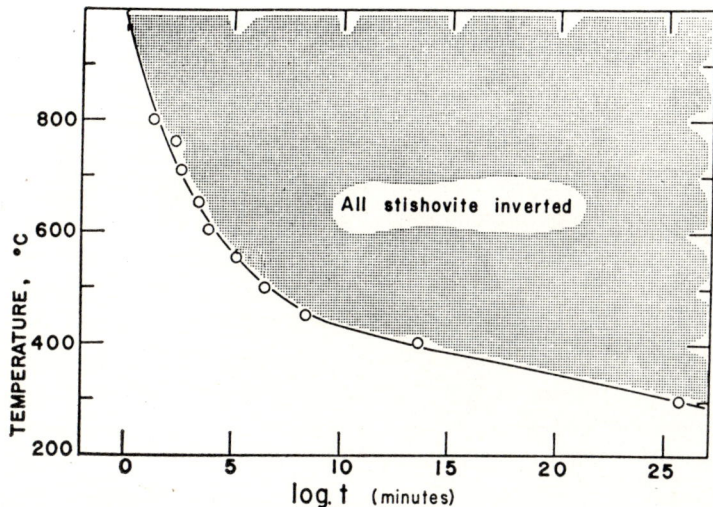

Figure 12. The logarithm of the time for total decay of stishovite to vitreous silica as a function of temperature, for Meteor Crater stishovite. For any stishovite to remain at Meteor Crater, the integrated cooling history, after the passage of the shock wave, must lie to the left of the polythermal inversion curve. (From Skinner and Fahey[230].)

and 498 °C and got a very high value, $> 10^{14}$, hence in the range which Primak, Szymanski, and Keiffer[185] reported for the high temperature annealing of radiation compacted vitreous silica. The activated step may therefore be similar, probably the breaking of a strained Si–O bond. On the basis of their data, Skinner and Fahey[230] give the time-temperature stability diagram shown in Fig. 12. From Dachille, Zeto, and Roy's[229] work taken in conjunction with this work of Skinner and Fahey,[230] it appears likely that the cristobalite found by Stishov and Papova[220] was a secondary product from the devitrification of the vitreous silica formed from the stishovite.

METEORITIC BLAST

Cosmic velocities of meteors are about 40 kM/sec.[232,233] Thus, their velocity relative to the earth's surface may range from 10–80 kM/sec, depending on their entry direction. Their entry angle would commonly be oblique. Masses below ∼10 tons are braked to terminal velocity by the time they reach the earth's surface; smaller objects far above the earth's surface. Moderate objects, although their surfaces ablate at incandescence in the upper atmosphere, are not heated greatly internally because of the short time involved, and the surface cools again as they descend at low velocity through the lower atmosphere. They may be quite cold when they reach the earth; one stony object dug up in Wisconsin a few minutes after a fall on a hot summer day condensed frost. Objects above 100 tons retain a large portion of their cosmic velocity; they may reach the earth's surface at 10–60 kM/sec. At 10 kM/sec, were the kinetic energy transformed into heat adiabatically, an iron object would become gaseous at 18,000 °C if ionization did not take place, 15,000 °C if it did! Its energy content 12,000 cal/g is an order of magnitude greater than that of a high explosive like TNT 925 cal/g, nitroglycerine 1486 cal/g, picric acid 1000 cal/g.[234] The normal gas volume for the iron would be ∼28,000 cm³/g compared to ∼700 cm³/g for conventional high explosives. Thus, even allowing for energy loss on penetrating the earth, a meteorite's explosive energy and power is an order of magnitude greater than a high explosive's! It forms a blast crater rather than the impact craters made by smaller objects. No meteoritic object 100 tons or greater has been found. Typical blast craters have a depth about 13% of their diameters. The largest one reported at Vredefort, S.A. is 140 kM diameter—others, Nordlinger-Ries, Germany (25 kM); Deep Bay, Saskatchewan (13.7 kM); Meteor Crater, Arizona (1.3 kM). The Wabar, Arabia crater 76 M diam. × 10 M deep must be at the low extreme for a blast crater. The Meteor Crater exposure seems to be a typical one and has been studied extensively, both scientifically and also explored by mining interests hoping to find large iron masses; none exist. Iron fragments are found as much as 5–10 miles away. In the area is a great deal of what has been called iron shale, solid rust brown material consisting of oxides of iron and nickel mixed with calcareous substances and other terrestrial materials, obviously not a weathering product. There may be metal fragments within. This must be a reaction product between dust produced by the blast and the meteorite, possibly in the liquid and gaseous or ionized state.

DURATION OF THE SHOCK PHENOMENA

It is of interest here to arrive at an independent order of magnitude estimate for the duration of the shock phenomena associated with the meteorite impact. None could be found in the literature, where the discussions given in the articles on the occurrences of the high pressure silica phases attempt to estimate the nature of the shock phenomena from the products. For this purpose Meteor Crater, Arizona is considered, for it appears to be the most exhaustively explored exposure; and, from the surrounding material, is very clearly a blast crater formed by a moderately large iron meteorite. The ratio of diameter 1300 M to depth 175 M, 7.5 is much larger than that found for emplaced explosives, chemical or nuclear, where the ratio is 3.5–4.[235,236,237] The ratio is the same for the Wabar crater, 76 M diam. × 10 M deep. It is therefore obvious that meteorites mushroom on impact before exploding, and they probably explode long before they are stopped. This whole process enhances lateral excavation. The depth scaling factor given for emplaced explosive charges would indicate a 1200 kT (of TNT) explosion, or $\sim 1.2 \times 10^{15}$ cal.[235,236] An object entering at mean meteor velocity 40 kM/sec would retain 30 kM/sec at earth's surface. Such an object would have to be 14 M diam. to possess the above energy. The range of velocities 10–60 kM/sec which such an object might possess would indicate objects in a range 20 to 11 M diam. It seems probable that explosion occurred before all the kinetic energy was converted to heat, as indicated by the many scattered large pieces (missiles). The assumption of $\frac{1}{3}$ being available for explosion seems reasonable. Then a 20 M object at 30 kM/sec is reasonable, but it would have been nearer 30 M diameter if its direction had been opposed to the earth's direction and its velocity had been at the lower extremum, ~ 10 kM/sec. For the discussion here, the diameter usually given, 20 M will be used. Maximum missile ranges given for emplaced explosives of this energy would be some 11–22 kM.[237] An abundance of material has been found within a 15 mi radius of the crater, hence in accord with this picture of the blast. For a missile 11 kM distant which travelled a low trajectory, neglecting air resistance, maximum height reached would have been 0.6 kM, time of flight 24 sec, and starting velocity $\frac{1}{2}$ kM/sec. This velocity is greater than terminal velocity for falling objects and faster than the speed of sound in air. Hence, considerable

energy loss would have occurred in flight, the fragments must have had several times the initial velocity given, and would have propagated shock waves
through the air.

From the behavior of emplaced explosives—that for shallow burial, relative crater dimensions do not alter appreciably with burial depth, and the
depths excavated are not much greater than the emplacement depth—it
would appear that the meteorite must have penetrated some 150 M of rock.
Since the object was ~ 30 M in diameter, even at its cosmic velocity initial
burial would have taken 10 msec, and 0.1 sec would be required to reach maximum depth. Following this would be the explosion which, had it occurred at
the missile velocities ~ 1 kM/sec, would have required ~ 1 sec to clear out
the crater. These times also accord with the mechanical behavior of the earth,
for the duration of seismic disturbances are of the order of magnitude
~ 1 sec.[238] Therefore it seems reasonable to describe the events as a series of
shock waves of duration of the order of magnitude ~ 1 sec. This is a 5–6 orders of magnitude longer duration than shock waves studied in the laboratory. The abundance of quartz and the relatively small amount of lechatelierite
may be taken as indicative that the material recovered from Meteor Crater
was not subjected to shock intensities far from 380 kbar; more heavily
shocked material was probably lost in the blast.

ORIGIN OF CRATER PRODUCTS

The sandstone specimens from the rim of Meteor Crater are described by
Sclar, Carrison, and Cocks[228] as showing the presence of frothy structures
and metallic spherules in the vitreous silica. The stishovite was present in the
acicular form indicating temperatures above 900 °C and pressures in excess
of 100 kbar during growth. They proposed partial fusion of silica occurred
much below 1713 °C because of the presence of water and that coesite crystal-
lized when the pressures fell below 100 kbar during passage of the shock
wave, with temperatures possibly remaining in excess of 900 °C. Then rapid
thermal decay to temperatures below 700 °C ensued after passage of the
shock wave, and only partial inversion of stishovite occurred. The above discussion of the formation of the crater shows that no such simple sequence of
events was possible, and the complexity of the events possesses sufficient
possibilities for understanding the synthesis of the products although it is not
possible to give the exact sequence. It is evident that there were several sets
of shock waves. Since seismic velocities are 4–5 kM/sec, they arrived before
the missiles which would have been at much higher temperature. The missiles
were projected with velocities several times that of the fastest rifle bullets,
about 0.1–0.2 times the shock wave velocities. Thus the arrival of the spherules and the formation of the associated structures is a secondary phenome-

non, although the sequence of shock waves and rarifactions would not yet have terminated.

PHASES IN LABORATORY SHOCK WAVES

McQueen, Fritz, and Marsh[239] reexamined Wackerle's[210] data after the discovery of stishovite, and concluded that the high pressure phase appearing in Wackerle's Hugoniots was stishovite. This writer does not agree with this conclusion; he regards the phase to be a relatively ordered dense array of oxygens in approximately octahedral symmetry but with the silicons disordered and the bonding quite irregular. Although the final description they give,

A dense silica glass, which in its short-range order is stishovite, is the most probable candidate for this phase. We would expect the distinction between crystalline and vitreous stishovite at these elevated pressures to be far less (even negligible) than the distinction that exists between vitreous silica and crystalline quartz at zero pressure. That this difference may not be completely negligible is indicated by a slightly better fit being obtainable with lower initial density.

would seem to leave little difference between our opinions, yet the course of transformation and the state of the final phase are quite different in the two hypotheses. They must consider the region 140–370 kbar to be a 2-phase region, yet they find grave discrepancies with this explanation. The 2-wave structure typical of such a region is absent; and there is no evidence of stishovite in the recovery products of either the high pressure region or the hypothesized 2-phase region. The similarity of the product of shocking quartz and vitreous silica, and the integrity of the product, would indicate a simple synthesis rather than the formation of stishovite which subsequently transformed into vitreous silica at the post-shock temperature. The recovery of unaltered quartz from the region 170–370 kbar, their "2-phase" region, would indicate that in the nearly uniaxial compression of the plane shock wave, despite the deformation, the oxygens remain closely associated with the silicon atom to which they are tetrahedrally bonded. At about 370 kbar the oxygens from a neighboring tetrahedron must approach sufficiently closely, and octahedral symmetry is achieved. At this point there must be extensive Si–O bond cleavage, and an appreciable fraction of the Si atoms must be in wrong positions for the rutile structure. It is not surprising that such a structure does not persist, for the ion radii ratio, even in stishovite, is at the limit of stability for rutile structures; and the oxygen ion size will be greater when there is not a silicon at the center of the octahedron. So many of the Si–O bonds have been cleaved and enough atomic movement has ensued that the quartz configuration cannot be restored when the shock wave has passed. Thus the compression has resulted in a direct vitrification of the quartz. The failure to attain appreciable compaction from either quartz or vitreous silica shocked into this pressure range must be associated with the Si–O network fragments being of too short a length to permit the compaction to be locked in, for the production of compacted material in lower intensity shock waves in vitreous silica shows there is sufficient time for this transformation; indeed, the radiation experiments to be presented below will show the compaction can occur in times 3 orders of magnitude smaller. Thus, the evidence indicates that in the intermediate pressure region, the network remains in tetrahedral coordination although twisting of portions of the network occurs. By 370 kbar, nearly octahedral packing is attained with considerable network fragmentation.

COMPARISON OF METEORITIC BLAST AND LABORATORY SHOCK WAVES

The distinction between the laboratory shock wave and the meteorite blast is that in the latter there occurs a repeated succession of shock waves so that finally enough diffusion can occur in a small proportion of the material to place the silicons in a favorable position to stabilize octahedral packing; and it is a very small portion indeed— ≪1% of the material is thus stabilized. Similarly, a small proportion of network fragments are in favorable orientation during some of the later in the sequence of shock waves to be stabilized in coesite configuration; and this too is a small proportion ∼1%. In the larger craters, the recovered material is more distant from the shock source and hence the time scale over which the shock waves pass this point is stretched. The smallest craters would tend to be formed by lower velocity objects, hence the blast effect would be less, and higher temperature products from nearer the blast center might be available from not having been scattered so far or shattered so greatly. However, since seismic data indicate[235, 236] the compressional wave intensity varies inversely with the 3.4 power of the blast energy, and the crater dimensions (from the explosives data) also vary with the 3.4 power of the blast energy, the shock intensities should be closely similar at similar positions of all crater walls. However, because of the large ratio of radius to depth, ∼3.7, evidence of greater intensities and temperatures and shorter durations should be available at the floor of the crater than at the rim. No reports on this subject were found. The possibility of sufficient difference in the high pressure behavior of porous rocks, possibly containing water, should be considered. In the lower range of shock intensities, the work of Ahrens and Gregson[240] on sandstones indicates agreement with the work of Wackerle and the work of Fowles on quartz, but no data on the high shock intensity region was found by this writer. However, this writer believes that the differences in the shock conditions in the meteoritic blast are far more significant.

VII. Radiation Compaction of Vitreous Silica

A. Introduction

DISCOVERY AND GENERAL BEHAVIOR OF QUARTZ AND VITREOUS SILICA

Discovery of the radiation compaction of vitreous silica is attributed to Primak, Fuchs, and Day[241,242,243,36,97] although radiation compaction of vitreous silica and glasses had surely been achieved much earlier by others without their appreciating it. Primak's experiments were begun after he learned from Simpson[244] about Berman's work[245] on the low temperature thermal conductivity of quartz exposed in British nuclear reactors. Fuchs[242] had been interested in studying the behavior of the refractive index of solids exposed in nuclear reactors. Primak argued that displacement of atoms could hardly affect so insensitive a property as the refractive index appreciably; he had neglected to consider the possibility of a phase change. However, quartz and vitreous silica were irradiated none the less. The changes found were large, too large to be accounted for on the basis of a mild disturbance of the structure or the introduction of absorption bands. Day[243] determined the density, and the change was found to correspond to the change in refractive index. Just a little later, Wittels[246] (who independently had learned of Berman's work and had begun an investigation of quartz) made a study of the behavior of the x-ray diffraction and the density of quartz exposed in a nuclear reactor. Primak[10] investigated the optical properties and density and their annealing. Other early independent studies were those of Lukesh[247, 248,249] and of Šimon.[163,164,250] The general behavior may be described as follows: on irradiation (near room temperature) near fuel in a nuclear reactor, quartz is gradually disordered to an amorphous state which is about 2.7% more dense than vitreous silica. Vitreous silica is very rapidly (with about $\frac{1}{7}$ the exposure required to disorder quartz) compacted to a density about 3% greater than vitreous silica. It then gradually expands by about 10% of the original change in density, to a final density about 2.7% greater than that of vitreous silica. Grossly, the final products obtained from quartz and vitreous silica are the same. Except for a few comments which may illuminate the process of compaction of vitreous silica, nothing more will be said here about the disordering of quartz.

OLDER STUDIES OF GLASS

Studies of radiation effects in glass are at least as old as studies of radio-activity. Curie and Curie[251] noted the coloration of glass and porcelain used to hold their radioactive solutions, and there were a number of later reports of such phenomena. Twyman and Brech[252] described x-ray induced coloration of vitreous silica and the annealing of this coloration. Little more will be said about this early work, or even much of the later work, on absorption bands; for most of it was interpreted incorrectly, and little of it is related to the compaction.

ION BOMBARDMENT

Koch[253] noted a reduction in reflectivity of glass surfaces subjected to ion bombardment. This item is of little scientific interest because the complex phenomena involved include film deposition and composition changes by selective sputtering, but for its being the inspiration for Hines' later investigations,[254,255,256] the first successful studies of radiation effects caused by low energy ion bombardment. Hines and Arndt[255] studied the effect of ion bombardment on vitreous silica and showed there was an increase in reflectivity which they explained by an increased refractive index as reported previously by Primak, Fuchs, and Day[97] for neutron bombardment.

MISCELLANEOUS OBSERVATIONS

Stewart[257] reported a deposit of about the density of cristobalite scraped from the interior of a vitreous silica discharge tube. It appears likely that this material was radiation-compacted vitreous silica. If so, his would be the first report of vitreous silica compacted by ion bombardment. Passing references to materials tests performed during the late war (1941–1946) and during the subsequent period of classified research on these subjects, appear in old progress reports, generally inaccessible; but no fundamental results from this work are known to this writer.

THE NEUTRON COMPACTION

Many aspects of irradiation studies were restricted from publication when Primak and Fuchs, early in 1951, began their investigations of the behavior of quartz and vitreous silica exposed in nuclear reactors. The first report of a change in optical properties appeared in July 1952, of the density in January 1953; and the first published report appeared in 1953. A summary of this early work was given by Primak.[258] Lukesh's[247] x-ray diffraction study of irradiated vitreous silica appeared in 1955. Šimon's studies[163,164] appeared shortly thereafter.

IONIZATION COMPACTION

It was generally considered that atomic displacement was required to produce density changes in vitreous silica. In 1962 Primak and Edwards[8] reported small negative dilatations caused by ionization. Primak, Edwards, Keiffer, and Szymanski[122] tried to explain them as an electrostatic effect. In 1958, at the Tashkent conference, Starodubtzev and Azizov[259] reported an expansion caused by gamma ray irradiation. Expansions had not been observed in Primak's laboratory. When the Russian report became available to them in 1963, Primak and Kampwirth[146] began an investigation of the effects of ionization on vitreous silica. They found the expansion to be associated with impurity. In the course of their studies they found negative dilatations far too large to be explained as an electrostatic effect. The results of their investigations had broad structural implications which are presented below.

RELATION TO COLOR CENTERS

Radiation-induced absorption in vitreous silica has been a morass from which few investigators who entered it have unmired themselves. Until recently, only one center had been well established: the alkali compensated aluminum center; and its behavior appeared to be inconsistent until Lell[260] showed how the compensating ion affected its behavior. Now the behavior of a germanium center is fairly well established; and largely through the work of Weeks and his collaborators, the E' center. Primak and Kampwirth[146] showed a relationship between the aluminum alkali center and the structural behavior. Since the E' center involves a non-bridging oxygen, it should be related to effects involving network cleavage, and evidence for this will be presented. Thus, there has been a little progress in relating color centers to structural changes since this author's last review;[261] but, for the most part, color center behavior has not been related to the structural behavior of vitreous silica. For a review of the color centers, the reader is referred to that by Lell, Kreidl, and Hensler.[37] There is no extensive review of the subject which summarizes the older as well as the recent data.

B. The Neutron Compaction

NEUTRON FLUXES

The compaction of vitreous silica in nuclear reactors was originally related to the fast neutron component of the radiation present there.[241] Most of the results which were reported were obtained in facilities close to fuel, and it is certain that the fast neutron-induced processes were the most significant. This does not mean the changes are caused by the primary fission neutrons or the flux over 1 MeV which some writers report. Primak[262] showed that for the usual reactor facilities, the flux of neutrons between 10^4 and 10^6 eV was the significant component. Since the flux density of neutrons in an interval of *ln E* does not vary greatly in nuclear reactors, the flux density of neutrons responsible for damage is roughly $\frac{1}{4}$ of the total flux density except where excessive thermalization has occurred. In that case, it would be about $\frac{1}{4}$ the flux density excluding the large thermal component.

DATA

A composite of results obtained in several reactors is given by Primak[10] and is reproduced in Fig. 13. It clearly shows the rapid compaction, the maximum, and the supervenient expansion. Primak correlated the relative damage rates with the property changes measured for graphite inserted into the same reactor cans. It is seen that some of the points obtained for vitreous silica on this basis do not fit well. He attributed the deviations to temperature effects:—annealing during irradiation. However, in later work, Primak and Edwards,[8] and Primak and Kampwirth[263] did not find appreciable temperature effects over the range of temperatures believed to have been attained in the irradiation cans. It is known now that ionization can cause both contraction and expansion (see Section 8). Thus, a correlation to fast neutron flux alone is not valid. As Primak showed,[264] the ratios of radiation fluxes may vary spacially by many orders of magnitude in a nuclear reactor. How the behavior of vitreous silica is affected is yet to be studied. Since appreciable annealing effects have not been observed, it may be argued that the rate of irradiation (i.e., the flux) will have little influence on the compaction considered as a function of dose. However, the measurements have been made fairly long after removal of specimens from reactor facilities, so that even this point must yet be held in question except for the ion bombardment evidence to be presented below. Under these circumstances it seems best to present data gathered in a single reactor facility. Such a set of data is available from Primak's investigations in Hole 7 of CP 5 and are given by Primak and Kampwirth.[263] The data were gathered by measurements of density and by interferometric measurements of changes in length. They are presented on a logarithmic scale in Fig. 14. It is seen that they are very accurately exponential over many orders of magnitude.

THERMAL SPIKES

Shortly after Wittels and Sherrill's data[265] on progressive irradiation of quartz became available and showed a period of accelerated change, Primak[266] compared this data with that for vitreous silica. He hypothesized that a thermal spike mechanism[267,268] was responsible for the compaction of vitreous silica and for the accelerated change in quartz. From the discussion

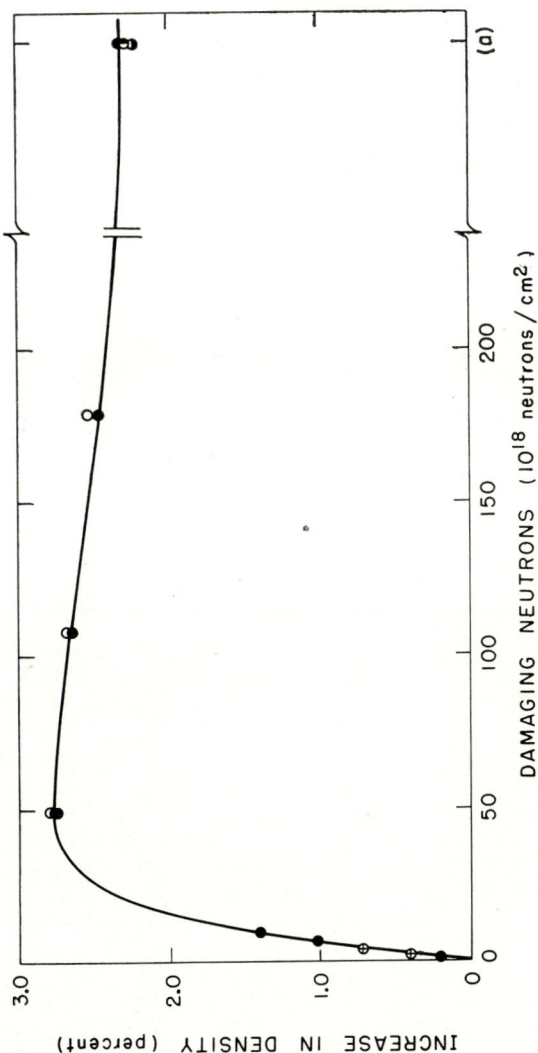

Figure 13. Change in density of vitreous silica on irradiation in nuclear reactors: open circles, calculated from the expansion; solid circles, from density determinations; crossed circles, from the expansion measurements given in reference 9; half-open circles give correct relative densities of what were originally a quartz sample (vertically divided circle) and a vitreous silica sample (horizontally divided); the solid circle at this dosage is from an accurate density determination made about two years later. The dosage at (a) is estimated at 250 to 400 on the scale. (From Primak[10].)

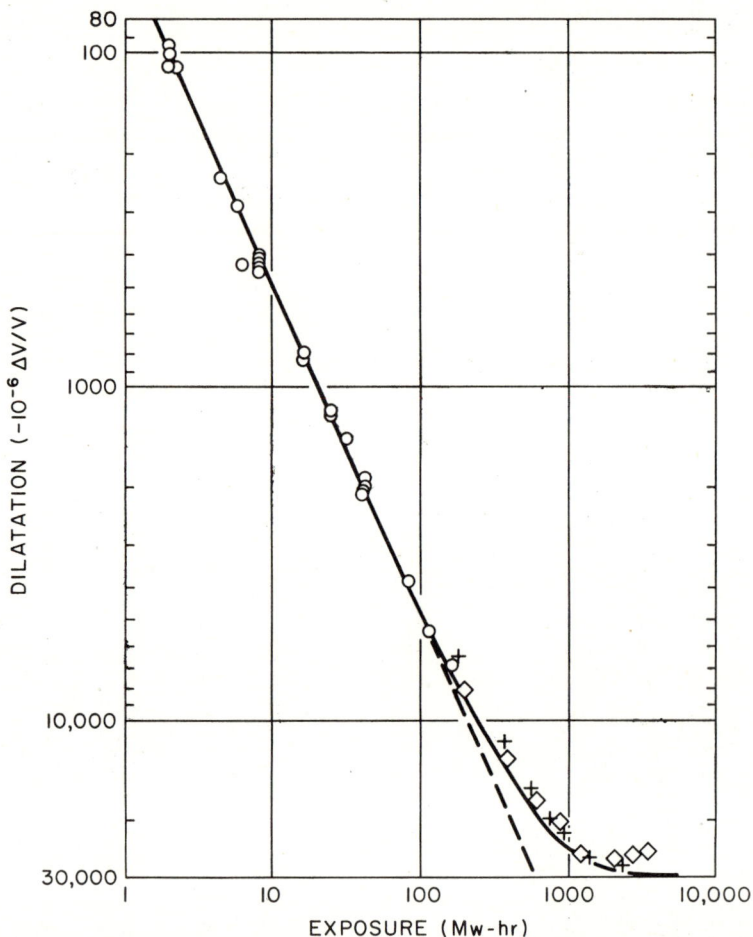

Figure 14. Compaction of vitreous silica in the vertical thimbles of CP-5: circles, at 40°–50°C; crosses, at 20°C; diamonds, at 90°C. The curve drawn is that of the true exponential dependence A $(1 - e^{-Bx})$ where A and B are suitable constants. (From Primak and Kampwirth[263].)

of the structural behavior of the silica network given above, it is obvious that the dominating feature of the period of accelerated change must be motility of network segments formed by cleavage, but the role of thermal spikes in the process has yet to be clarified. Within the next two years, Primak's thinking along these lines developed further. Certainly by 1957, when his paper[10] on quartz and vitreous silica was being prepared, he had formulated the basic hypothesis which was presented with slight modifications in subsequent papers. This was not based upon a comparison of the behavior of quartz and vitreous silica, but upon the behavior of vitreous silica alone. If the course of compaction is considered to be a simple exhaustion of compactable material, then the linear exhaustion period can be obtained from the dose required to produce $[1 - e^{-1}]$ of saturation. This was about 30×10^{18} energetic neutrons/cm². From the neutron scattering cross section it is easy to compute the number of scattering events involved:

$$N = 3.5 \times 10^{-24} \times 30 \times 10^{18} \, n,$$

where n is the number of atoms/cm³. The number of atoms affected by each scattering event is then n/N which is about 10^4. Because the diffusion of heat involves an exponential decay, this quantity sets very close limits—within half an order of magnitude—for the time of the process. It is about 10^{-11} sec. The energy associated with such a spike is the energy which can be expended in elastic collision; it is assumed that ionization is not sufficiently confined to make an appreciable contribution to the energy of this region. The further interpretation was based on Seitz' investigation of the dissipation of energy by an energetic particle.[269,270] In this theory, it is assumed that above some threshold energy no appreciable energy is expended in elastic collision; while below this threshold, no appreciable amount is expended in ionization. The behavior of graphite indicated the threshold for vitreous silica should be about 20 keV. This determines the energy density or "temperature". Primak[271] has now re-examined the behavior on the basis of the investigations of Lindhard and his associates (which have just recently become available). [273,274,275] Since the ion bombardment data are involved, further discussion is deferred until these data are presented.

SUPPORTING EVIDENCE

This was the original theory for the radiation compaction of vitreous silica. The first supplementary evidence came from Primak and Szymanski's[183] determination of the activation energy distribution for vitreous silica irradiated in a nuclear reactor. They pointed out that the low activation energy side of the distribution could have arisen from a high temperature annealing occurring for a very short time, $\sim 10^{-9}$ sec, at a high temperature $\sim 2500°C$, if the annealing laws found at long times could be extrapolated to these short times. Later when other compaction phenomena became familiar, Primak[276] compared the conditions calculated for the thermal spike with those known to produce compaction under static and under dynamic conditions, and found the conditions of pressure and temperature calculated for the thermal spike to be reasonably consistent with those required to produce the compactions observed in other ways. The summary given in Table 9 is taken from material used to prepare the paper by Primak, Edwards, Keiffer, and Szymanski.[122] According to this interpretation, the gross aspects of the neutron compaction accord with what is observed under rather less cataclysmic conditions. The unique feature is the short time in which the state is attained. It appears that the compaction is to be classed among the very fast reactions.

TABLE 9 State of a thermal spike[a] at quenching following a neutron scattering event (according to ref. 122)

Energy	20 keV
Number of atoms	10^4
Overall length	50–80 oxygen diameters
Radius	6–12 oxygen diameters
Time from scattering	$(1/2) \times 10^{12}$ sec
Temperature	5,000–10,000°C
Pressure	3–7 kbar

[a] Between spherical and cylindrical.

STRUCTURAL INVESTIGATION OF NEUTRON COMPACTION

Neutron compacted vitreous silica was subjected to x-ray examination by Lukesh[247] who noted differences from the diffraction curves for vitreous silica. Primak[5] compared Lukesh's curves with those published by Warren and concluded the distribution of Si–Si distances was increased while their mean value was decreased. The O–O distances were hardly affected. He concluded that the x-ray data indicated that the deformations consisted mainly of adjacent Si–O tetrahedra being bent or twisted with respect to each other. Independently, Šimon[164] had made his own investigation and had reached the same conclusions. In view of the care of his x-ray work, and his computations, and his previous experience in investigating the pressure compaction of vitreous silica in this manner, his work deserves special respect. He pointed out[166] the similarity of the changes observed in the pressure compaction and the neutron compaction and went on to show the behavior of the 9.1 μ infrared absorption band, considered to be related to bending of adjacent tetrahedra with respect to each other, was similar for the pressure and neutron compacted materials. The work on the neutron compaction has a special significance because of the homogeneity of the product as compared to the product of pressure compaction. Thus, it was demonstrated conclusively that the greater range of the distribution of Si–Si distances is intrinsic to the compacted state and not an artifact resulting from an admixture of materials. The vitreous silica remains intact on neutron compaction, and it is well suited for optical absorption measurements. Šimon was able to make precise measurements of it in the infra-red, and it was with this material that the displacement of the 9.1 μ absorption band was first determined for compacted vitreous silica. Only later did he obtain the less precise measurements (given above) for the pressure compacted vitreous silica.

Addendum

Significant results have been obtained by others; e.g., Mayer and his collaborators,[277,278] and by some Russian investigators.[279] This work has not been treated here because it is concerned mainly with the disordering of quartz, a subject which is largely beyond the scope of this monograph. Lungu's work[280] is of greater interest in connection with the supervenient expansion and is treated below (see page 75).

C. Ionization Compaction

Historical

The first report of the ionization compaction of vitreous silica resulted from an attempt by Primak[8] to determine the displacement threshold in vitreous silica by the usual method involving electron bombardment. He applied the photoelastic method for measuring the dilatation,[209] a very sensitive method which he had developed in an investigation of lithium fluoride made in collaboration with Delbecq and Yuster.[282] The method can be used to determine small dilatations quickly in isotropic or suitably oriented cubic material when the radiation is directed and its range is considerably less than the thickness of the specimen. Optical finishing requirements are not severe. Primak found no evidence of a threshold (like Arnold and Compton[283,284] before him using the optical absorption as an index), and Primak and Edwards[8] then went on to explore other aspects of the ionization compaction. They found it to be caused as readily by soft x-rays. They also discovered an ionization expansion for neutron compacted vitreous silica, a subject which is discussed at length in Section IX (see page 139).

Impurity Effect

After they had discovered the ionization expansion of pressure compacted vitreous silica (treated in Section IX) Primak, Edwards, Keiffer, and Szymanski[122] attempted to explain the radiation expansions and contractions in silica; but except for this, the ionization compaction received no further attention until Primak and Kampwirth[146] began to check Starodubzev and Azizov's[259] report of an expansion caused by gamma ray irradiation. Primak and Kampwirth's statement about it is,

The effects of gamma rays had never been studied in our Laboratory, but in the many measurements of the density, dilatation, and length of vitreous silica after irradiation in reactors, with positive ions, with electrons, or with x-rays, only contraction had been observed.

They subjected their vitreous silica to gamma irradiation; and, again, found only a contraction. Then they recalled the contrasting behavior of Corning 7943 and "OH-Free" vitreous silica in the work of Weeks and Lell[144] and began an examination of several low OH vitreous silicas: Corning 7943, In-frasil, and Vitreosil. Since they had found no peculiarity associated with the use of gamma rays, they continued their studies with electrons because of the greater dose rate which could be achieved. They used 0.3–0.6 MeV elec-

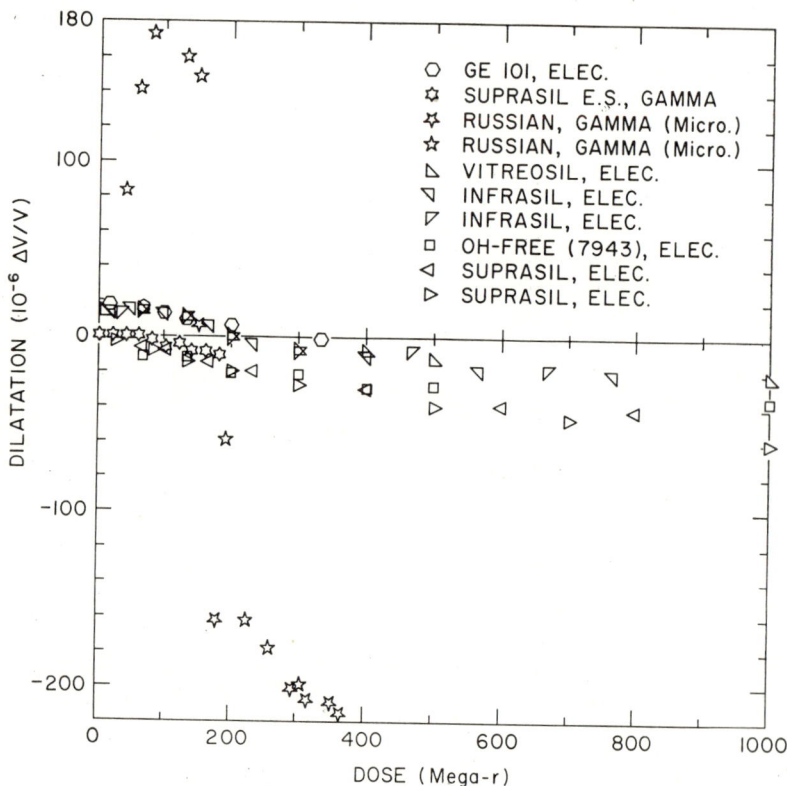

Figure 15. Dilatation of various vitreous silicas caused by ionizing radiation. Russian gamma-ray data are taken from Starodubtsev and Azizov[259], measurements made with a microscope. Suprasil gamma-ray data were taken inter-ferometrically of end standards (E.S.). The remainder were photoelastic measure-ments of specimens thicker than the range of the 0.6 MeV electrons used, and the mean (over the range) dilatation was measured and plotted against the mean (over the range) ionization. The abbreviations used in the legend are: ELEC for electron bombardment, E.S. for interferometric measurements of end standards, GAMMA for gamma-ray irradiation, Micro. for length measurements with a microscope (presumably mounted on some type of comparator).
(From Primak and Kampwirth[146].)

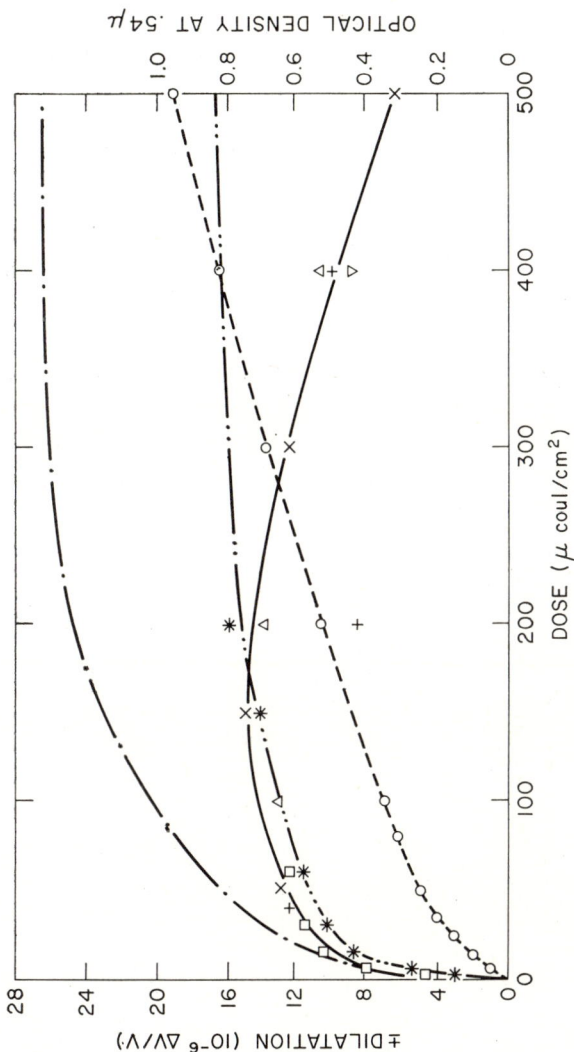

Figure 16. Resolution of the expansion and contraction of the coloring vitreous silicas: (solid line, the positive dilatation of the coloring vitreous silicas; crosses, X's, triangles, results of three progressive irradiations of Infrasil; squares, five specimens of Infrasil used for short irradiations); (dash-double-short-dash curve with asterisks, optical density of Infrasil); (dashed curve with circles, negative dilatation of Suprasil); (dash-single-short-dash curve, construction of the supposed positive dilatation of the coloring vitreous silicas assuming the negative dilatation upon which is superposed is the same as that of Suprasil's). (From Primak and Kampwirth[146].)

trons because the range was suitable for the photoelastic method, and it was a good operating region for their van de Graaff machine. Infrasil and Vitreosil color because of their aluminum content, whereas the Corning 7943 does not. They found that the coloring vitreous silicas showed an expansion, whereas Corning 7943 behaved much like Suprasil (which has a high OH content); and another vitreous silica, Optosil (which colored slightly) showed a decreased contraction. As in the Russian report,[259] they found that the expansion soon saturated; and then contraction ensued, apparently at the same rate as the contraction in the non-coloring vitreous silicas. Thus, it appeared that the expansion and the contraction were independent and at the start occurred simultaneously. In Fig. 15 is shown their data and the Russian data. In Fig. 16 their resolution of the expansion and contraction is shown.

RELATION TO COLORATION

Primak and Kampwirth[146] report the initial coloring of the vitreous silica took place very rapidly, as did the expansion. Both saturated early, the coloring more sharply. The coloring of vitreous silica and quartz was demonstrated by the work of Mitchell and Paige[285,286,287] and others to be largely associated with the alkali-compensated aluminum center. Some small contribution may also be made by other trivalent ions like Fe^{+++}. Compensation may also be made by H^+. Whether alkaline earth ions may contribute is not discussed in the literature, but Mg^{++} is found[145,146] in spectroscopic analyses of the coloring vitreous silicas. Bambauer[288,289,37] showed that the radiation coloration behavior of quartz is greatly affected by the compensating ion, notably that it is inhibited by H^+ and is most intense for Li^+ and Na^+; and Lell[260] showed the same to be true for vitreous silica. Thus, Primak and Kampwirth's failure to find a 1:1 correspondence between the coloration of the vitreous silica, known to have been compensated by a mixture of ions, is, as they pointed out, no evidence against their association of the expansion with the aluminum center. Instead, it indicated to them that the dilatation was a better measure of the radiation behavior of this center than the absorption; for the dilatation continued to measure changes in configuration of centers which did not show optical absorption. Their explanation of the expansion was a simple one—that the trapping of an electron or hole in the vicinity of an Al–O link in the network weakened the bond and rupture ensued.

DILATATION FORMALISM

To obtain a quantitative relation between the radiation and the effect, Primak, Edwards, Keiffer, and Szymanski[122] proposed the following *ad hoc* procedure: to count the dilatation by giving it in units of the oxygen ionic volume. The justification was that it would be difficult to accept a much larger unit because such volumes are not available in the vitreous silica structure; it would be difficult to use a much smaller unit because efficiences for some processes which had been observed would then exceed 100%; i.e., a chain reaction would have to be postulated whereas experimental evidence pointed to individual events. The silicon volume is neglected in all these calculations because it is, relatively, so small. It may be noted that a similar *ad hoc* procedure has given good correlation for the alkali halides where independent means of determining the numbers of centers are available. Although the procedure can be justified only for obtaining a rough estimate, in fact it appears to give correlations which are much better. The oxygen ionic volume for this purpose was taken by Primak and Kampwirth[146] to be one which provide a void space of two oxygen ionic volumes for each six oxygen ions present in the network. Thus the fully packed solid would possess a density just below that of coesite, and quartz would be intermediate. This oxygen ionic volume is 17×10^{-24} cm^3; and because it will be referred to quite often in the discussion below, it is given an abbreviation, O.V., for use as a unit or in text; and, in equations, the symbol V_O will be used for it.

STRUCTURAL FORMALISM

In addition, Primak, Edwards, Keiffer, and Szymanski[122] gave a structural formalism incorporating these ideas. On the average, in a section of the network, the void space would be surrounded by about 6 oxygens. Then in the 3-dimensional network such a void space would be surrounded by 14–20 oxygens. Since each oxygen is shared by several such regions of the network, the distributed ratio of void space to oxygen is about $\frac{2}{6}$ for each. In the compaction, the network became kinked in places, and the kink displaced a void volume of 1 O.V. This structural concept is similar to ideas expressed by Bridgman and Šimon.[9] Although, as mentioned above, the fact that such a single distortion cannot in general be performed in a 3-dimensional network (a more realistic hypothesis will be formulated below), relegates this hypothesis to merely a formalism; it is of interest to explore it a little further because it gives a much clearer picture of the magnitude of the compaction effects than the realistic atomic hypothesis. The 3% which is the maximum compaction found for neutron irradiation (and which it will be shown below has a special significance in the pressure compaction) is a kink in about $\frac{1}{6}$ of the loops (the network surrounding a void space). This corresponds approximately to each kinked loop being surrounded by unkinked ones. If every loop is kinked to displace an O.V./loop (i.e., 1 kink/loop), the density becomes that of quartz; while if there are 2 kinks/loop, the density becomes that of coesite.

IONIZATION ENERGY

The next step in determining the efficiency of the process is to determine the mean energy expended per ionization. No experimental determinations of this quantity are available for vitreous silica. For air (gaseous), the experimental value for the mean ionization energy is about 34 eV. In water it is considered to be about 20 eV, while in ice it may be a little higher. F-centers are formed very efficiently in potassium bromide loaded with H^+ and it is considered that nearly every ionized electron is trapped as an F-center. The mean energy required to form an F-center there has been determined to be about 35 eV. The mean counting energy in sodium iodide scintillations is about 100 eV, but there are, certainly, other ionization processes which are not counted. A value about 2.2 times the band gap has been considered to be a good value for the mean ionization energy.[280] However, vitreous silica has no proper band structure, but the energy of the fundamental absorption might be a reasonable substitute; this might be about 10 eV. On the other hand, the threshold energy required to form some centers in the oxides have been reported[284] to be as high as 60 eV, but it is likely that there are other less energetic processes which would lower the mean ionization energy. Thus, a value of 30 eV for the mean ionization energy for vitreous silica is a reasonable one, but the correct value may be a little lower, or as much as twice as high.

EFFICIENCY OF IMPURITY EXPANSION

Primak and Kampwirth[146] reported the aluminum content of their Infrasil to have been 7×10^{-5} by weight or 3.4×10^{18} atoms/cm^3. From Fig. 16, the expansion saturates at a dilatation of 27×10^{-6}. This corresponds to about 0.5 O.V./aluminum atom, excellent agreement for such a calculation, and further support for their hypothesis for the expansion and its correlation with the aluminum center. They give 3.57×10^{-6} per $\mu C/cm^2$ as the initial rate of dilatation, and the energy dissipated in ionization by 0.6 MeV electrons as

$$25.6 \times 10^{18} \text{ ev per } \mu C/cm^2.$$

Since 25×10^{-6} was the dilatation corresponding to 3.4×10^{18} aluminum atoms, the initial mean energy for effecting dilatation was therefore 57 eV/ aluminum atom or 120 eV/O.V. The major uncertainties in correlating these numbers with the amount of ionization are the values of: the mean energy of ionization, the mean volume expansion per center, and the fraction of aluminum centers participating. From the above discussion, the values used here for the first two would appear to be known within a factor of 2. The behavior of the aluminum centers in the present application is unknown, and a special uncertainty may be attached to those compensated by hydrogen. These do not appear to contribute to the coloring; and if the presence of H^+ causes segmentation of the network at an Al–O–Si link much as H^+ is supposed to at a Si–O–Si link, these centers would not contribute to the expansion. In the coloring vitreous silica studied by Primak and Kampwirth, it has been estimated that about half of the aluminum centers are compensated by H^+. Then, if H^+ compensation segments the network, the radiation expansion per aluminum center would be 1 O.V. and the mean energy would be 120 eV/ aluminum center. Thus our knowledge of the fraction of aluminum centers participating is also uncertain by a factor 2. If suitable specimens could be obtained, this would be the easiest of the three quantities to fix experimentally.

The radiation expansion associated with the aluminum centers in vitreous silica is thus seen to have a very high efficiency initially: $\frac{1}{4}$ to $\frac{1}{2}$ of the electrons produced in ionization are trapped at these sites. Since the mean distribution of aluminum atoms is such that they would be separated by about 2 loops of the Si–O network, this distance would seem to be approximately the mean free path of ionized electrons. It may be assumed that every electron formed in the loop in which the aluminum is located is trapped, and a smaller number of those formed in adjacent loops.

For those unfamiliar with this subject, it may seem as if too much space has been given to a very crude calculation. The precision of this calculation is actually not worse than other calculations on similar subjects. For example, in calculations using absorption bands, incidental uncertainties are not much different from those found here, and uncertainty in the oscillator strength and symmetry of the centers may introduce an uncertainty several times as great as that in the unit of expansion here; while overlapping absorption bands and background absorption adds further uncertainty to those calculations.

THE FRACTIONAL POWER DEPENDENCE

The impurity effect is a complexity of interest here mainly because it shows some of the dynamic behavior of the network and illustrates the efficiency calculations. The compaction appears to proceed independently of it as indicated in Fig. 16 and as will be seen below in the annealing behavior. Primak and Kampwirth[263] found the ionization compaction did not obey an exponential dependence. They were able to follow it only until a decade below saturation, and thus the saturation behavior does not appear in their work. Over the range of compaction in which the neutron compaction was linear, the ionization compaction followed a fractional power dependence on dose. For irradiation with 125–600 keV electrons in air, the dependence of com-

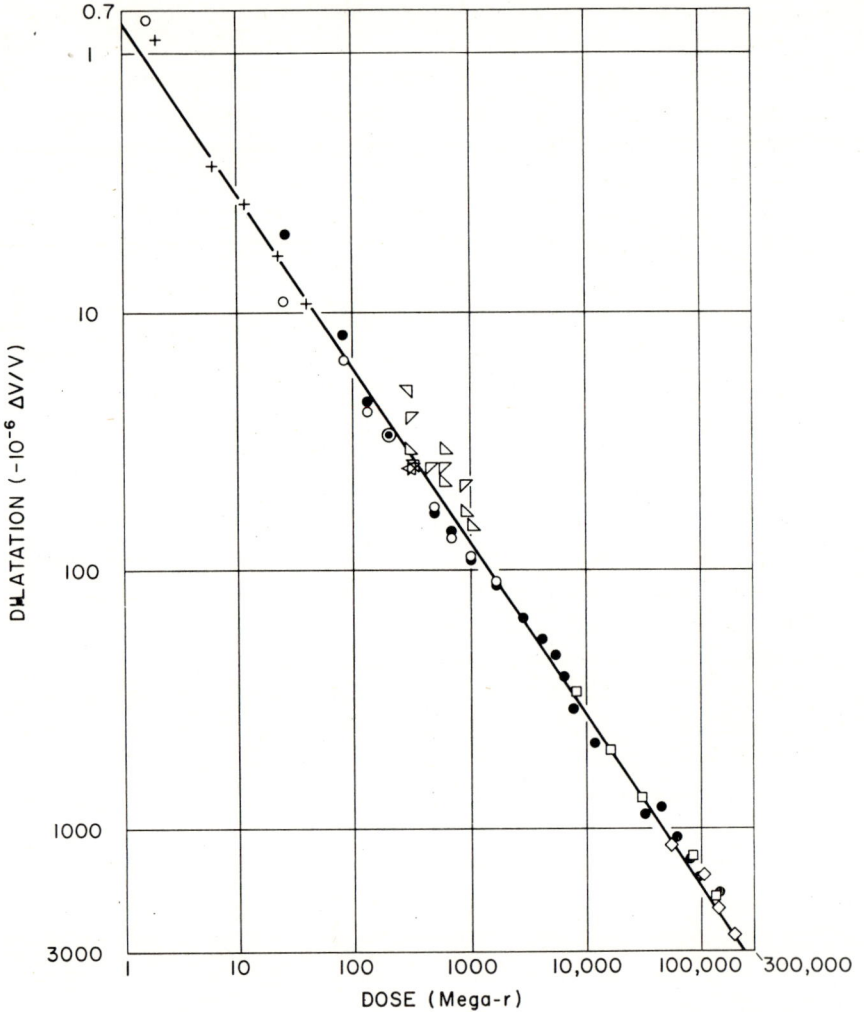

Figure 17. The dilatation of Suprasil at the point of maximum damage along the range of electrons plotted against the dose at this point: circles, actual measurements; round spots, calculated from the mean dilatation (both for progressive 0.6 MeV electron irradiations of specimen 2883); squares and diamonds, respective progressive 0.3 MeV irradiation of two specimens; crosses, respective single 0.6 MeV irradiations of five specimens. Triangles are comparative points for gamma irradiations of end-standards; the quadrants are for the respective temperatures 7°, 25°, 50°, and 95°C. The left half-diamond is for 75°C. The line is drawn for a slope of 0.66 ($\frac{2}{3}$ power dependence). (From Primak and Kampwirth[263].)

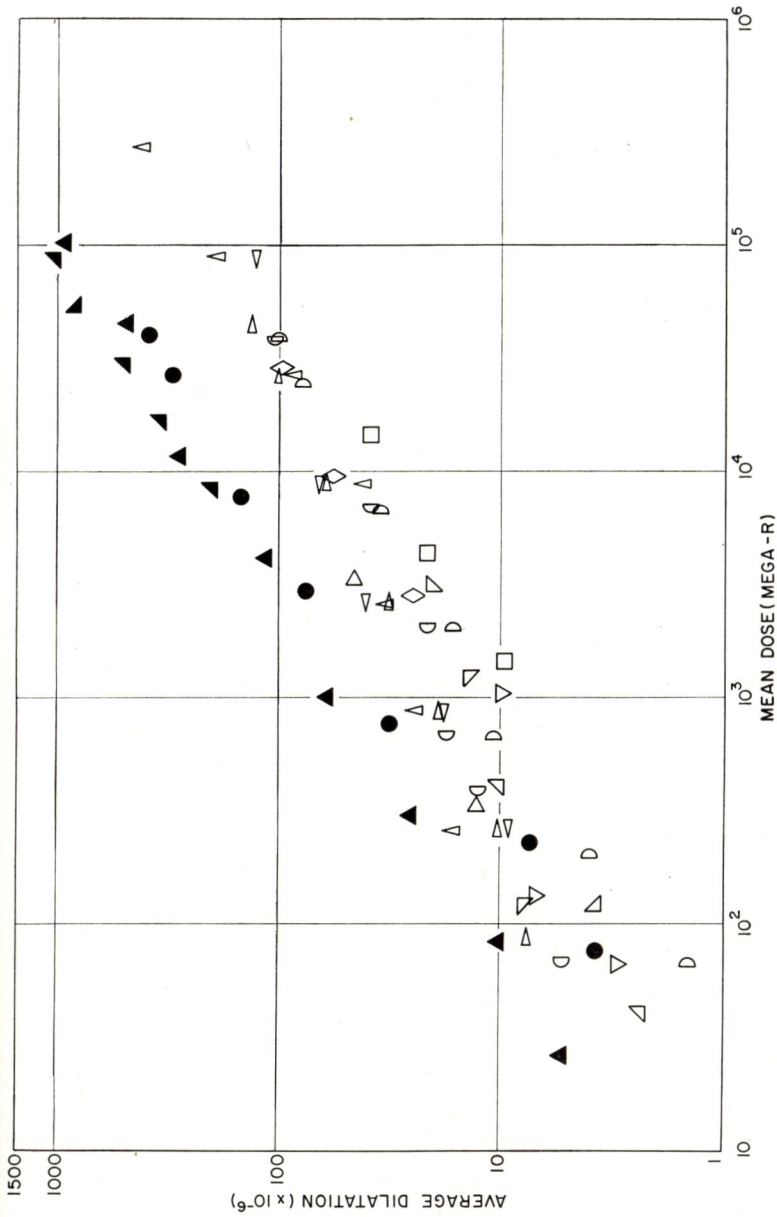

Figure 18. The mean (along the range) dilatation of vitreous silica subjected to bombardment by electrons of various energies, in air, and, in vacuum, plotted against the mean dose. Irradiations in air are represented by solid symbols, in vacuum by open symbols; different orientation of symbols indicates different specimens subjected to progressive irradiations; the code for different energies (keV) is: squares, 40; diamonds, 60; arrow points, 80; circles, 125; half-circles, 150; right triangles, 300; equilateral triangles, 600. (From Primak and Kampwirth[263].)

paction was as the $\frac{2}{3}$ power of dose. This also appeared to be the dependence for gamma irradiation of samples immersed in flowing water. Experiments were also conducted in vacuum with electrons of various energies, some as low as 30 keV. The latter data showed greater scatter; and the dependence may have been a somewhat smaller fractional power, perhaps the $\frac{1}{2}$ power of dose. The two groups of results are shown in Figs. 17 and 18.

EFFICIENCY OF IONIZATION COMPACTION

A fractional power is not a natural dependence for an effect associated simply with an agent. Therefore Primak and Kampwirth were greatly concerned about its being an artifact arising from experimental errors. A major concern was the measurement of charge incident on a good insulator. The electrical behavior of insulators is of general interest, and a separate section is devoted to it below. They also considered effects of annealing, errors in measuring dilatation, and secondary radiation. Finally, they concluded the dependence was largely intrinsic although experimental error may have caused a small alteration from the true dependence. The experimental result for the dilatation as a function of dose is:

$$\delta = \xi D^{\alpha}$$

where ξ and α are constants and α is between 0.5 and 0.7. The differential equation is:
$$d\delta/dD = \alpha\xi^{1/\alpha}\,[\delta^{(1/\alpha)-1}].$$

This does not include saturation behavior. Thus for α over the range $\frac{3}{4}$ to $\frac{1}{2}$, the rate of dilatation depends on inverse powers of dilatation covering the range $\frac{1}{3}$ to 1. For α having a value $\frac{2}{3}$, as shown in Fig. 17, ξ is 0.38×10^{-6} cm³ per $\mu C/cm^2$, and using the conversion value 1540 O.V./cm³ per eV mm/ $(\mu C/cm^2)$,
$$dD/d\delta = 4.3 \times 10^6\ \delta^{1/2}$$

in eV/O.V. At the beginning of the data $\delta = 10^{-6}$, the mean energy of compaction is 4000 eV/O.V.; by mid range, $\delta = 10^{-4}$, it is 43,000; and at the end of the data given it is about 230,000. Thus, at the beginning of the data, compaction is occurring for every 150th ionization, while at the end of the data it has been reduced to $^1/_{5000}$.

INTERPRETATION OF FRACTIONAL POWER DEPENDENCE

Primak and Kampwirth[263] discussed the behavior of the ionization compaction in detail. The lack of an energy dependence over this range of electron energies showed it was not a displacement effect. The intensity of ionization (transient charge concentration) is too low for any ordinary effect involving primary interaction between charged centers. The dilatations at which the fractional power dependence is first seen are too small for any ordinary exhaustion to be occurring. The local energy deposited is too small to excite a region in the manner seen in neutron irradiation. They concluded the effect was caused by individual ionizations and was related to the state of ionization. Although the constants have a different physical meaning, the differential equation obtained for such a process is the same as for neutron irradiation. They tried modifying the differential equation in various ways and found that although it was easy to alter the behavior in the two decades below saturation, altering the 4 decades below that from linearity was not possible. They concluded from these attempts that the fractional power dependence is not caused by a competition between recombination and an increasing distance between sites available for compaction, nor does it represent an exhaustion, nor an annealing. The effect is like a strain or a hardening. Succeeding compaction events in the same region became more difficult or less probable.

STRUCTURAL INTERPRETATION

In the room temperature region, Primak and Kampwirth[263] found no temperature dependence for the ionization compaction. It was difficult to understand why a process whose probability is so low and which involves a rearrangement of structure is not thermally activated. Since saturation behavior is not evidenced, sites suitable for the process must be ionized many times before the process occurs. They therefore considered it likely that the rate controlling factor for the ionization compaction was the process of locking it in; that ionization weakened or segmented the network and permitted structural movement; but whether a new structural arrangement was locked in, depended on other suitable motion in the network. For the fractional power dependence to extend to compactions as small as those found experimentally, the single compaction event must affect a large volume of the solid. Since saturation is not seen, it does not exclude further compaction from this region; it only makes compaction more difficult. At this writing, the explanation offered is that the compaction causes a redistribution of microscopic network stress associated with abnormal bond angles. A similar effect was described above for the α–β-transition in quartz (see pages 18, 22, 23, 26).

EFFECT OF IONIZATION INTENSITY

Primak and Kampwirth[263] did not observe a change in efficiency of compaction when electron current was increased by a factor 5. Compaction for gamma ray irradiation appeared to have the same efficiency although ionization intensity was an order of magnitude lower. However, for compaction with 140 keV protons (which, as will be shown below, appears to be an ionization compaction) the efficiency was found to be some 8-fold greater while the ionization intensity was some 100-fold greater. At this intensity of ionization, ionization is occurring in adjacent loops of the structure. The network might thus be greatly weakened and segmented, as well as highly excited; and this could facilitate both rearrangement and locking in.

Ionization in a Nuclear Reactor

The intensity of ionization in a reactor is very great. Primak and Edwards[210] found a slightly greater rate of compaction for very short exposures in the nuclear reactor CP-5. This may be evidence for a contribution from ionization compaction when the efficiency is still relatively high. It will be shown below that the effect of ionization at greater exposures is no longer to cause compaction but to cause its release (see Section IX, pages 107 et seq.).

Network Cleavage in Ionization Compaction

The introduction of E' centers by ionization is direct evidence of cleavage of the Si–O network by ionization and must cause an expansion. It is to be noted that compared to the efficiency of cleavage at Al–O bonds, the efficiency of cleavage at an Si–O bond is very low and that compaction swamps out this effect completely.

D. Ion Bombardment

Introduction

Interest in ion bombardment of glasses has stemmed from a number of sources. Low energy ion bombardment (and electron bombardment) has been a problem in the operation of vacuum electronic devices because of surface charging, gas trapping and evolution, and alteration of surfaces. These problems are summarized by Carter and Grant.[241] They are not of major interest here because the work has been with multicomponent glasses, and many of the effects are associated with, or greatly modified by, the non-network ions. The mechanisms for charge storage and transport, and the gas permeability, particularly as the temperature is raised, are quite different for vitreous silica. This field of investigation is virtually a virgin one for vitreous silica.[292] The range of ion energies of greatest interest here is the keV to MeV region. It was chosen for investigation originally because, (1) it is a range of energies provided conveniently by a variety of machines; e.g., mass spectrometers, Cockcroft-Walton machines, and Van de Graaffs; and (2) it is the range of energies of primary ions produced by the energetic neutrons in nuclear reactors; and, hence, where a great deal of the data of radiation effects was accumulated, and about whose behavior so much curiosity has been engendered. The first serious investigation of glass bombarded with ions of this energy, as mentioned above, were those by Koch[253] and by Hines.[254] These investigations are of little interest here because they were of multicomponent glasses; and, also, they involved many extraneous complexities. The first investigation or real interest is the one by Hines and Arndt[255] who studied the effect of 7.5 keV He$^+$ and 38.3 keV Ne$^+$ ions on the reflectivity of vitreous silica. The changes were found to correspond to an increase in refractive index of 0.01, the same as that reported by Primak, Fuchs, and Day,[97] and by Primak[10] for exposure in nuclear reactors.

STRESS RELAXATION BY SURFACE CRAZING AND BY PLASTIC FLOW

When Primak[293] began his studies of the dilatation of vitreous silica by ions in the energy range 50 keV to several MeV, he saw a rich variety of phenomena. Of the destructive phenomena, the Lichtenburg discharge was known previously and is discussed below. The surface crazing, although it must surely have been observed before, does not seem to have been described. Examples of surface crazing are shown in Fig. 19. Primary crazing consisted of typical polygonal craze areas, mostly rectangular, about 1 mm across. Further irradiation produced areas as small as $\frac{1}{4}$ mm across, and eventually some exfoliation. Most of the areas showed a set of Newton's rings, each area having curled upward, indicating a greater shrinkage of the upper regions. The curling was different for protons than for helium ions, indicating a different distribution of negative dilatation with depth. When the beam energy (ion range) was decreased, the surface crazing became fainter; and by the time the range was but 1–2 microns ($\sim$150 keV) crazing could no longer be seen.

In most of the crazing experiments only a portion of the surface was bombarded by the ion beam. Not only did crazing occur, but also a depression was seen in the bombarded area. Thus the vertical as well as the horizontal shrinkage was apparent. A depression was seen even when the ion range was small and surface crazing did not occur. A local deformation associated with radiation-induced dilatation had been sought by Smith, Leivo, and Smoluchowski[294] in the alkali halides, but had not been found there. It had surely occurred in Hines and Arndt's work,[254] but they did not observe it. Primak[293] found it in quartz, an elevation being produced, as would be expected, because irradiation causes it to expand. Local surface deformation was not found for some other oxides, as magnesium oxide. Ordinarily the stress is distributed over the whole specimen in accord with the laws of elasticity, and local deformation is not seen at the boundary of the ion beam.

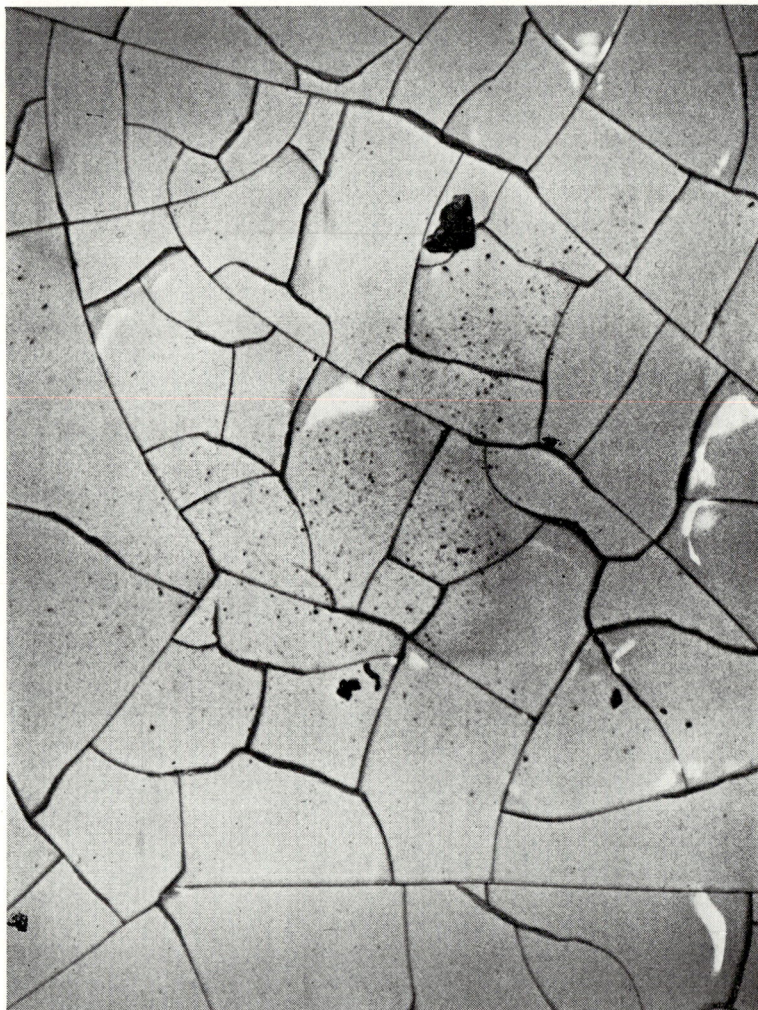

Figure 19. Typical example of surface crazing described by Primak[293] as seen under the microscope with a 10 mm objective. The crazed areas are $\frac{1}{4}$—$\frac{1}{2}$ mm across.

Its occurrence in vitreous silica and in quartz is thus a unique radiation effect: a radiation-induced plastic flow. The measurements indicated that when crazing was absent, the depression in the case of vitreous silica was greater than $\frac{1}{3}$ the dilatation. But this work should be re-examined because Primak was uncertain of the ion ranges. The evidence he gives for the elevation in quartz is clearer because there was little difference in elevation produced on Z- and X- cut surfaces despite the radiation-induced expansion being twice as great for the X-direction.

Before presenting further evidence for a radiation-induced stress relaxation involving plastic flow, it is necessary to consider another effect found by Primak, the dispersed depolarization. Optical properties of the ion bombarded surfaces are very complex. The reflectivity measurements made by Hines and Arndt were a very crude approach. A more subtle approach is by ellipsometry. Polished vitreous silica has been studied by Yokota, et al.[295] and by King and Downs;[296] irradiated vitreous silica by Schroeder and Dieselman.[297] These authors have treated the propagation of the electromagnetic wave on the assumption that the medium is isotropic, which frequently is not the case; Primak[293] calculated the birefringence for one irradiated specimen to be in excess of 1 μ/mm. The refractive index of the vitreous silica increases on irradiation by an amount which corresponds closely to that expected for the increase in density; it is not caused by the development of a strong absorption in the ultraviolet as is the case for lithium fluoride[298] and magnesium oxide.[193] Media with an increased surface refractive index have interesting properties for the propagation of electromagnetic radiation which are best known for the behavior of the ionosphere. Osterberg and Smith[208] have investigated the surface transmission in the case of glasses. Schineller, et al.[300] attempted to make an optical wave guide by irradiating vitreous silica. Their analysis of the radiation effect is certainly incorrect, as will be apparent from the discussion below, and their specimens should be reinvestigated because of the possibility that the crazing phenomenon may have been present in them. Primak[207] noted a dispersion of depolarized light internally reflected from the irradiated face, and he treated the phenomenon as interference. None of the descriptions of the optical behavior of the irradiated vitreous silica surfaces are adequate. Primak[293] utilized the dispersed depolarization to evaluate the refractive index change in the surface layer semiquantitatively, and he showed that the disappearance of stress birefringence as irradiation progressed was not annealing of the radiation-induced changes, but rather a stress relaxation.

Primak's[293] original experiments were with protons and helium ions 50–140 keV. The stress-birefringence associated with the contraction of the bombarded surface of the vitreous silica blocks increased to a maximum and then began to decline to nil even though an increasing refractive index in the irradiated layer was evidenced in the dispersed depolarization phenomenon. Measurements of greater precision from later work are given below. Primak calculated the mean stress in some of the irradiated layers and found it to be many-fold the normal breaking strength, 6500 PSI, a finding which is affirmed here although the figure he gives, 10-fold, may be somewhat high because his ranges may be somewhat small. However, even the high figure he gives is but 7% of breaking strengths measured for vitreous silica fibres at room temperature.[202]

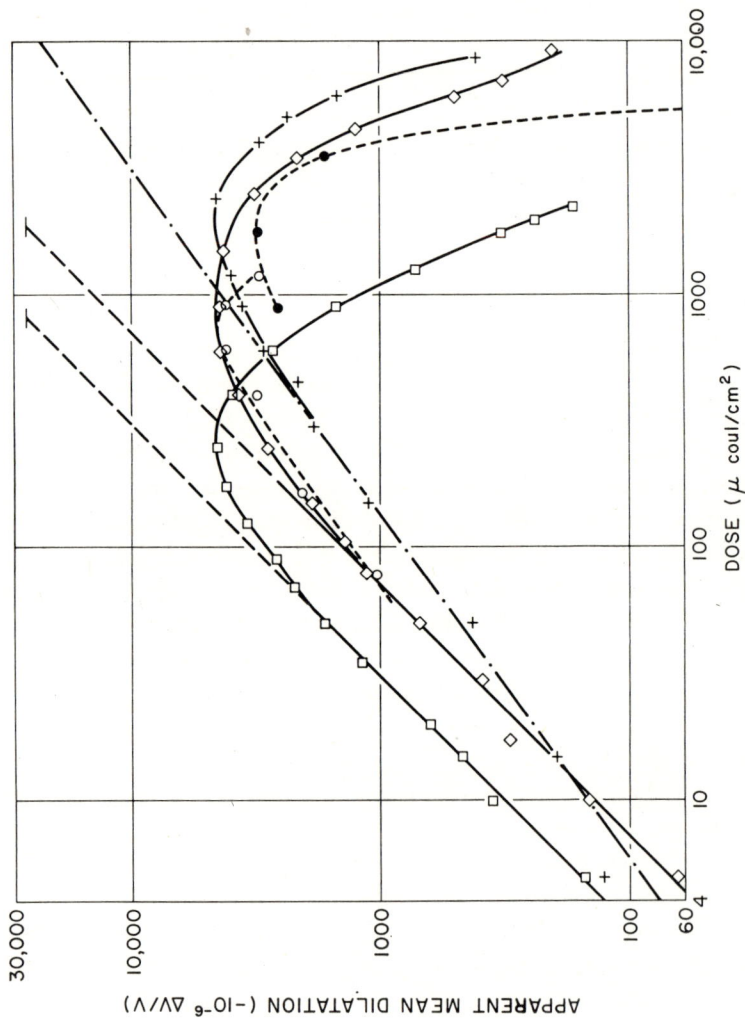

Figure 20. The mean dilatation of Suprasil bombarded with He $^+$ 140 keV (squares), D $^+$ 140 keV (diamonds), H $^+$ 140 keV (crosses), compared with H $^+$103 keV (circles) at much greater current densities ($\sim$20$\times$) reported by Primak.[293] The dashed lines have a slope of unity and are extended to the presumed saturation of the dilatation; the dot-dash lines, a slope of 0.71. (From Primak and Kampwirth.[263])

COMPACTION BY H⁺, D⁺, He⁺

Primak and Kampwirth[263] proceeded to determine dilatation as a function
of incident charge for 140 keV H⁺, D⁺, and He⁺. Their hope that the dependence on dose would be established before the effects of stress relaxation
appeared was realized, as shown in Fig. 20. The dependence for D⁺ and He⁺
was linear, while for H⁺ it was the 0.7 power. This was interpreted to mean
that the compaction by 140 keV H⁺ was almost entirely an ionization effect.
Since the initial rate for D⁺ was about the same as for H⁺, it was concluded
that the deuterium case was also largely one of ionization compaction; but
now enough local energy was supplied to counteract inhibition of the locking
in of compaction. The efficiency was twice as great for He⁺ as for D⁺; and
it was therefore concluded that half of the compaction occurred by other
mechanisms, ones involving local thermal excitation as described for neutron
compaction. These conclusions are reviewed below because of their further
investigations (see page [X-41]).

THRESHOLD FOR THE COMPACTION PROCESS

Primak and Kampwirth,[271] and then Primak,[272] continued these studies of
ion bombardment to obtain further data for the light ions and to obtain data
for neon and argon ions. Although these investigations are yet in an early
stage, the results are so significant that they will be given in some detail.
Primak integrated the Lindhard stopping powers as follows:

$$E_{v>TH} = \int_0^E \frac{S_{v>TH}(E)}{S_T(E)} \, dE,$$

where S is the stopping power, E is energy dissipated by the moving ion, the
subscript v is used to indicate the energy associated with collision processes,
the subscript Th is used to indicate a threshold, and the subscript T the total
energy dissipated through collision and electronic excitation. Although these
calculations of energy dissipation should be more reliable than range calculations, there is yet considerable uncertainty because the electronic stopping
power is poorly known. If the compaction is through a massive thermal spike,
as was suggested above for the neutron compaction, the only significant
scattering events are those in which a large amount of energy is transferred.

If a quantity which is proportional to the energy dissipated in collision
processes is plotted against it on logarithmic paper, a line of slope unity is
obtained. For a quantity proportional to the energy dissipated in processes
above some threshold plotted against the energy dissipated in all collision
processes, a curve is obtained. Primak's results are shown in Fig. 21. For a

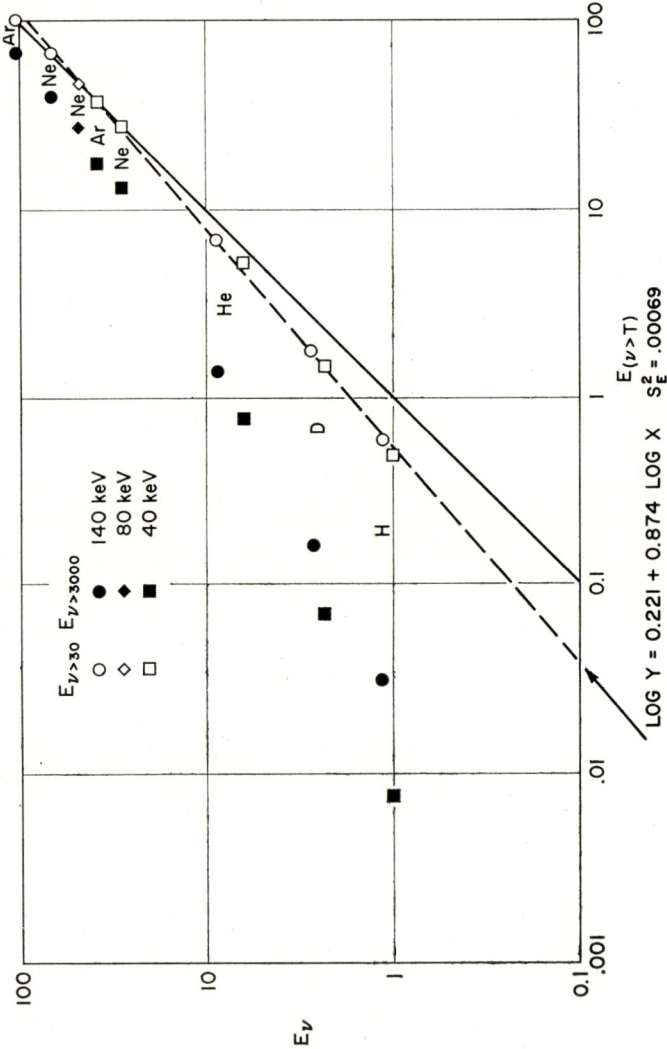

Figure 21.   The total energy dissipated in vitreous silica by atomic collisions plotted against the energy dissipated in vitreous silica by atomic collisions in which an energy greater than a threshold value T is transferred. The full line corresponds to the threshold of zero (slope unity); the dashed line is a logarithmic least squares fit to data for a threshold 30 eV.

30 eV threshold, the curve is nearly a straight line with a 13% difference in slope from that for no threshold. This procedure can therefore be used to obtain the threshold energy for the effect. It is of special value for studying the dilatation of vitreous silica, because compaction caused by ionization renders the usual procedure employing fractional MeV electrons useless. Despite the scattering of their data, no matter how they treated it, the slopes obtained by Primak and Kampwirth[272] and by Primak[303] indicated a threshold very much less than 30 eV. In contrast, when Hines and Arndt's refractive index data[255] for crystal quartz was treated in like manner, a threshold of about 25 eV was indicated. These results, present-

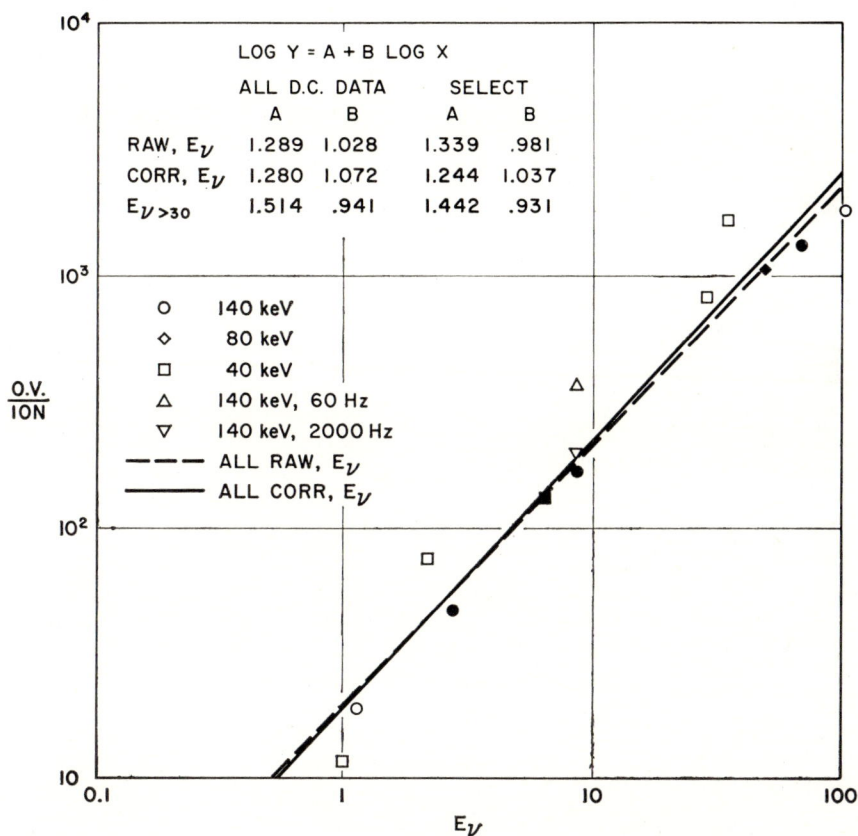

Figure 22. The total dilatation associated with ions incident on vitreous silica plotted against the energy dissipated by the ion in atomic collisions. The ions employed can be obtained by comparing the abscissae with the ordinates of Figure 21. The dashed line is a logarithmic least squares fit for a line of slope unity; the full line, a logarithmic least squares fit.

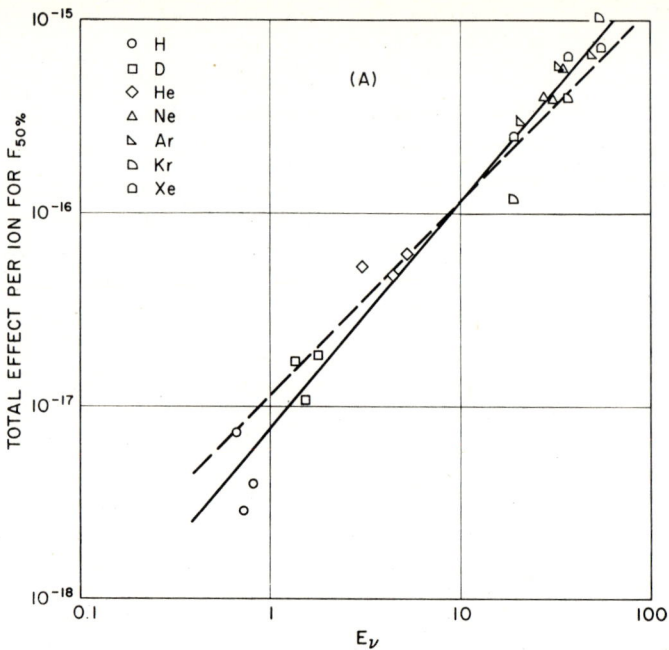

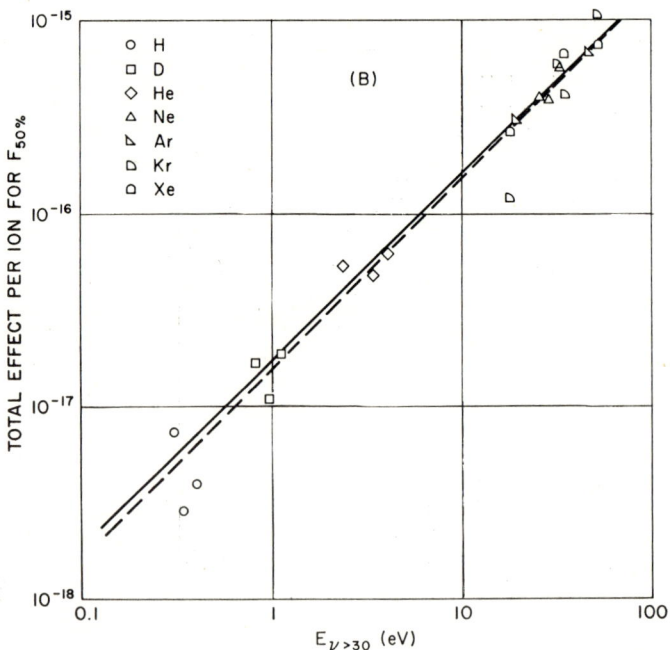

Figure 23. The refractive index data given by Hines and Arndt[255] for ion bombardment of quartz treated in a manner similar to that employed in Figure 22. The total effect was obtained by dividing their $F_{50\%}$ by their layer thickness. The dashed line is a best fit for slope unity, the full line a logarithmic least squares fit. (A) is for nil threshold, (B) is for a 30 eV threshold.

ed in Figs. 22 and 23, can be interpreted as indicating the compaction is
through a single thermal spike, but for the long ranges of the ions.

THERMAL SPIKES IN ION BOMBARDMENT*

The neutron compaction involves the stopping of silicon and oxygen ions.
According to the Seitz hypothesis, only below ~ 20 KeV are the collision
processes significant. Ranges for such ions were not available when Primak
made his early calculations; and he took the results of an inquiry by James
[301,302] in which it was suggested that in this region of the stopping, elastic
encounters occurred in every plane of atoms traversed. On this basis, Primak
took the range to be about 200 atomic distances. Curiously, this gives a range
of 0.049 μ as compared to 0.047 μ for a calculation of the range of a 20 KeV
neon ion (whose mass is close to the mean oxygen, silicon masses) by Lindhard's method,[273,274,275] an agreement beyond the precision of either calculation. Since the dose rate (the only certain experimental quantity available
for the process) indicated that $\sim 10^4$ atoms were involved in each compaction
event, the radius of the region would then be about 4 atomic distances. The
thermal spike is thus an elongated one, more appropriately treated as a
cylindrical than as a spherical one.[123]

Primak[303] undertook a reinvestigation of the thermal spike hypothesis.
The simple thermal spike may be described in terms of the quantities: T temperature rise, T_m maximum temperature rise, r radius, t time, α subscript for
a designated radius, i subscript for the point of inflection of temperature and
energy, V volume to some designated radius, P pressure, Q energy in calories
per unit length, E energy in eV, H energy in ergs, R range (microns), ζ^2 exponential factor $r^2/4x^2t$, N number of atoms to some designated radius,
A conversion constant $Q/\varrho = E/AR$, x^2 thermal diffusivity, γ Grüneisen constant, ϱ density, c heat capacity, n oxygens per cm^3. The cylindrical thermal
spike is:

$$T = \frac{Q}{c\varrho} \frac{1}{4\pi} \frac{1}{x^2t} \exp(-\zeta^2). \tag{1}$$

The maximum temperature is oe the certral axis:

$$T_m = \frac{Q}{c\varrho} \frac{1}{4\pi} \frac{1}{x^2t} = E/4\pi ARx^2t. \tag{2}$$

For a cylindrical thermal spike, the inflection in the temperature and the inflection in energy occur at the same radius. Quantities of interest in describ-

---

* This section was revised January, 1972 to correspond to the author's recent
investigations.

ing the spike are:

$$\zeta_i^2 = \tfrac{1}{2},$$

$$r_i = \sqrt{2x^2 t},$$

$$V_\alpha = \pi r_\alpha^2 R = \frac{1}{A}\,\zeta_\alpha^2\,E/T_m,$$

$$N_\alpha = 4\pi n x^2 t \zeta_\alpha^2 R = \frac{n}{A}\,\zeta_\alpha^2\,E/T_m,$$

$$t = N_\alpha/4\pi n x^2 t \zeta_\alpha^2 R,$$

$$P = \gamma H/V. \tag{3}$$

The mean pressure over some toroidal cross section of the thermal spike is:

$$\bar{P}_{1,2} = \gamma\,\frac{Q}{4\pi x^2 t}\left\{\frac{e^{-\zeta_1^2} - e^{-\zeta_2^2}}{\zeta_2^2 - \zeta_1^2}\right\}, \tag{4}$$

and must be adjusted for units; e.g., to give kilobars:

$$\bar{P}_{1,2} = 0.042\gamma\varrho c T_m f(\zeta_1,\zeta_2). \tag{5}$$

The function $f(\zeta_1,\zeta_2)$ from the axis to the inflection point is:

$$f\left(0,\sqrt{\tfrac{1}{2}}\right) = 0.7869\ldots \tag{6}$$

Primak and Kampwirth[17] presented evidence that in 20% of the thermal spike a different behavior occurs. Therefore the function from the inflection point to a radius encompassing a volume five times as great is of interest; i.e., when $V_x = 5V_i$:

$$f\left(\sqrt{\tfrac{1}{2}},\sqrt{2.5}\right) = 0.2622. \tag{7}$$

For most purposes, it has been customary to define the thermal spike as within the radius of the inflection temperature. For a cylindrical spike this encompasses 39% of the energy.

When the thermal spike hypothesis for the compaction of vitreous silica was proposed, the thermal conductivity of vitreous silica at elevated temperatures had not been determined, but it was rising with temperature over the range in which it was known. Primak therefore attempted to determine the effect of a variable diffusivity on the characteristics of the thermal spike and concluded that although the temperature distribution within the thermal spike was modified somewhat by becoming more uniform, the heat flow from the thermal spike, hence its pertinent characteristics, were controlled by the external medium. In his reinvestigation he was able to apply modern computing equipment to the problem and considered it in two ways:—first as a two medium problem with the thermal spike possessing a higher thermal diffusivity than the external medium; and second, by a method due to Boltzmann, as a continuous medium problem with the thermal diffusivity varying as a power of temperature. The results confirmed the conclusion reached earlier. He also considered the variation in energy dissipation along the range; and found it did not affect the results significantly.

Several determinations of the thermal conductivity up to 1200°C have become available in recent years and are assembled by Goldsmith, et al.[374] In the region approaching red heat and above, the results rise remarkably rapidly, in excess of the 4th power of temperature; and there are large discrepancies among them. These could be accounted for if there were a contribution from radiative transfer, particularly from contacting surfaces, as sample dimensions, quality of surfaces, and nature of the contacting materials would all affect the results. Several additional determinations have been published during the past decade.[375,376,377] Several of these investigators concluded that a contribution from radiative transfer was present, and one investigator sought to demonstrate this by studying inhomogeneous materials.[377]

In the thermal spike of radiation damage, radiation should be largely in spectral regions in which the neighboring material is opaque; hence, no large rise in the thermal diffusivity should occur. Thus, the thermal spike should be only slightly modified from that for constant diffusivity. For the precision required here, it is considered sufficient to compare calculations obtained for a simple thermal spike, and the values of the constants are taken to be heat capacity 0.27 cal/g deg, diffusivity 0.008 cm²/sec, density 2.2 g/cm³, Grüneisen constant 0.03, and 4.4×10^{22} oxygens/cm³. To calculate the pressure, the heat capacity of interest is that within the thermal spike, not that external to it; and 0.3 cal/g is used. The formulas for the thermal spike taken to the point of inflection then become:

$$t = 4.52 \times 10^{-18} \, N_i/R,$$
$$r_t = 0.1265 t^{1/2},$$
$$T_m = 1417 \, E/N_t,$$
and
$$P = 7.46 \times 10^{-4} \, T_m f(\zeta) \tag{8}$$

for the condition which would be quenched in were the energy dissipated uniformly along the thermal spike. This will be called the simple mean thermal spike.

The formalism which was presented for counting events in vitreous silica can be used to obtain a result for the energy expended per event. Since the dilatation is about 2.9% at saturation, 2.9% of the total number of atoms in the thermal spike are the number of ionic oxygen volumes (O.V.) which are to be counted for the effect. According to the Seitz approach, about half the energy is dissipated in elastic collisions. Thus 10 KeV is to be associated with 2.9% of 10^4 oxygen atoms. This gives the result, 34 eV per displacement. Similar results are obtained if the energies are calculated by the Lindhard theory. Thus, for a neon ion of 140 keV energy, 67 keV expended in elastic collisions is associated with 2.9% of 40,000 oxygen atoms, which gives 53 eV/O.V. The energy per atom in the thermal spike is such that the energy per counted event (or displacement as those using Seitz's method refer to it) corresponds to the magnitude usually taken for the displacement energy. The same result is obtained from more elegant calculations. It is the basis for analyses such as that by Schineller, et al.[300] Because of the accident that the saturation dilatation is a 3% compaction, such a calculation provides no test of displacement theory nor of the thermal spike hypothesis; it is just some interesting numerology.

If the dilatation is used to count the compaction processes, the quantity to be related to the energy dissipated by the ion is the integral of dilatation over the range of the ion. If no stress relaxation has occurred, this quantity can be obtained experimentally from the strain in the attached material; because theoretically and experimentally, the strain is a linear function of the thickness of the medium. Primak and his collaborators[209,306] have developed methods of measuring it precisely photoelastically. Specimens 10–12 mm square (D) and 2–4 mm thick (W) are used. Birefringence measured through the depth D of the specimen in a direction perpendicular to the face varies linearly along the width W. When $R \ll W$, the dilatation is

$$\delta = 4.92 \times 10^{-3} \frac{W}{D} \frac{z}{R},$$

where z is the difference in retardation for white light, extrapolated to opposite edges, and given in degrees rotation of the analyzer of the de Senarmont compensator. For the typical specimen $W/D = \frac{1}{3}$, and 1 deg corresponds to 1.64×10^{-7} cm^3/cm^2. Although he could not measure it here because of the stress relaxation, Primak assumed saturation to be the same as for the neutron compaction, $\delta = 0.029$. Then, the fraction of saturation is

$$F = 0.0566/R.$$

Primak used the Lindhard ranges. For the lightest ions, the ranges were underestimated because the electronic stopping was overestimated; for the heavier ions, the ranges were overestimated because the Lindhard calculations gives the range along the path of the particle. The range corrections are 5–30%, and various parts of the calculations are affected differently. At our present state of knowledge the corrections are hardly significant and should not affect our conclusions. The quantities of interest are the yields and efficiencies. The yield is simple $\delta R/zV_0$ in O.V. where V_0 is 1.7×10^{-23}. Introduction of the incident ion charge and the ion energy gives the remaining quantities needed to calculate the characteristics of the simple mean thermal spikes according to Eqs. 8. The results are given in Table 10A.

Because the ranges are not involved in calculating the temperature, examining it affords the simplest comparison of these data. The fluctuations appear to be quite random. The data are those utilized originally on a logarithmic scale to determine the threshold (see just above). Here on a linear scale a decided scattering in seen. The most reliable data give a value near 1800° for T_m, and thus the thermal spike may be considered to range from about 1250°C to about 1850°C. The yields which would correspond to T_m being 1800°C are given and are well within the precision of the data; this corresponds to an identical value ~ 45 eV for the energy required to cause a compaction of 1 O.V. by any of these ions. If the energy dissipated at a particular point along the range is introduced into Eqs. (8), the temperature and other characteristics at a given time will vary along the range. Such a thermal spike calculated for a 140 keV Ne$^+$ ion is shown in Fig. 24.

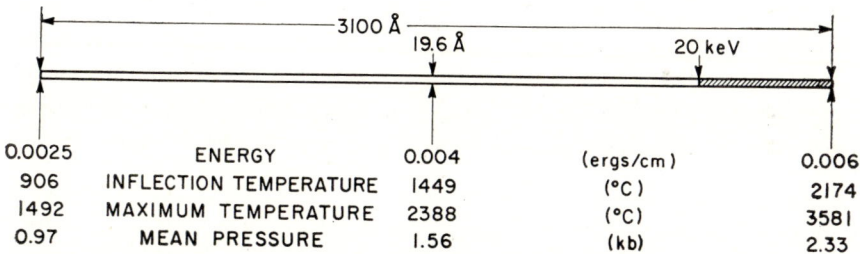

0.0025	ENERGY	0.004	(ergs/cm)	0.006
906	INFLECTION TEMPERATURE	1449	(°C)	2174
1492	MAXIMUM TEMPERATURE	2388	(°C)	3581
0.97	MEAN PRESSURE	1.56	(kb)	2.33

Figure 24. Formal representation of the thermal spike associated with the stopping of a 140 keV Ne ion in vitreous silica; the whole, based on the Lindhard theory; the shaded, based on the Seitz theory.

The characteristics of the thermal spike conceived originally to explain the results of the neutron compaction (see Table 9) involved times $\sim 10^{-11}$ sec and dimensions ~ 50 atomic radii as the condition at quenching. This was a comfortable volume and long enough time to consider the effect as a thermal one. This is not true for the characteristics given in Table 10A. The ranges of the ions are so great that the radii of the thermal spikes are but a few atomic diameters (~ 5 for the Ne thermal spike). The thermal constants give times for the quenching of the volume affected that are but a few atomic vibrations (~ 5 for the Ne case). The same kind of compaction is found for He$^+$

8*

TABLE 10A　Simple mean thermal spike characteristics

Ion	Yield (O.V./ion)	Oxygens affected (N_i)	Range (μ)	Energy, Total Nuclear (keV)	Efficiency (eV/O.V.)	Thermal Spike				Yield for $T_m = 1800$ O.V./ion
						t_i (10^{-15} sec)	r_i (Å)	T_m °C	P kbar	
				— 140 keV —						
Ar	2233	79,750	0.155	103.3	46	2326.0	19	1835	1.20	2276
Ne	1656	59,143	0.307	68.8	42	871.0	12	1648	1.08	1516
He	225	8,036	1.06	8.54	38	34.3	2.3	1506	0.98	188
D	59	2,107	1.594	2.74	46	5.98	0.98	1843	1.20	60
H	26	929	1.174	1.135	44	3.58	0.76	1732	1.13	25
				— 80 keV —						
Ne	1316	47,000	0.179	48.5	37	1190.0	14	1462	0.95	1069
				— 40 keV —						
Ar	2046	73,071	0.046	34.4	17	7180.0	34	667	0.44	758
Ne	1038	37,071	0.091	28.9	28	1840.0	17	1105	0.72	637
He	166	5,929	0.482	6.44	39	55.6	3	1539	1.01	142
D	92	3,285	0.790	2.29	25	18.8	1.7	988	0.65	50
H	16	571	0.604	0.976	61	4.23	0.83	2420	1.58	22

TABLE 10B Distribution of events

Ion	Range (μ)	$E_{\nu>6}{}^a$ (keV)	Broken[b] Links (No.)	Compaction[c] (O.V./ion)	Oxygens[d] Affected (No.)	Concentration[e] of Broken Links (%)	Spacing[f] of Affected Oxygens (Å)	Spacing[f] of Broken Links (Å)	Spacing of[f] Compaction (Å)
					– 140 keV –				
Ar	0.155	102.6	17,100	2233	79,750	46.5	0.019	0.091	0.69
Ne	0.307	68.2	11,367	1656	59,143	14.4	0.052	0.27	1.85
He	1.06	7.72	1,287	227	8,107	15.9	1.31	8.24	46.7
D	1.594	2.21	368	59	2,107	17.5	7.56	43.3	270.0
H	1.174	0.832	139	26	929	14.9	12.6	84.7	452.0
					– 80 keV –				
Ne	0.179	47.9	7,983	1316	47,000	17.0	0.038	0.22	1.36
					– 40 keV –				
Ar	0.046	34.2	5,700	2046	73,071	7.8	0.0063	0.081	0.22
Ne	0.091	28.4	4,733	1038	37,071	12.8	0.025	0.19	0.88
He	0.482	5.86	977	166	5,929	16.5	0.81	4.94	29.0
D	0.790	1.86	310	92	3,286	9.4	2.40	25.5	85.9
H	0.604	0.714	119	16	571	20.8	10.6	50.8	378.0

a Nuclear energy dissipated in events in which more than 6 eV is transferred calculated according to the theory of Lindhard et al.[273,274]

b $E_{\nu>6} \times 1000/6$.

c From the experimental data.

d The compaction/0.028. Note some calculations given above use 0.029.

e 100 × Broken Links/Oxygens Affected.

f Along the range.

and D^+ ions; and even for protons, for which the behavior is somewhat different, the same values for T_m and P are calculated. For these ions t is a fraction of an atomic vibration and r_i is less than an atomic diameter. Whether the thermal conditions developed in the thermal spike would give the observed compaction is yet unanswered. When Cohen and Roy's[168] results for the pressure compaction as a function of temperature and pressure (Fig. 6) are extrapolated linearly from 850°C where they terminate, they give a 3% compaction for zero applied pressure at 1400°C. However, vitreous silica quenched from 1400°C (perhaps quenching of macroscopic specimens is too slow) shows a 0.1% compaction. Mackenzie[173] reported that 15 kbar pressure was required to produce 3% compaction at 2000°C. To resolve these difficulties, the atomic behavior is examined.

It was pointed out above that there are two major factors in the compaction process. First is the movement of oxygens into the larger void spaces; and second, bond cleavage in the network to permit a strand of the network to alter its configuration. Of course, a quenching of the compacted configuration must then ensue: the altered configuration is the normal one for the excited condition; the compaction occurs on cooling. No role is designated for the displacements. They must anneal under the conditions for most of the observations. The displacements may cause some secondary phenomena which are yet to be explored, but the primary effects are assigned to the excitation and bond cleavage. The energy required for cleaving an Si–O bond should be ~ 6 eV, and such a threshold is not in conflict with the threshold determination presented just above. The distribution along the range, of the quantities of interest here, are given in Table 10B. It is seen that the compaction occurs in only a fraction ($\sim \frac{1}{6}$) of the instances of bond cleavage. For this reason the possibilities of the precondition for compaction being bond cleavage or an electric field condition are rejected. It is concluded that the precondition is vibrational excitation, akin to the precondition in the thermal compaction. The distinguishing behavior of the radiation compaction must result from the greater fragmentation of the network and the greater stability of the cleavages, the latter resulting from ionization and the occasional displacement.

Because the transition from a reduced power dependence of the compaction on dose occurs between H^+ and D^+, their behavior is a key to understanding the process. The smallest unit of the solid in which the compaction can be described is that encompassing the void space, hence 14–18 oxygens in the mean structure. Bond cleavage has been assumed to require ~ 6 eV. It is seen in Table 10B that such energies are deposited at every 3rd to 4th such unit along the range, and this is given as the incidence of bond cleavage. Since the energy is deposited not in the bond but in the atom, and since dissipation may occur by other means than bond cleavage (especially for large angle scattering), the spacing of cleaved bonds will be somewhat greater than that given in the Table on this account; on the other hand, there will be bonds in the structure cleaving at lower energies, and this will contribute to decreasing the spacing. Further, the lifetime of these cleaved bonds has not been considered. Although the description cannot be more than semi-quantitative, it does serve to describe the mechanism. The compaction now requires the favorable juxtaposition of vibrational energy relative to the cleaved bonds. For protons the incidence of cleaved bonds is reduced to every 5th to 8th unit encompassing void space. The behavior of protons appears to be an admixture of corpuscular and ionization compaction, but with the corpuscular compaction still behaving in the manner found for the heavier ions, despite its infrequency along the range.

For Ne^+ and Ar^+, as can be seen in Table 10B, the density of the deposited energy is sufficient to cleave every bond in every unit along the range and for part of a unit outward. Yet the efficiencies found for them are the same as those for deuterons and He. In the mechanism of compaction presented here, compaction does not occur at these pressures in the loops in which bond cleavage has taken place, hence it could occur only peripherally. More likely, the compaction which is fixed is not developed at this time, but only after the excitation has spread outward. This aspect of the process is reminiscent of the aging of a thermal spike. However, in the present view, the compaction results not from the thermal conditions alone, but is facilitated and controlled by the bond cleavage, the configuration being fixed by recombination. This mechanism could lead to a difference in peripheral and central compaction, the explanation selected by Primak and Kampwirth[304] for the supervenient expansion of pile-exposed vitreous silica.

The mechanism proposed here solves the problem of the unrealistic thermal conditions in the thermal spikes associated with the light ions. The present hypothesis still involves massive conversion rather than isolated atomic events—a requirement of the dose data. Thus it is still a spike hypothesis, albeit, not a thermal spike; it is a bond cleavage spike.

E.   Miscellaneous

CHARGE STORAGE AND BREAKDOWN

For the ion and electron bombardments described here, the problems of charge storage and breakdown have not been studied in detail, and only qualitative observations are available. Under the usual conditions of bombardment in high vacuum, when the beam overlaps an edge, ionization by the beam, scattered ions, and secondary electrons is sufficient to form an electrical path along the edge provided that it is connected electrically to the target electrode. Primak and his co-workers[263] have set specimens on skimmed molten Wood's metal; on solidification it gave suitable support as well as thermal and electrical contact. When the edge is not irradiated, or when the specimen is insulated from the support (as by double backing tape or set on wax), a Lichtenberg discharge may occur,[8] and evidence for its occurrence may be seen in the microscope in oblique, dark field, or vertical illumination. (photograph shown in Fig. 25). In photoelastic examination, an irregular strain pattern may be seen after such a discharge; and the dilatation calculated from the birefringence is low, showing stress relaxation has occurred. Some glasses are more subject to breakdown than others, and this has been attributed to their higher leakage resistance under bombardment. Hines[255] placed a thermionic emitter in the target Faraday cup of his accelerator to discharge the surface. In a poor vacuum, Primak and Edwards[8] used a dilute plasma excited with a few thousand volts A.C. To provide an electrical path in another case, they painted the edges of the specimen and the mounting wax with a silver pigmented conducting lacquer. Primak and his co-workers[263] found that ionization in air was adequate to provide an electrical path for most vitreous silica specimens electron bombarded in air, but was inadequate for one which had been subjected to a long exposure in a nuclear reactor.[304] Whether the breakdown potential or the leakage resistance had been altered is unknown. Charge storage appears to be increased,[307] but what effect this has is not known. Primak and Kampwirth[263] found that vitreous silica specimens subjected to electron bombardment in vacuo while sitting on a grounded aluminum backing plate developed a strong adhesion to the plate; and when removed, were attracted to other objects. Unreported additional details are presented here. To develop frictional resistance as great as that found for displacing the specimen on the target holder, a 10 kg load had to be applied to a 1 cm^2 specimen placed on a similar surface. To obtain a normal force of this magnitude electrostatically, the upper surface of a 3 mm thick specimen would have to be charged to $\sim 10^6$ volts, hardly possible with incident electrons $\sim 10^5$ eV! Such a potential would have deflected the beam; yet no difference was found for the rate of ionization dilatation when specimens were completely silvered except for the bombarded top surface. It is therefore concluded that the charge on the unsilvered specimens was transferred to their bottom surfaces and that the electrostatic force was developed across the very small gap and the oxide coating of the specimen holder. Since this distance was very small, the forces could be obtained from charges corresponding to voltages $\sim 10^3$, typical of those maintained on insulators by mild electrification processes. Similar electrostatic adhesion phenomena have

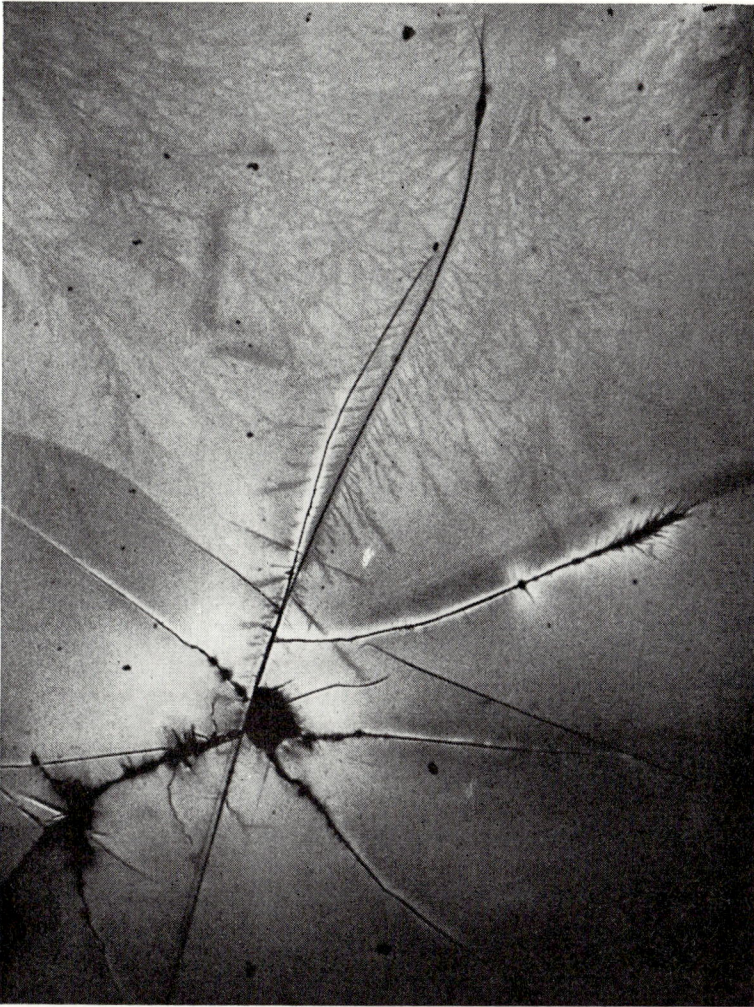

Figure 25. Microphotograph (35 mm objective) of a Lichtenberg discharge produced during a 1 MeV proton bombardment of vitreous silica. The area shown is about $\frac{1}{2}$ cm across.

found technical application recently.[308] Such charges would have no significant effect on the measurements considered here. In small Suprasil specimens, this transient charge appeared to be largely dissipated in several hours. No effect on the dilatation was seen for these specimens, but transient dilatations were found in studies of the impurity associated expansions,[146] and of release of neutron compaction[304] (see pages 145 et seq.).

Glasses have not been a favored material for the study of charge storage.[309] The phenomena are more complex than those in waxes and plastics, the surface conductivity and accumulated homocharge is a more severe problem, the leakage is greater, and they cannot be sectioned easily. The electrical resistance in ionizing fields was treated by Fowler.[310] Following the destruction of several large shielding windows by Lichtenberg discharge upon mild mechanical shock, there was a flurry of research,[311,312,313,314] but this languished when it was found that providing a relatively thin cover glass of less sensitive glass solved the practical problem.[315] Charge storage in these cases arose from the predominantly forward scattering of the Compton effect.[316,317] Gross,[318] and also Hardtke,[319,320] found that the irradiated glasses exhibited thermoelectric behavior. Few observations were made with vitreous silica, and these do not illuminate the problems of interest here. Primak and Kampwirth's observation[304] that neutron compaction enhanced the sensitivity of vitreous silica to Lichtenberg discharge on electron bombardment, indicates an investigation of charge storage phenomena in various vitreous silicas should be made.

FURTHER COMMENTS ON STRESS RELAXATION

All specimens showing radiation-induced dilatations in nuclear reactors develop internal stresses because self-absorption makes the internal flux density non-uniform. If the dilatation saturates, it would appear that the stresses should be relieved at saturation; but Primak and Edwards[8] found that the stresses developed in vitreous silica were not relieved at saturation. Instead, they passed through zero in the neighborhood of the maximum compaction and then reversed during the period of the supervenient expansion as shown in Figs. 26A and B. They did not begin to decrease again until long after the dilatation had become nearly constant, beyond the extremum of Fig. 26B. Primak[293] pointed out that this effect was caused by stress relaxation (plastic flow was meant) during compaction. The present significance of this observation is the small stress at which plastic flow occurred during neutron irradiation; in contrast to the large stress developed before it was observed with proton, deuteron, or helium ion bombardment; and the failure to observe it in electron bombardment. This indicates that the mechanism for the plastic flow involves cleavage of the Si–O network, leaving the segments free to rearrange, release the stress, and then reconstitute the network by recombination. Fragmentation of the network is very extensive in neutron bombardment; it is more isolated in light ion bombardment; and it is rare in electron bombardment. Earlier, Mayer and Lecomte[278] reported that for vitreous silica fibres under mechanical stress, compressive and extensive,

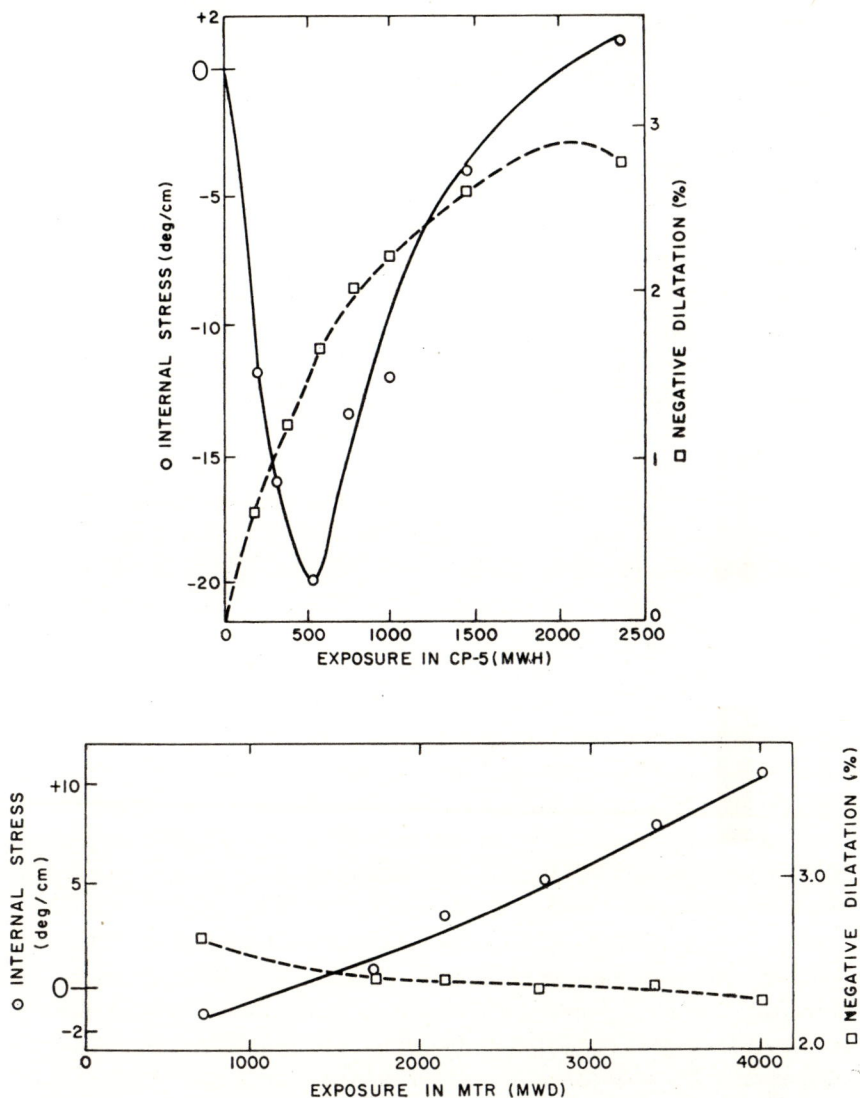

Figure 26.   (A) Internal stress at edges of cylinders irradiated in a CP-5 fuel element thimble. (B) Internal stress at edges of silica specimens $\frac{3}{16}$ in. sq. $\times 1.187$ cm long irradiated in the MTR. The stress scales in (A) and (B) are not identical but correspond to ~ 1 kg/cm^2 for $1°$/cm; the exposure scales are very different and not quite comparable for the two reactors but for (B) may be taken as contracted about 3-fold compared to (A); i.e., the effect found after 2000 MWH (CP-5) corresponds to that after 300–1000 MWD (MTR). The dilatation is plotted as squares for comparison. (Redrawn from Primak and Edwards[8].)

(material, dimensions, stress, mechanical arrangement, reactor environment, all unstated), in a fast neutron flux $2 \times 10^{12}/cm^2$, the creep rate at 60 °C was increased (approximately) to its value at 600 °C in the absence of radiation.

RADIATION DISORDERING

The products of irradiation have been described here as a compacted vitreous silica, a higher density but more disordered vitreous phase than vitreous silica. There has been some controversy on this subject. One aspect is easily dismissed: the assumption[322] that an increase in density implies an ordering. This view appears to have arisen from observation of the behavior of quartz and vitreous silica reaching a common intermediate density on irradiation, and has no structural basis whatsoever. The second comes from several different lines of investigation which do have either a structural basis or structural implications. The first was a report by Wittels and Sherrill[265] which described the observation of α-quartz lines in neutron compacted vitreous silica which had been annealed. This is discussed below (see page 125). The second is from the work of Primak.[10] He found that specimens of quartz which had been disordered by exposure in a nuclear reactor beyond a certain point, but which still possessed anisotropic optical properties (birefringence and rotatory power) were further disordered on annealing and reached the density of ordinary vitreous silica. Some quartz not irradiated quite as long also disordered further on annealing but reached a density just a little greater than that of vitreous silica. The diffuse halos obtained in x-ray diffraction of these specimens were a little sharper than for similar specimens of vitreous silica. No examination for homogeneity was made. However, it is evident that phases which are more ordered than vitreous silica can be made; but it is also evident from the x-ray diffraction data for irradiated vitreous silica that they do not form in the radiation compaction near room temperature. Further evidence on this subject has been obtained by Primak and Edwards.[8] They irradiated an inhomogeneous vitreous silica (Ge 101). The kind of inhomogeneity displayed by this material was discussed above and described as a residue of structure from the crystal quartz starting material and a varying composition associated with the surfaces of the grains which were fused (see pages 33, 40). Primak and Edwards did not find noticeable change in the inhomogeneity after irradiation for the period required to compact the specimens (these were the specimens in which the regular behavior of the radiation-induced internal stress was first observed) but there was a marked decrease in birefringence of the birefringent zones after irradiation for a period comparable to that required to disorder quartz. After subsequent post-irradiation annealing, the inhomogeneity increased, but it was yet considerably less than before the irradiation. This is further evidence that the radiation behavior is a disordering process. Billington and Crawford[324] attempted to adduce evidence on this subject from the measurements of low temperature thermal conductivity and heat capacity but were unable to reach definite conclusions.

CRYSTALLIZATION AND DEVITRIFICATION

This subject is presented here rather than under the heading of thermal annealing because of reports of direct formation of crystalline material on irradiation and the possible implications of these findings for the thermal spikes.

Wittels and Sherrill[265] reported the observation of α-quartz lines in the x-ray diffraction patterns of neutron compacted vitreous silica which had been heated. Billington and Crawford[323] state the results were for very thin wall capillary tubes, but the original description was quite ambiguous over which specimens, irradiated crystalline phases or irradiated vitreous silica, were involved. Billington and Crawford wonder whether the large surface to volume ratio might have affected the results because Primak and Szymanski[183] found that the density of neutron compacted vitreous silica returned to that of ordinary vitreous silica on heating. It should be noted that the heating of 16 h at 960° employed by Wittels and Sherrill could have caused devitrification, especially if some contamination were present. However, Roy and Busmer's investigations[325] show that exposure in a nuclear reactor does affect the course of phase changes among the crystalline phases of silica in a complex manner. Thus, additional studies would be very desirable.

Wittels and Sherrill[265] described the formation of polycrystalline material formed by the heating of neutron disordered quartz. Crawford and Wittels[326] state that porosity may develop on heating crystal plates which had been exposed in a nuclear reactor. Mayer and Lecomte[278] studied the phenomena further and described the product formed by heating material from the midstage of the radiation disordering of quartz as amorphous and anisotropic. In view of Weissmann and Nakajima's work,[327] the subject is classed here as one requiring further investigation. However, it is really a problem in the disordering of quartz rather than one in the compaction of vitreous silica and therefore beyond the scope of the present inquiry.

Corning 7940 (High Purity Fused Silica) which had been exposed in the LITR (nuclear reactor) was examined by Weissmann and Nakajima[328] by transmission electron diffraction and electron microscopy. They found evidence of numerous very small α-quartz regions. They had also examined irradiated quartz[327] and found evidence of inhomogeneity in its electron density. The concern here is with two matters: their observations and their explanations. They considered the inhomogeneity to be caused by a segregation of silicon in the quartz and attempted to explain the density change in this manner. A careful examination of their calculation shows it implies a loss of oxygen. Experimentally, no such weight losses are found on irradiation; and there is no direct evidence of any appreciable segregation of silicon, although Gossick[329] has considered the possibility of a plasma resonance center analogous to the colloid centers in alkali halides. Weissmann and Nakajima[328] attempted to explain the radiation-induced increase in density of vitreous silica as caused by the formation of the quartz crystallites. Even their own evidence does not support such an explanation, for they found that the crystallites became apparent toward the end of the supervenient expansion, whereas the compaction occurs very rapidly in the early stages of irradiation. It thus seems most reasonable to associate the crystallites with some secondary phenomenon. Crystallites have not been found in direct x-ray examination.[330] Weissmann and Nakajima found them in greatly thinned specimens prepared by the action of a HNO_3–HF–H_2O jet. It will be recalled that this reagent was employed by Fahey[231] to separate the phases of silica because of their vastly different solution rates in it. Thus two possibilities arise: that in their thinning operation Weissmann and Nakajima concentrated a phase present in small amount; or that the phase was highly distorted by the surrounding network, and the strain was relieved by differential solution. However, the facts that the phase was not seen in the unirradiated material and that there was an increase in both the quantity and size of the crystallites during irradiation, shows it appeared as a result of the irradiation. At this time, it appears best to consider the effect as a radiation-induced crystallization associated with thermal spikes in regions which have been subjected repeatedly to such treatment. If this interpretation is correct, the effect is analogous to that found in shock wave compaction where crystallization is not seen in material subjected to single laboratory shock waves, but is seen in low concentration in the extended sequence of shock waves produced by meteoritic blast. A radiation-induced crystallization may be quite a complex sequence of events as indicated by Roy and Busmer's[325, 331] experiments on the effect of exposure in a nuclear reactor on phase changes in silica; there may be forerunner high pressure phases. In summary: the concentration of crystallites formed on exposure in a nuclear reactor must be quite low since they have not been observed in bulk specimens, and the crystallites cannot have a great effect on the density because the density is decreasing when they are developing. The effect should be studied further; and the effect of impurities, particularly OH content, should be investigated.

Anomalous Properties

The low temperature anomaly in vitreous silica is greatly reduced on compaction. Westrum[332] gives data on the reduction of the low temperature specific heat by neutron compaction. Strakna[333] studied reduction of the ultrasonic loss peak, and Clark and Strakna,[334] the low temperature heat capacity, by neutron compaction. White and Birch[335] give data for the thermal expansion. Flubacher, Leadbetter, Morrison, and Stoicheff[336] follow Smyth's approach[125,126] and relate the anomalous heat capacity to several Einstein modes. They state that less than 2% of the normal modes being optical modes will account for the anomalous heat capacity. These are probably transverse modes of the Si–O–Si link, as has been discussed above (see page 31). The fact that they are so greatly inhibited by several per cent compaction (i.e., in the early stages of compaction) indicates their origin. In presenting the structural formalism (see page 95), the irregularity of the network was not considered. In analogy to the treatment of quartz (see page 18), it is reasonable to associate larger amplitude unsymmetrical oxygen vibrations with larger loops, and these loops would most easily participate in compaction in the manner described above for the kind of motion which occurs in the α–β-transitions. If the optical modes were associated with such loops in the network, compaction would eliminate them. The hypothesis developed by Strakna[333] and by Clark and Strakna[334] is erroneous for it is based on an incorrect model for the structure of vitreous silica, a linear Si–O–Si bond. Also their assumption that Westrum's[332] second quartz samples represents saturation of effect is erroneous; saturation would require an irradiation an order of magnitude greater, and the heat capacity would then be indistinguishable from that of irradiated vitreous silica. White and Birch[335] point out that the anomalous properties are reduced by introducing non-network impurities and argue that this effect is also an inhibition of the optical modes. According to the hypothesis presented here, the effect is produced by the impurities preferentially occupying the larger loops. It would be very desirable now to determine how network cleaving impurities affect the low temperature anomalies and whether the radiation behavior is influenced.

Applications of Radiation Compaction

Virtually no applications, either positive or negative, have been made of the radiation-induced property changes of vitreous silica. For two applications which have been suggested, the effects have not been described accurately. Schineller et al.[300] have suggested that the radiation induced change in refractive index may be used to construct an optical wave guide. They propose proton irradiation and attempt to correlate the effect (incorrectly) with the number of displacements, whereas it has been shown here that the effect appears to be largely an ionization effect. From their description, it appears that some mechanical effect (stresses or crazing) may have been present in their devices, in addition to the change in refractive index. Ionic sputtering has been suggested as a means for polishing and figuring glass.[337,338] These writers do not appear to have taken into account the concomitant radiation effects: changes in composition, changes in volume, changes in refractive index, induced strain; which would develop an optical element whose stability would not meet the severe optical requirements for which the process was intended. Malitson, et al.[339,340] have been concerned about radiation-induced changes in refractive index in optical elements subjected to space travel, but have examined only multicomponent glasses. Lungu has investigated vitreous silica fuel elements. His interpretations have been based upon structural models which have been rejected here. However, his experimental results have some bearing on the supervenient expansion and are discussed below (see page 150).

VIII. Thermal Release of Compaction

INTRODUCTION

There are several fairly detailed studies of the thermal annealing of neutron compacted vitreous silica from the stage of supervenient expansion, but with material which by present standards must be considered inadequately defined. Our whole consideration of the thermal annealing will have to be based on these studies because there are no other detailed studies. There are less detailed data for pressure compacted vitreous silica. There are no data for the early stages of neutron compaction, for shock compaction, for meteoric blast compaction, or for polishing compaction. The thermal compaction data intrinsically contain thermal annealing information, but the subject has never been studied from that point of view.

The first observers of the compaction, Primak, Fuchs, and Day,[241] and Bridgman and Šimon,[9] both heated the compacted vitreous silica and observed a release of compaction. Primak and Szymanski[183] performed a series of isothermal annealings of old (stored for a long period after irradiation) neutron compacted vitreous silica from near the peak of the compaction. The original material was probably GE 101 vitreous silica, and it had been irradiated in a test hole in a Hanford reactor. The densities given for the particles indicates it to have been from the period of the supervenient expansion; the radiation dose corresponds to a point close to maximum density. Primak, Szymanski, and Keiffer[185] later published isothermal and step annealing data for specimens definitely from the region of the supervenient expansion. The original work of Primak and Szymanski was on material which had been crushed to 60 mesh grains prior to irradiation. The later results published by Primak, Szymanski, and Keiffer was for clear laboratory tubing drawn to ampules in which other materials were irradiated, and long after irradiation it was crushed to 45 mesh grains. The annealings were performed in glass tubes, pyrex for some of the lower temperature annealings, clear vitreous silica for the others. The densities were measured after annealing by suspension in a heavy liquid whose density was adjusted by regulating its temperature. Several methods were used for determining the density of the liquid, but all were referred to hydrostatic weighings of a bob in the liquid and in water. The results will be treated together for they display no noteworthy differences.

THEORY OF THERMAL ANNEALING

The nomenclature used here follows. A set of isothermal annealings is obtained by taking a specimen and heating it at a given temperature. Heating may be interrupted for measurement; but when resumed, it is resumed at the same temperature. Step annealing consists of performing isothermal annealings at a particular temperature; then the same specimen is used to perform a set of isothermal annealings at a higher temperature. It was shown by Primak[184] that these are very different experiments: that in isothermal annealing the original state of the material is studied; in step-annealing how the original state was modified by the previous annealing.

Primak and Szymanski[183] observed annealing from about 300°C to about 1000°C, at which temperature the original density had been restored. This long range of temperature for annealing cannot be described by singly activated processes, as was pointed out by Vand, and by Neubert and his collaborators. Primak and Szymanski analyzed their data by a method originally due to Vand,[341] which had been adopted by Neubert,[342,343] and whose theory was further developed by Primak.[344] The usual treatment assumes independent processes are occurring, and it will be shown that this is probably the case for the annealing of compacted vitreous silica at the higher temperatures. The annealing for a single process is

$$p = p_0 e^{-kt}$$

where p_0 is the original concentration, t is time, and k is the rate constant which may be given by the modified Arrhenius expression

$$k = A e^{-\varepsilon/\tau},$$

where τ is the energy per molecule, Boltzmann's constant times the absolute temperature, and ε is the activation energy, which will here be given in eV. The properties of the function

$$\theta = \exp\left(A t e^{-\varepsilon/\tau}\right)$$

and its derivatives with respect to t, θ; and with respect to v, θ', are very interesting (see Primak's papers[184,344] for these) and are the key to the whole development. When there is not a single process, but a distribution, a property which is a suitable measure of the processes is given by the integral

$$P(\varepsilon) = \int p_0(\varepsilon)\, \theta\, (\varepsilon, t)\, d\varepsilon.$$

It was pointed out by Vand that θ is nearly constant for most of its range; and over the range of ε where it does vary, the distribution $p_0(\varepsilon)$, if sufficiently broad, may be considered to be constant. There are different ways of giving an approximate solution to the problem, the simplest being Primak's. The p_0 for a suitable average value $\bar\varepsilon$ is taken out of the integral:

$$P \cong p_0(\bar\varepsilon) \int \theta\,(\varepsilon,t)\,d\varepsilon.$$

Since the time derivative of the integral in this equation is unity, it follows that,

$$\dot P \cong -\frac{\tau}{t} p_0(\bar\varepsilon) \int \theta\,d\varepsilon = -\frac{\tau}{t} p_0(\bar\varepsilon).$$

Thus, by differentiating the experimental data, a segment of the original activation energy distribution can be obtained. Primak calculated $\bar\varepsilon$ as

$$\bar\varepsilon = \gamma\tau + \tau \ln At.$$

The first term—the product of Euler's constant, the absolute temperature, and Boltzmann's constant—is a small correction and has usually been neglected. It is equivalent to the difference between the most probable and the average values. The second term is a very significant quantity in all annealing experiments and has been designated

$$\varepsilon_0 \equiv \tau \ln At.$$

It is the most probable activation energy for annealing occurring at a particular temperature and time. This relation is what causes the kinetics nearly linear in $\log t$ when processes are distributed in activation energy. If p_0 were constant, the property plotted against $\log t$ would be linear; and it is the deviations from linearity that indicate the features of the distribution. Because of the logarithmic dependence on time, and because it is usually impractical to observe annealing for more than 3 or 4 decades of time, only a small segment of the distribution is revealed in any isothermal annealing; a series of isothermal annealings at different temperatures must be made to find the whole distribution. The annealing behaves in the following well known manner: at any temperature, when the property is plotted against a linear time scale, it appears to slow down to practically nil; then, when the temperature is raised, it seems to start afresh; and this behavior is displayed over a large range of temperature.

It is obvious that the distribution is closed: it can extend over only a limited range of ε, for otherwise an infinity is introduced; and similarly, it is obvious that the distribution cannot be truly continuous, it is only quasi-continuous. How continuous is it? Actually, because the exponential func-

tion is so greatly non-orthogonal, even a sophisticated application of mathematical technique cannot resolve a lightly populated distribution or even
several rather widely spaced discrete activation energies, and it is readily
shown that attempts to do this are mathematically unjustifiable.[344,345] Any
resolution of this kind must be justified (i.e., the activation energies identified
and evaluated) on a physical basis or by isolating the processes experimentally. In a disordered solid like vitreous silica, many slightly different configurations exist; and hence, for physical reasons, it may be assumed that the
distribution is densely populated.

The isothermal annealing data give the original distribution of processes
undergoing annealing. They do not give any information about the kinetics.
In particular, A, the frequency factor, has to be established in another way.
Primak and Szymanski[183] pointed out that the segments of the distribution
obtained at different temperatures will not fit properly unless a proper value
is chosen for A. In this way they decided a value of 10^9/sec gave about as
good a fit as could be obtained. Later Primak, Szymanski, and Keiffer[185]
showed it was easier to plot the data in integral form. The property (not its
slope) is plotted against ε_0, the most probable activation energy, for various
values of the frequency factor. The property which was used was the fractional residual density change. According to the structural formalism presented above, the negative of the dilatation would be the proper measure of
the compaction. However, the quantities used by Primak et al.[183,185], based
on the per cent change in density, do not give appreciably different results
because of the small density changes involved. It was quite evident that for
annealing temperatures below about 650°C, the appropriate value for the
frequency factor was low, below 10^8; while for the higher temperatures, the
appropriate value was high, above 10^{13}.

The determination of the frequency factor from the isothermal data was
marginal and might have been overlooked but for their examination of the
step annealing data. Indeed, their original purpose in treating the isothermal
data in integral form was to show that their conclusions obtained from analysis of the step annealing data also appear in the isothermal annealing data.
For the step annealing, the behavior of a single process may be described:

$$p = p_0 \left[\prod_{j=1}^{n} \theta_j(t_j, \tau_j) \right] \theta(t, \tau),$$

where the $\theta_j(t_j, \tau_j)$ are the final values of θ_j in the previous n steps of annealing. The expression now becomes,

$$P = \int p_0 \left(\prod_{j=1}^{n} \theta_j \right) \theta \, d\varepsilon;$$

and as before

$$\dot{P} \cong -\frac{\tau}{t} p_0(\bar{\varepsilon}) \int \left(\prod \theta_j \right) \theta \, d\varepsilon$$

$$\cong -(\tau/t) \, I p_0(\bar{\varepsilon})$$

where I is the integral. An approximation for this integral in gamma functions may be given when $n = 1$; but, in general, it is best to evaluate it for the experimental conditions for various values of A by using numerical methods in a digital computer. Primak, Szymanski, and Keiffer[185] found that employing a wrong value for A caused a dramatic discontinuity between the segments of the activation energy distribution function revealed by the steps of annealing. As might be expected, the discontinuity was largely at the beginning of the new step of annealing where the influence of the previous annealing was most prominent. There was little question but that a value of $A \sim 10^8$/sec was required for the annealing at low temperatures (below 600°C), and a value $\sim 10^{14}$ was required for higher temperatures of annealing. They also showed that altering the order of reaction from $\frac{1}{2}$ to 2 had no appreciable effect on the results of the calculations. A representation of their distribution is given in Fig. 27.

Annealing may also be conducted by varying the temperature according to a known law; usually a linear one is employed. Such annealing was named tempering by Vand, and we continue this nomenclature. Since τ is now a function of t, the integration is affected; and the functions obtained are no longer exponentials but are the exponential integrals familiar in the theory of radiative transfer through absorbing media. Such data are obtained in differential thermal analysis and in thermoluminescence, but since no such data will be presented here, the interested reader is referred to Primak's papers[184,344] for further information. However, it may be wise to note that the theory shows that the positions of peaks occurring at the same activation energy will appear at different temperatures when tempering at different rates. Many investigators have observed the variation of the temperature at which peaks occur without appreciating the reason for it. All such data should be corrected for the tempering rate. This is most easily done by completing the analysis to derive the activation energy distribution. There is another kind of annealing which appears very commonly in the literature: step annealing in which only one point is taken at each temperature. Some authors call this isochronal annealing when the length of time of the steps is made a fixed value. There is no significance to the fixed heating period in a case like vitreous silica where the value of A is not constant. The results of Primak, Szymanski, and Keiffer[185] show that it is a mistake to make the annealing times too short, because the influence of the previous annealing will cause

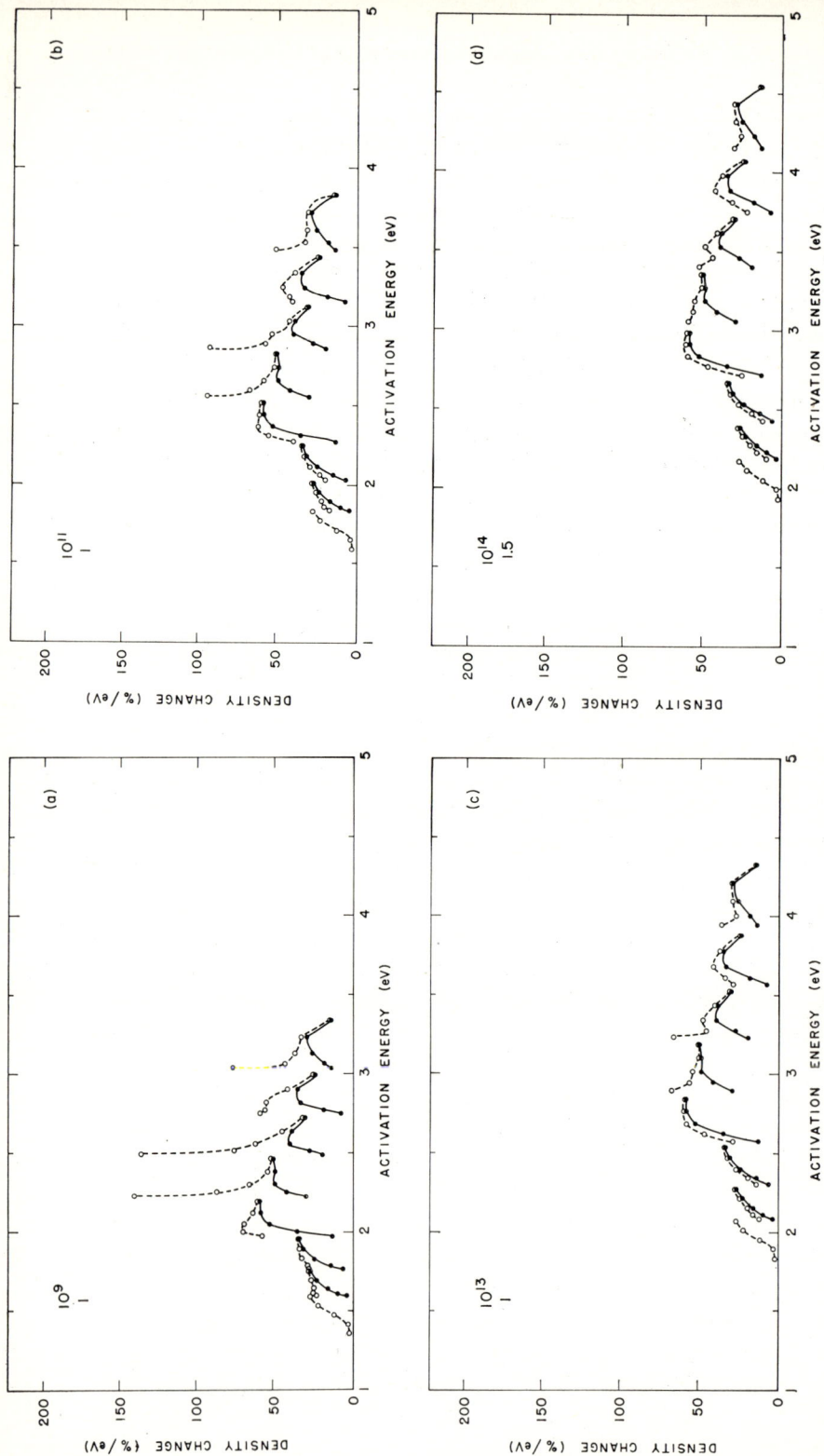

Figure 27. Activation energy distributions calculated for stepannealing of neutron compacted vitreous silica with the assumption of first-order kinetics and frequency factors I times the distributions. (From Primak, Szymanski, and Keiffer[185].)

inconsistent results. When the frequency factor is as low as 10^8/sec these times should be 2 hours or more. When the frequency factor is as large as 10^{14}, a time $\frac{1}{2}$ to $\frac{3}{4}$ hr may be satisfactory. Most of the data which have been gathered in this manner have been for heating times which are too short. The disadvantage of making a measurement for only one time at each temperature is the loss of information about the frequency factor.

ANNEALING OF PRESSURE COMPACTED VITREOUS SILICA

In their paper which first identified the pressure compaction of glass, Bridgman and Šimon[9] gave isothermal annealing data for compacted B_2O_3 glass. These data show room temperature annealing and characteristics of an activation energy distribution. Only a few observations were made on vitreous silica or on a specimen compacted at room temperature. The compacted material was reported as 17.5% increased density (14.9% compaction) but the actual density given for the starting material, 2.2 g/cm³, is incorrect. The density given for the compacted material, 2.61 g/cm³ corresponds to 18.6% density increase, 15.7% compaction. No appreciable room temperature annealing was found. After heating at 430°C for 1 hr, the density increase was reported to have been reduced to 7.9%, but since the data are not given, this figure could not be checked. Keiffer, Szymanski, and their students[182,122] performed step annealings of vitreous silica compacted at room temperature. Their compacted vitreous silica began to anneal not far above room temperature (~ 100°C) and was $\frac{3}{4}$ completed by 650°C. The per cent compaction annealed plotted against temperature was nearly linear. The annealing behavior indicated an activation energy distribution. Preliminary calculations by Keiffer gave a frequency factor $\sim 10^8$/sec. Mackenzie[172] studied the annealing of vitreous silica compacted at somewhat higher temperatures. He, too, found behavior characteristic of an activation energy distribution and noted the near linearity in $\log t$ without appreciating its significance. The manner in which these data are presented makes it difficult to give a quantitative comparison with other data. Also, the data are spotty (rather than systematic), and compaction conditions are not stated. Thus, it would be difficult to make an independent analysis. However, the following qualitative observations may be made: (1) annealing began at temperatures below the compaction temperature; (2) annealing was first observed at ~ 200°C, a higher temperature than that observed by Keiffer et al.[182] for room temperature compacted vitreous silica; (3) annealing was not completed at as low a temperature as that observed for room temperature compacted vitreous silica by Keiffer et al. These conclusions must be qualified: (4) the data is for highly compacted material, and the effect of compaction on the annealing has not been investigated; and (5) specimens were quenched at high pressure during compaction so there might be some slight admixture of low and high temperature compacted material. Cohen and Roy's[168,170] work in which pressure was released at high temperature and then cooled is additional confirmation of (3), for their specimens possessed large compaction despite their having been held at 600 °C for a period following compaction at that temperature. Thus the structure of the material compacted at low temperature must be different from that compacted at high temperature, even though the compactions may be the same (see page 157).

ANNEALING OF SHOCK- AND THERMAL-COMPACTION

There does not appear to be any information on the thermal annealing of the shock-compacted vitreous silica. The implications of the ionization release of compaction to be described in Section IX indicates annealing will be at relatively high temperature (see page 140).

The annealing aspects of the thermal compaction were discussed in Section IV, devoted to thermal compaction (see pages 61, 64). It will be recalled that a linear behavior in log t appeared there also.

IONIZATION EXPANSION AND COMPACTION

There are no systematic studies of the annealing of the ionization induced dilatations. It was pointed out in Section VII that the radiation-induced dilatations of vitreous silica are complicated by the presence of an element of independent expansion accompanying the compaction when certain impurities were present (see page 91). Primak and Kampwirth's[146] investigation of this effect is the only study of an impurity effect in the annealing of vitreous silica. The expansion associated with the aluminum center showed a room temperature annealing which was found to be logarithmic in time and 30–50% was released/yr. Their results are given in Table 11. The thermal annealing of compaction for different specimens was different. They considered it might have been related to the temperature of compaction, but our considerations here indicate the possibility of an impurity or structural effect will have to be considered also; the specimens which annealed more readily had a high OH content. The coloration and its associated expansion annealed in a lower temperature range, and this permitted a resolution of the annealing of the expansion from that of the compaction, as shown in Fig. 28. These experiments were step annealings of 30 minutes duration. It is well known that the absorption in vitreous silica anneals in the temperature range with which Primak, Szymanski, and Keiffer[185] associated the low frequency factor, and in which Keiffer, Szymanski et al.[182] found annealing of most of the room temperature compaction in their specimens. On the other hand, a major portion of the neutron compaction does not anneal until much higher temper-

TABLE 11 Spontaneous annealing of the mean positive dilatation and the mean optical density of 0.6 MeV electron-bombarded Infrasil[a]

Dose (μC/cm^2)	Date of measurement	δ ($\times 10^{-6}$)	Optical density 0.54 μ	Optical density 0.225μ
2	3 Jan. 1967	4.56		
	30 June 1967	3.6		
	% change	(27%)		
50	1 Oct. 1965	12.1	0.63	1.17
	30 June 1967	9.3	0.56	0.99
	% change	(30%)	(13%)	(18%)
2000	6 Oct. 1965	−15.3	0.98	1.26
	7 July 1967	−19.0	0.92	1.11
	% change	(24%)	(7%)	(14%)

[a] From Primak and Kampwirth.[146]

atures. The ionization compaction caused by electrons anneals at a lower temperature than the neutron compaction. This may be taken as an indication of the temperature at which the processes of compaction occurred. Levy[307] showed that even though the optical absorption may have annealed in the neutron compacted vitreous silica, configurations which form the absorption centers persist, for these specimens are readily made absorbing again with a small ionization dose. He also showed, by studying differences of the absorption curves during annealing and re-establishing absorption, that the absorption in the region he studied involved contributions from overlapping absorption bands. However, there was no attempt to resolve the effect and relate it to the dilatation in the manner done by Primak and Kampwirth.[146]

MECHANISM

The structure of vitreous silica is such that it is unnecessary to be concerned with diffusion effects in the annealing of the compaction. The low temperature process may therefore be considered merely as an improbable process, one which is activated many times before compaction is released, and it may be much like the untangling of a snarled rope: untangling one portion becomes the key for untangling another portion. This qualitative picture assumes quantitative significance in some of the effects observed when compaction is released by ionization (see page 149). The role of bond cleavage in this process has not been assessed, but it may be amenable to investigation by suitable modification of some of Levy's[307] techniques. The high frequency factor associated with the high temperature processes, and its occurrence in the temperature range where plastic flow becomes evident, in-

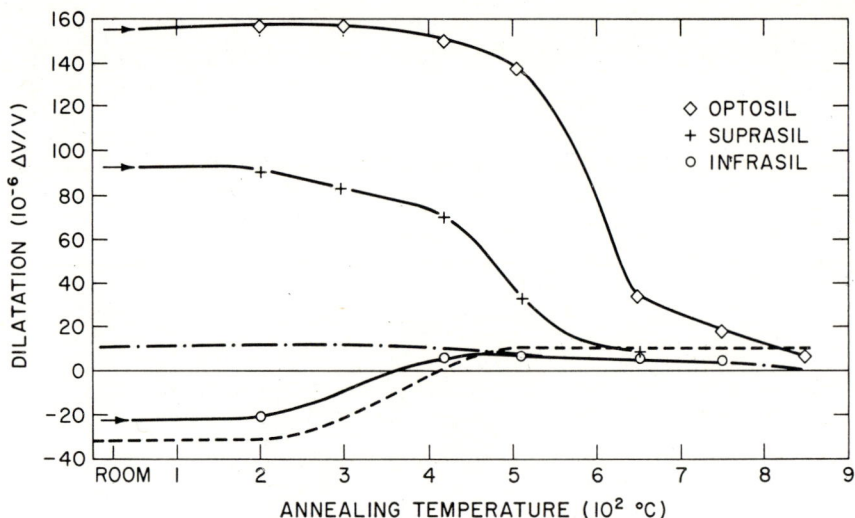

Figure 28.   Resolution of the expansion and contraction of the coloring vitreous silicas: (solid line, the positive dilatation of the coloring vitreous silicas, crosses, X's, triangles, results of three progressive irradiations of Infrasil; squares, five specimens of Infrasil used for short irradiations); (dash-double-short-dash curve with asterisks, optical density of Infrasil); (dashed curve with circles, negative dilatation of Suprasil); (dash-single-short-dash curve, construction of the supposed positive dilatation of the coloring vitreous silicas assuming the negative dilatation upon which it is superposed is the same as that of Suprasil's). From Primak and Kampwirth[146].)

dicates a kinetics controlled by bond cleavage. By a temperature of 1000°C, bond cleavage becomes so prominent that there is no difficulty for short segments to rearrange themselves to the ordinary vitreous silica configuration; a true equilibrium configuration is achieved in relatively short times as shown by Douglas and Isard.[149] That this also applies to other than thermally compacted vitreous silica is shown by the highest temperature annealing data reported by Primak and Szymanski[183] where a density lower than that of the original vitreous silica was found for a specimen which had been heated at 1000°C.

IX. Ionization Release of Compaction

INTRODUCTION

The release of compaction by ionization was first noted by Primak and Edwards.[8] They found that neutron-compacted vitreous silica expanded when bombarded with electrons or when irradiated with x-rays. Primak, Edwards, Keiffer, and Szymanski[122] later reported results of irradiating pressure-compacted vitreous silica in a nuclear reactor and with x-rays. They found an extremely rapid and efficient release of compaction, and they attempted to find a mechanism for it. Primak and Kampwirth[180,304] further investigated both pressure compacted and neutron compacted vitreous silica and also made a few measurements of shock-compacted vitreous silica. The investigation of the pressure compacted vitreous silica was conducted with small grains whose density was determined by suspension in a heavy liquid. The grains were very convenient for thermal experiments. In the investigation of the neutron compacted vitreous silica, rectangular blocks were used; and the measurements were made by the photoelastic method, with a sensitivity $\sim 10^{-6}$. At this sensitivity a variety of effects were observed which could hardly be investigated by measuring density. The behavior of the pressure compacted vitreous silica is described first, and the complexity displayed by the neutron compacted vitreous silica afterward.

PRESSURE COMPACTED VITREOUS SILICA

Primak, Edwards, Keiffer, and Szymanski[122] reported the radiation induced expansion of pressure compacted vitreous silica was the most rapid radiation induced dilatation which had been observed. It was some 1400 times faster than the mean rate of dilatation observed in the neutron disordering of quartz, some 200 times faster than in the neutron compaction of vitreous silica. They developed the structural formalism given above (see page 95) to calculate its efficiency and concluded it was also the most efficient expansion which had been observed, greater than 1 O.V./ionization. Because of its magnitude and efficiency, it could not be explained as a displacement effect, nor as an electrostatic deformation, nor as a thermal spike effect, nor as a photoelectric or other recoil effect. They concluded it had to be "a rapid transient effect associated with the local distortion or energy deposition of the ionization event." They concluded,

It would be interesting to compare the ionization expansions for pressure-compacted silica, partially thermally annealed pressure compacted silica, and pressure-compacted silica prepared at various temperatures.

The investigation proposed by Primak, Edwards, Keiffer, and Szymanski was performed by Primak and Kampwirth[180] utilizing soft x-rays as the ionizing agent. Primak and Kampwirth found that the release of compaction followed a log t (t, time) relationship, that it increased with temperature, and varied with the amount of compaction. It was decreased by prior annealing, and was less when the compaction had been accomplished at a higher temperature or for shock-compacted material. On the basis of these observations, they concluded it was a cooperative effect involving radiation and thermal processes and that it could be used to obtain information about the state of compaction and how the compaction was supported.

The thermal annealing for their specimens, pressure compacted at room temperature, was negligible at 100°C. However, even at 15°C, during exposure to x-rays, a marked positive dilatation ensued. The amount of dilatation experienced in 1 or 2 hr of irradiation increased for the first few per cent compaction, but then it changed little for greater compaction. Thus, the behavior of other variables was most easily seen for compactions of a few per cent or greater. The amount of dilatation experienced by the room temperature, pressure compacted vitreous silica in a 1 or 2 h irradiation was roughly proportional to the absolute temperature, indicating it to be thermally activated; and to the radiation dose, indicating it to be a radiation effect. The intimate relationship of temperature and radiation was further revealed by the behavior of specimens irradiated after thermal annealing at 200°C. The dilatation which occurred during thermal annealing was roughly proportional to the amount of compaction present originally; but the radiation effect was markedly lower for the higher compaction, indicating the importance in the radiation effect of that part of the compaction which is thermally annealed easily. This importance was emphasized by the behavior of specimens compacted at higher temperatures: the amount of radiation-induced dilatation for the shock wave compacted vitreous silica and for vitreous silica pressure compacted at 400°C was but a small percentage, 10% for the former and 20% for the latter, of that found for vitreous silica pressure compacted at room temperature. Because of this intimate relationship between temperature and radiation, the temperature of preparation, and the prior thermal annealing, Primak and Kampwirth called the effect a radiation-annealing effect. The radiation-annealing which occurred in a 2 h period was sufficiently regular in its behavior to give a good graphical display, and such graphs are shown in Figs. 29 and 30.

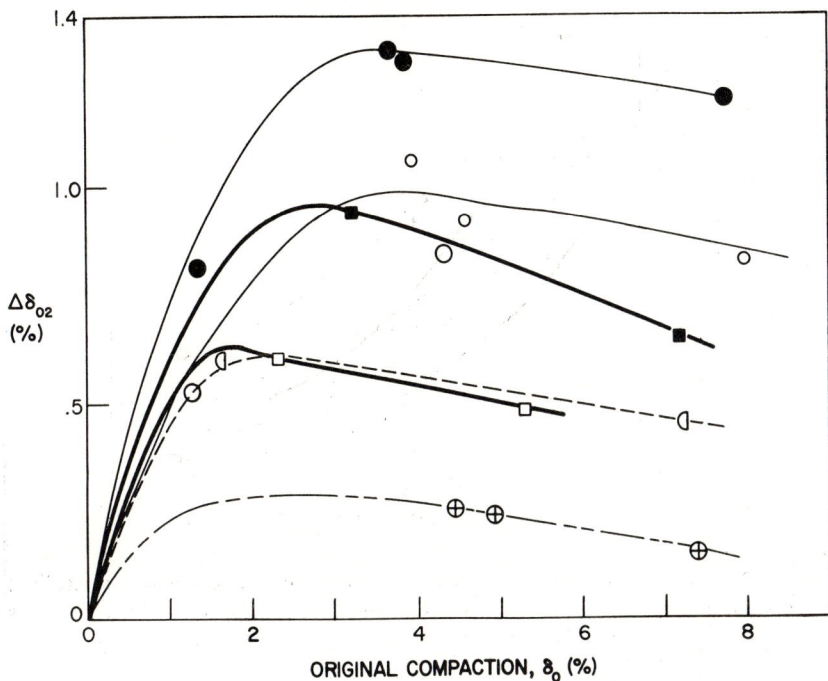

Figure 29.   The per cent compaction radiation annealed in 2 h. The prior thermally annealed specimens are referred to their values after annealing. The code is: small circles, from Primak et al.[122]; half-circles, at 22 mA x-ray tube plate current; quartered circles, at 11 mA; squares, prior thermally annealed at 200°C. Filled points irradiated at 103°C; except as otherwise qualified, irradiations were at 45 mA and 15°C. (From Primak and Kampwirth[180]).

The data displayed in Fig. 29 clearly shows the marked inhibition of the absolute amount of radiation annealing at about 3% compaction. It will be recalled that in the structural formalism, the mean distribution of compacted loops is such that they are completely surrounded by uncompacted loops up to about 3% compaction. Above 3%, adjacent loops must be compacted. This will assume a special significance when the locking in of the compaction is considered. No sudden inhibition is really involved as can be seen when the fractional annealing is examined, as shown in Fig. 30. From the smallest values studied, as compaction was increased, it became more refractory to radiation annealing. For the most rapid radiation-annealing they observed, Primak and Kampwirth calculated the mean energy for release as 3 eV/O.V., indicating an ionization releases several compacted units. If this interpretation has any physical basis, it may indicate that the compacted

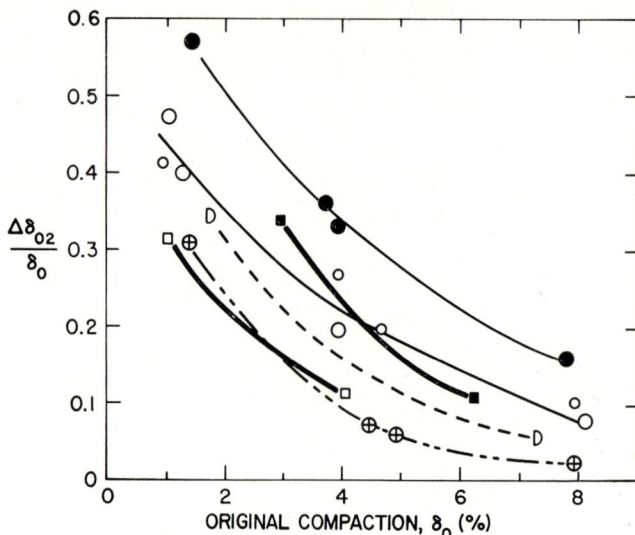

Figure 30. The fraction of the compaction released after 2 h radiation annealing. The prior annealed specimens are referred to their values after annealing. Coded as Figure 29. (From Primak and Kampwirth[180].)

elements support each other in the pressure compaction; or as described by Primak and Kampwirth, they are locked-in by their strain fields overlapping. The high efficiency has another implication: the ionization does not at first have to occur at a particular point in the network. From the amount of compaction which can be released at this efficient rate, it is easily calculated that in the structural formalism, ionization is effective at a distance of $1\frac{1}{2}$ loops of the network; ionization may be effective even though it occurs as much as $4\frac{1}{2}$ Si–O tetrahedra away from a particular point in the network. This may be taken to indicate the segment length which is undergoing reorientation, or the dimensions of the overlapping strain fields in this description.

The logarithmic radiation-annealing was followed by Primak and Kampwirth, in one instance, to 70% annealing of compaction; and there was no indication it was decreasing although a small peak below 30% annealed showed a portion was more easily annealed than the rest. If the results are to be interpreted in the activation energy formalism, the distribution is not one present *a priori*; it is created by the radiation. This distribution must refer to segments of the network which rearrange to normal configuration. The segmentation must be absent *a priori* and must be created by the ionization cleaving or weakening the network, but the reorientation must be the rate controlling factor. In the vitreous silica compacted at room temperature, the compaction must consist of deformed portions of the network locking each other in, but with little reorientation. When compaction is performed at high temperature, the network must readjust to a less strained configuration. This is an annealing, but it is not an annealing to the configuration observed in the absence of pressure: under pressure, the annealing is to a state associated with that condition of constraint. Nevertheless, when pressure is released, the resultant configuration proves to be more stable than that obtained at lower temperature so that despite the presence of radiation, a higher activation energy is involved. Similarly, the simple behavior described here, of the ionization cleaving the network to permit thermal reorientation, (or in the strain field description, unbalancing the strain field) becomes less effective when the compaction increases and contiguous loops are deformed; the locking-in has become more complex and the reorientation more difficult.

The mean values of the radiation induced activation energy distribution during periods of annealing were calculated by Primak and Kampwirth from the slopes of their logarithmic annealing curves and are shown in Fig. 31.

From the fact that the radiation-annealing was affected by the amount of compaction while the thermal annealing was not, Primak and Kampwirth concluded that the radiation-annealing was a more selective process. Their statement of this was that in thermal annealing, the whole network was equally subject to annealing; but that in radiation-annealing, only certain portions of the network were vulnerable. What may cause this selectivity? In radiation-annealing there is a selection of processes not only by their activation energy, but also by their location relative to an ionized site (it has been customary to call this a hole although the meaning of this term in an amorphous insulator is not clear) or trapped charge. The frequency factor for the radiation-annealing has not been determined (indeed, it would be difficult to suggest how to evaluate the frequency factor for a transient activation energy distribution), but it is probably low; the charge would have to be trapped for an appreciable time (possibly even as long as 10^{-5} sec) before annealing occurred. The investigations of Keiffer, et al.[346,347,348] demonstrate that pressure compaction enhances the ease of forming E' centers, a sign of network cleavage. It may be assumed that holes and trapping occur in portions of the network which are badly strained; according to the discussion above, in portions of the network where compaction is locked least securely. Undoubtedly this is the selection mechanism of the radiation-annealing. The selected sites will not be fixed points in the network; for, as compaction is released, other sites are the ones most strained. The release then becomes progressive; and the analogy previously given, of untangling a snarled rope (see page 137), assumes a further realism. The complexities of the behavior of neutron compaction to be presented below make this analogy even more realistic.

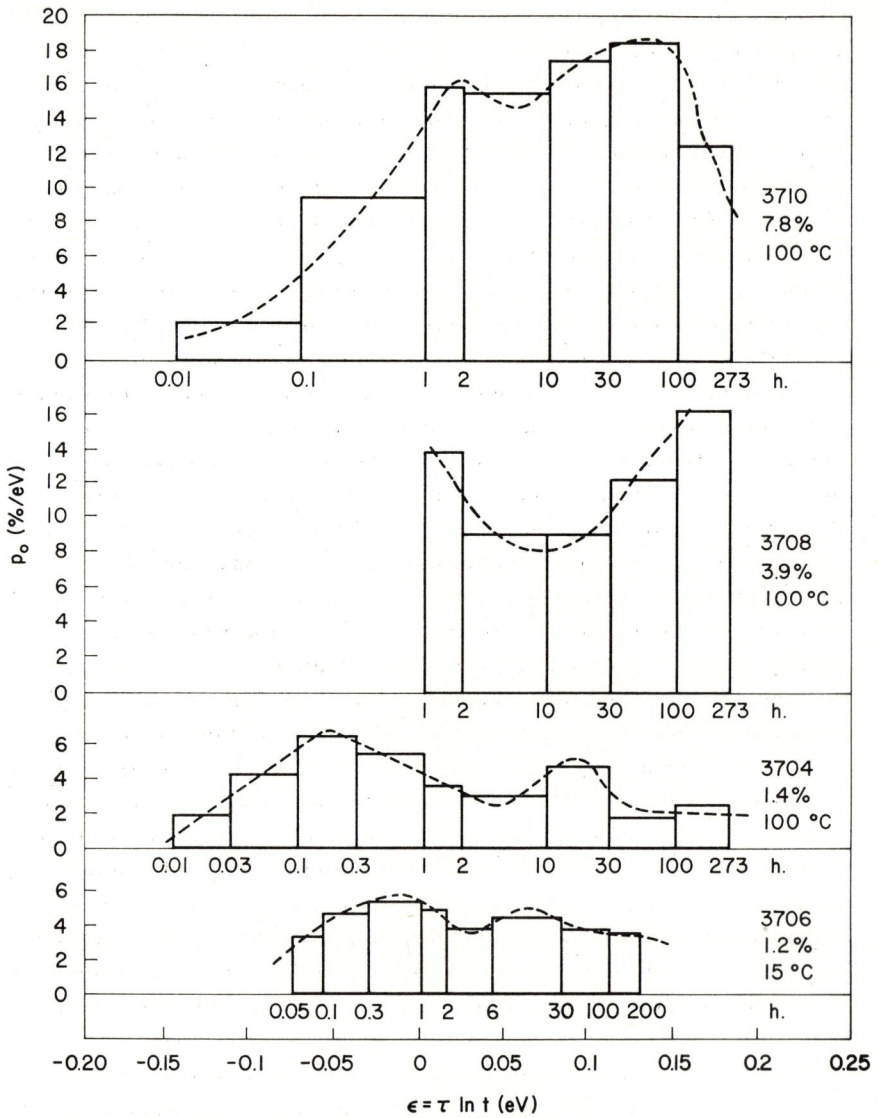

Figure 31.   Activation energy distributions calculated for specimens subjected to extended radiation annealing plotted against the relative activation energy (the actual activation energy is displaced by the quantity $\tau \ln A$ associated with the frequency factor). (From Primak and Kampwirth[180].)

Neutron Compacted Vitreous Silica

Primak and Edwards[8] subjected a number of specimens of neutron compacted vitreous silica (which had accumulated in their laboratory from other investigations) to a period of electron or x-ray irradiation and found that those which had been exposed in Hole VT7 (a hollow fuel rod) in the nuclear reactor CP5 for more than 8 Mw-h of reactor operation showed an expansion; specimens exposed less than 2 Mw-h showed a contraction. Some of these specimens were coloring vitreous silica (Homosil) and some were non-coloring (Suprasil). After Primak and Kampwirth[146] had found that an element of radiation expansion was associated with the coloration, they reinvestigated

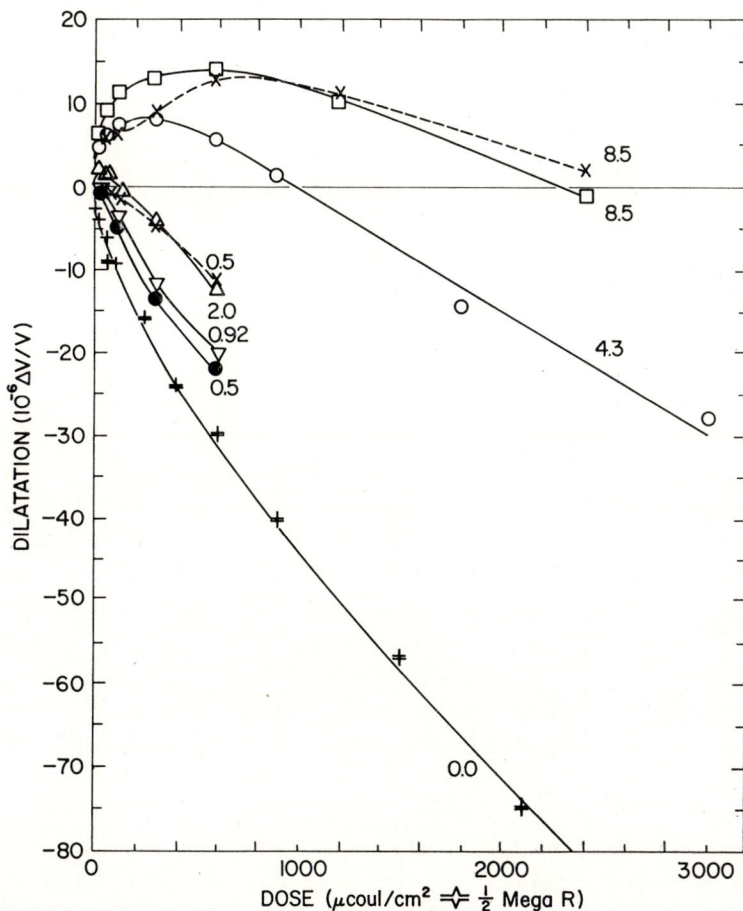

Figure 32.   The effect of electron (0.6 MeV) bombardment on pile exposed vitreous silica. The numbers on the curves are the pile exposure in MW · h in hole VT-7 of CP-5. The dashed curves are for Homosil, the others for Suprasil. (From Primak and Kampwirth[304].)

the behavior of the neutron compacted vitreous silica.[304] Fig. 32 clearly shows the nature of the effects. Even the shortest exposure in a nuclear reactor introduces an element of expansion. It is observed by a decrease in the normal contraction. If the exposure is long enough, the normal ionization compaction is overwhelmed; then a net expansion occurs. This element of expansion behaves in a manner analogous to the expansion associated with the coloring, the impurity expansion (see page 91); it may eventually be saturated; and then net contraction ensues. It thus seems reasonable, as for the impurity expansion, to assume expansion and compaction are occurring relatively independently. For small reactor exposures, the expansion associated with coloring seems to be an additional independent element; for longer reactor exposures, some unidentified complexity in behavior may be appearing; but it was not investigated.

These results were for short reactor exposures. The behavior of specimens with longer exposures is shown in Fig. 33. The logarithmic scale is for the purpose of presenting data covering a long range; it has no mathematical significance. The ionization expansion possesses several phases. There is seen a stage of velocious expansion which seems to saturate early, and then a slower expansion follows to beyond the highest dose investigated by Primak and Kampwirth.[304] They refer to this as principle expansion; and since there was no evidence that the principle expansion did not proceed from the start, they refer to the velocious expansion as pre-evident rather than precedent. The mean energy calculated for the pre-evident expansion was 32 eV/O.V., hence an O.V. is released for each ionization. Pre-evident expansion could revert, at least partially, in several days. Because of its efficiency and the reversion, they associated it with network cleavage. The magnitude of the maximum pre-evident expansion was not large; it was about 5×10^{18} O.V./ cm^3 after a few hundred Mw-h exposure in VT7 of CP5. At 5 Mw-h it was 1/20 of this. The principle expansion required $\sim 10^4$ eV/O.V.

RECUPERATION

The most curious of the phenomena observed by Primak and Kampwirth[304] was the recuperation phenomenon shown in Figs. 33 and 34. It was curious because it consisted not only of a recovery of pre-evident expansion, but it also caused an increase in the rate of principle expansion. They considered the pre-evident expansion played an important role in this effect. If their interpretation of the pre-evident expansion being associated with the trapping of charge is correct; then, according to the previous discussion, the trapping would occur preferentially at strained Si–O–Si sites. After a period of ionization expansion and after reversion involving recombination, the most strained sites would be other than those in the previous irradiation period.

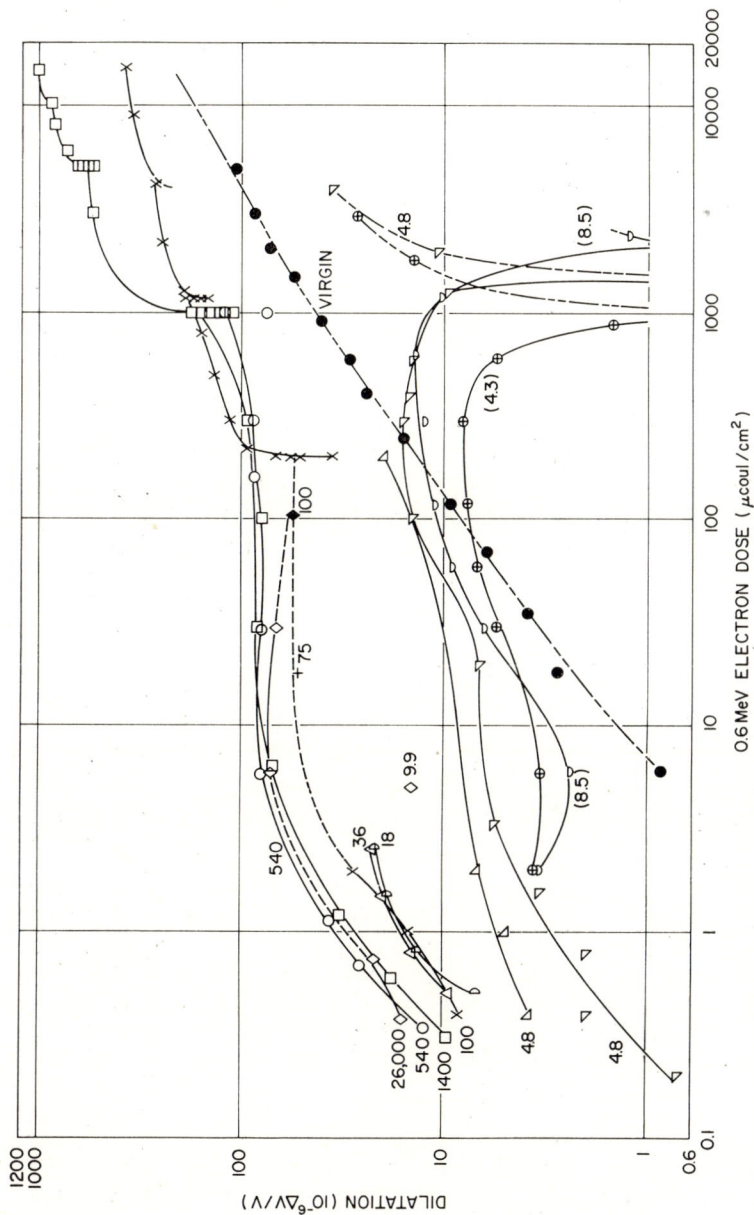

Figure 33. The effect of electron (0.6 MeV) bombardment on pile exposed vitreous silica. The numbers give the exposure (MW · h) in a vertical thimble of CP-5. The dashed curve is a section over which there are insufficient data to draw a reliable curve. The double dash curves are contraction, the remainder expansion. The 4.3 and 8.5 curves are also given in Figure 32. The solid diamond is the first point at which Lichtenberg discharge was noted in this specimen, but it may have begun by the previous point. All the specimens were Suprasil. (From Primak and Kampwirth[304].)

10*

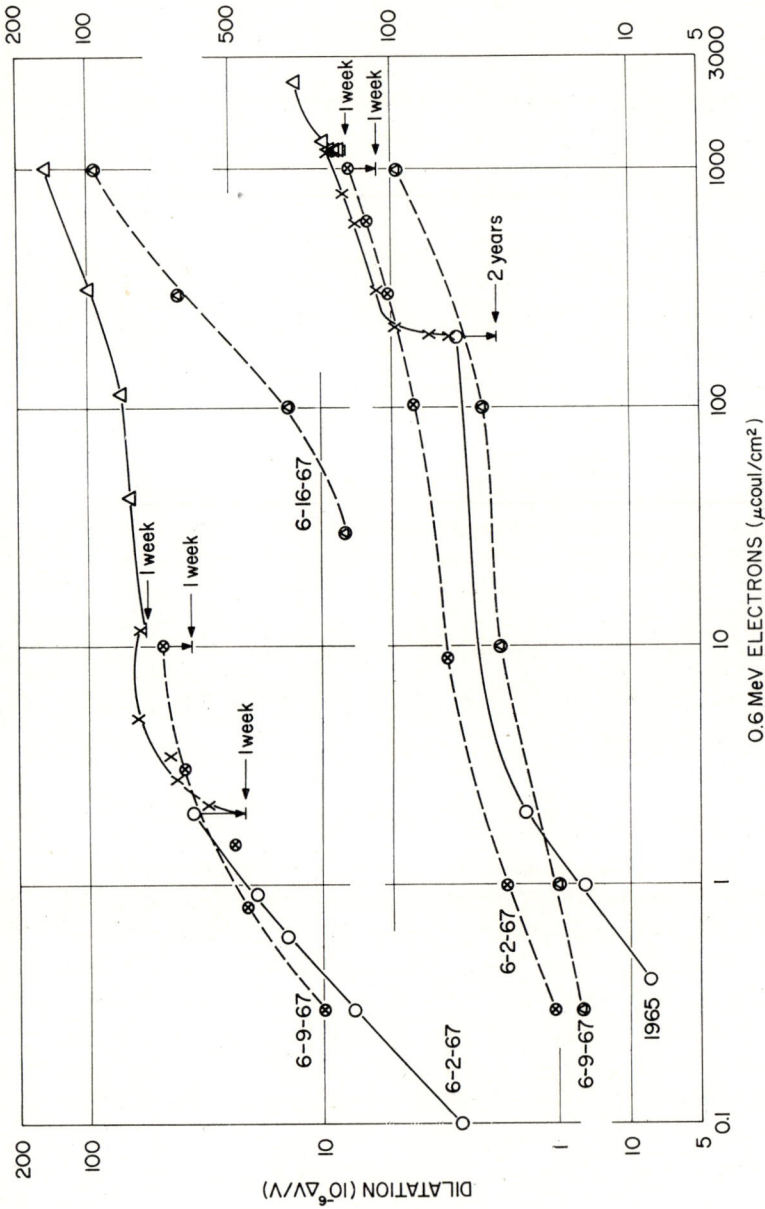

Figure 34. Two sets of data showing the recuperation effect. Both specimens were exposed simultaneously for 100 MW·h in CP-5. The circles are for the 1st period of electron bombardment, x's the 2nd, and triangles the 3rd. The dashed curves are for the dilatation observed in that period of electron bombardment, and the points are circled to avoid confusion. The electron bombardments were usually performed in less than 6 h, although the longer ones extended into another 6 h period on the following day. The arrows give the dilatation observed on remeasuring the specimen after the interval noted. (From Primak and Kampwirth[304].)

The spacial distribution of strain would thus be different than it was during the previous irradiation period, and the whole process would start anew; the pre-evident expansion would occur at different sites in the present period of irradiation.

SUPERVENIENT EXPANSION

When Primak and Edwards[8] discovered the ionization expansion of neutron compacted vitreous silica, they suggested that it might be the explanation of the supervenient expansion. After Primak and Kampwirth[304] investigated the ionization expansion, they reviewed this suggestion and concluded that the supervenient expansion was not an ionization expansion. They saw no reason why such an ionization expansion should occur during the ongoing neutron irradiation which was sweeping the whole solid with thermal spikes several times during the period of the supervenient expansion; any ionization expansion would be reversed constantly . Further evidence could be obtained from the dose; but it is difficult to provide a reliable estimate of dose because there is no set of data for the supervenient expansion and ionization expansion from a single reactor facility; and it is dangerous to mix data from different reactor facilities because of the great variation of ionization in reactors.[264] However, if the comparison is made with existing data,[263] then the dose for 0.1% supervenient expansion is about 10^{11} r, while for 0.1% ionization expansion it is about 5×10^{9} r. This preliminary comparison shows the expected poor correlation, but another comparison should be made when better data become available.

Primak and Kampwirth[304] suggested that the supervenient expansion was an indication of structure in the thermal spike: that in the central higher temperature regions a lower and more difficultly annealed compaction developed than in the cooler surrounding region subject to higher stresses and shock effects. They found support for it in Mackenzie's results[173] for the high temperature pressure compaction. The ionization expansion involved radiation-annealing of the outer region. The supervenient expansion consisted of the whole region being swept through by the cores of the thermal spikes. The characteristics of a classical thermal spike corresponding to this hypothesis may be calculated for a 140 keV neon ion from the data given in Table 10. As before, the dose rate gives 44,740 oxygen atoms affected by the stopping of this ion; but this is now N_α which according to this hypothesis is $5N_i$. The remaining characteristics are: $V_\alpha = 1.02 \times 10^{-18}$ cm^3, $n_\alpha = 10.3$Å, $r_i = 4.6$ Å, $t = 1.76 \times 10^{-13}$ sec, $T_m = 20,000°C$, $z_i^2 = \frac{1}{2}$, $z_\alpha^2 = 2.5$, $\overline{P_{0i}} = 13$ kbar, $\overline{P_{0\alpha}} = 4.3$ kbar (see pages 111–119). The physical picture presented here is an inner core which is less than a loop of the structure—one which is about two Si–O tetrahedra in diameter, while the outer diameter consists of the Si–O tetrahedra on the opposite side of the loop; and the phenomena are completed in just a few atomic vibrations—less than the time required to establish a thermal state. This is a far cry from the thermal spike originally conceived by Primak! It is more akin to a dynamic phenomenon. If this interpretation of the supervenient expansion is correct, it means that the final state is achieved only among those tetrahedra along the path of the moving particle, and the only additional compaction occurring is in the adjacent loops. The latter compaction would have to be about 10% greater than the core compaction according to a macroscopic calculation. Primak and Kampwirth's hypothesis of the supervenient expansion could be tested by determining the principle expansion for specimens at different points in the period of the supervenient expansion. If the principle expansion remained, it would show the supervenient expansion to be another effect, thus disproving their hypothesis. Such data are not yet available. The one specimen from this part of the neutron irradiation which Primak and Kampwirth attempted to study was destroyed by a Lichtenberg discharge toward the end of the period of pre-evident expansion (see page 119). Primak and Szymanski[183] comment on the activation energy distribution they obtained from annealing of the neutron compaction, that the lower end of the distribution could have arisen from a high temperature process, 12,000°K for 10^{-12} sec. Such conditions are not available for the thermal spikes associated with the compaction in Section VIII (see pages 111–119), but these conditions are present in the thermal spikes calculated just above. Thus, a comparison of the activation energy distributions revealed at lower temperatures by newly irradiated specimens along the supervenient expansion region would be significant. No such data are available.

ADDENDUM

Fission fragment damage in a UO_2–SiO_2 vitroceramic was investigated by Lungu, Rîbco, and Beleutǎ.[349] They treated the results as related to the vitreous silica matrix. There are difficulties in interpreting the results in the present context: the original impurity content of the matrix, the impurity introduced on irradiation, and the final composition of the irradiated product. The data as presented by Lungu et al. (see Fig. 35) show a very large supervenient expansion, 1%, while the maximum compaction was but 2%. The report indicates that the irradiations were performed at a much higher temperature than in any other work presented here. Thus, they raise the question whether some thermal annealing or radiation annealing effect may be involved in the process of the supervenient expansion. On the other hand, they represent damage by much heavier ions, hence a much more intense thermal spike than that developed by the silicon and oxygen ions scattered

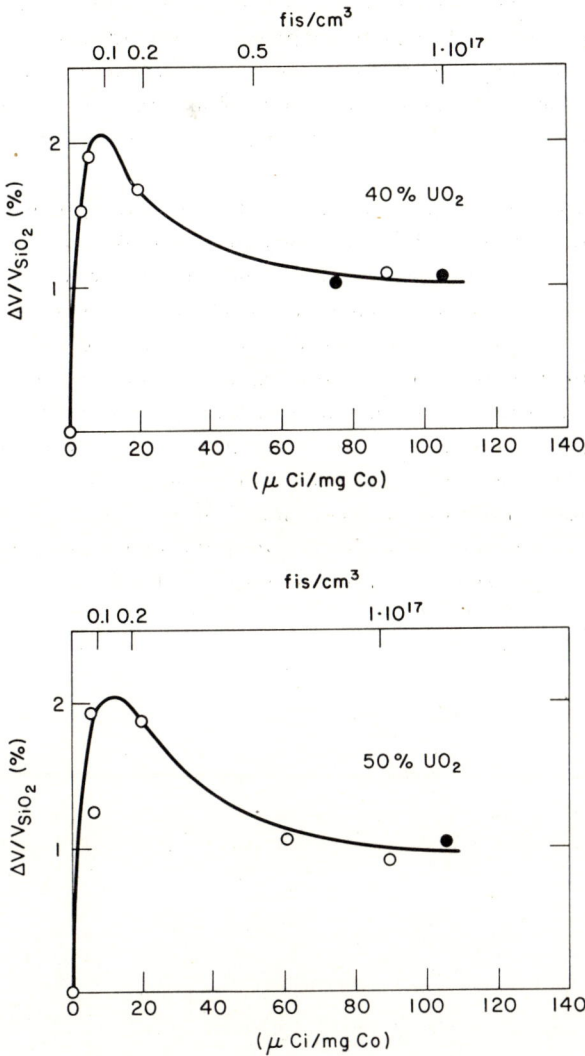

Figure 35.   Dilatation of SiO_2–UO_2 vitroceramics (reported as volume change divided by SiO_2 volume) inserted into vitreous silica ampoules *in vacuo* and irradiated in a dry vertical channel of the VVR-S reactor in a high temperature irradiation capsule at a neutron flux $1.3 - 1.6 \times 10^{13}$ n_0/cm^2 sec. The integrated flux was determined with a cobalt monitor, hence the units μ Ci/mg Co ($\cong 3 \times 10^{17}$ n_0/cm^2). The open circles were obtained by density measurements, the shaded circles from dilatometrical determinations of changes on annealing. (From Lungu et al.[348].)

by neutrons, and point to the desirability of studies with heavier ions if the means could be found. If the latter explanation were the explanation for the major effect, it would support the suggestion made above that the supervenient expansion is an annealing within the central region of the thermal spike, of compaction developed in the peripheral regions of prior thermal spikes.

Lungu[350] reported length changes for vitreous silica rods which were irradiated in the light water Bucharest swimming pool reactor. The maximum dilatation calculated is somewhat larger than that reported by Primak and his co-workers, and the supervenient expansion appears later. Sufficient experimental details to evaluate this work are not available; questions about the dose units, the possibility of aelotropic expansion, influence of kind of vitreous silica, the irradiation temperature, are among those to be answered. If the results are accepted as valid and comparable to others considered here, they may indicate an effect caused by a different ratio of radiation fluxes, possibly relatively more ionization in Lungu's work causing a less prominent supervenient expansion. It would be very desirable to investigate the behavior of well defined materials in a variety of radiation facilities.

X.   The Nature of Vitreous Silica*

ORDINARY VITREOUS SILICA

In this inquiry into its compacted states, we have learned that vitreous silica is a very surprising substance. By ordinary standards it is a very inert and stable material, quite constant in its properties. Yet its structure is remarkably labile. This combination of constancy and lability is a consequence of the Si–O binding, neither covalent nor electrovalent, but mid-way between.[350] Broken bonds form again readily, characteristic of electrovalent binding, but the constraints of the covalent character of the binding result in an open structure which is not readily rearranged, and it is thus stable in a disordered form. The covalent character of the binding also leads to a normal bond angle for Si–O–Si, ~140°. This prevents the formation of a disordered continuous 3-dimensional Si–O network. Breaks in the structure are encountered every 4th to 20th Si–O tetrahedron when traversing the structure. The frequency of these breaks and the electrovalent character of the binding permits the development of a statistically equivalent structure after a sequence of treatments which insure the original structure can no longer exist. The breaks in the structure are often an impurity site.

From the literature, it would seem that most of the bulk properties are only little affected (less than 1 %) over the range of compositions available in commercial vitreous silicas. However, recent work has shown some of the small differences can be related to the method of manufacture and to composition. The notable investigations of Jack and Hetherington and their co-workers were discussed above. Other related studies are those by Salmang and von Stoesser[351,352] by Douglas and Isard,[149] and by Brückner.[186,353,354] Some newer work, Fraser's[156] is discussed below.

Like the other silica structures, the structure of vitreous silica is a function of temperature. It is typical of the silica structures that the void space surrounding an oxygen is unsymmetrical. Thus, as the temperature is raised, the vibration of the oxygens is unsymmetrical; and the Si–O–Si bond angle changes. In the case of the crystalline forms where coherent displacement can occur, phase changes are evidenced when the movement is sufficient to alter the symmetry. In vitreous silica, coherent displacement is not possible.

---

* Revised February, 1970.

153

But by 600–800°C, the network segments can begin to move with respect to each other by activated processes. The new configurations can be quenched, and the vitreous silicas so obtained are quite stable at lower temperature and are denser the higher the temperature from which they were quenched. This was described as the thermal compaction process. If the process starting from high temperature is considered, the structure becomes rigid by 800–600°C. Yet the change in the normal bond angle continues as the temperature is lowered, as shown by the behavior of the crystalline forms. It is thus evident that all vitreous silica at lower temperatures is in a compacted state. The implications of this observation are too extensive to consider them in detail here. The prime structural characteristic of the compacted state so attained is that the network is in a state of stress and in a state of strain. All the bonds are stretched slightly, characteristic of a somewhat higher temperature. This is the state of strain and must be more accentuated for the weaker impurity bonds, making them efficient electron traps, than for the Si–O bonds. The impurity expansion by ionization and the formation of E' centers are taken as evidence of this state of stress.

TABLE 12   Per cent changes in density and selected acoustical properties of vitreous silica[a] caused by thermal compaction[b]

Temperature[c]	Density	Density[d]	Shear velocity[e]	Shear modulus	Poisson ratio
	ϱ	$\dfrac{\Delta\varrho}{\varrho}$	$\dfrac{\Delta v}{v}$	$\dfrac{\Delta m}{m}$	$\dfrac{\Delta v}{v}$
(°C)	(g/cm³)	(%)	(%)	(%)	(%)
		Corning 7940			
900	2.2009	0	0	0	0
1100	2.20207	+0.053	−0.188	−0.504	4.23
1250	2.20330	+0.109	−0.400	−0.688	6.49
1400	2.20360	+0.123	−0.413	−0.703	7.13
1500	2.2031	+0.100	−0.378	−0.652	6.91
as supplied	2.20125	+0.016	−0.121	−0.228	1.88
		Vitreosil			
as supplied	2.20240	0	0	0	0
1100	2.20270	+0.014	−0.100	−0.188	0.762
1250	2.20467	+0.103	−0.294	−0.487	3.73
1400	2.20555	+0.143	−0.338	−0.533	5.14

ᵃ Where several values are given by Fraser, the arithmetic means are given here.
ᵇ Data taken from Fraser.[156]
ᶜ Soaking temperature prior to quenching ("fictive" temperature).
ᵈ Dilatation is equal to the negative of the density change for these small density changes.
ᵉ Since $v = \sqrt{m/\varrho}$, it follows that $\Delta v/v = 1/2\,[(\Delta m/m) - (\Delta\varrho/\varrho)]$.

The description given here, that the material is compacted but that the bonds are stretched may seem inconsistent; but since the material is unsupported, it could not be otherwise. Geometrically, this can occur because the network linkages are not linear, the bond angle decreases on compaction, and is partially compensated by the network motility in a manner corresponding, in part, to the change in the helical angle of the Si–O network in quartz when the temperature is altered.

The amorphous character of vitreous silica insures its being isotropic. However, the fact that the linkages are always at an angle to any direction, the motility effect, and the unsymmetrical distribution of void space make for large anharmonic behavior and cause an unusually small Poisson ratio. The Poisson ratio is among the more sensitive properties of vitreous silica as shown by the work of Fraser, presented below (see Table 12).

ORIGIN OF COMPACTED STATES

The compacted states develop in either of two ways, or in a combination of them. Either the substance is excited, causing a statistical movement of oxygens into the void space, and this is quenched; or the substance is greatly compressed, also resulting in a mean displacement of oxygen into the void space. Some alteration in structure of the network is now required to lock in a new configuration. There is no problem in visualizing the process when it occurs above about 750°C, or under irradiation, for then the network is fragmented by the thermal or radiation processes, and a slight twisting of network segments relative to each other can occur by a process described above as motility (see pages 16, 23). This mechanism accounts for the maximum compaction found in radiation processes and places certain kinetic restrictions on them. The process of accommodation facilitated by cleaving the network is one which releases stress there. Thus, the greatest compaction which such a process can support is in every other loop of the network. As was described above, this corresponds to $\sim 3\%$ compaction. The existence of the supervenient expansion thus shows that the radius of compaction in the spike associated with heavier-ion bombardment is somewhat greater than two loops of the network, a conclusion reached above on other grounds. This mechanism also accounts for the decreasing efficiency of compaction by ionization as the compaction proceeds: for cleavage occurs most readily in the compacted, the most stressed portions, of the network.[346,347,348] This is no longer an ordinary saturation process, but one in which the affected portion of the material has a preferred interaction with the agent, and thus the compaction is inversely proportional to the number of sites compacted, as found by Primak and Kampwirth.[263]

The process of accommodation by which the pressure compaction is locked in at temperatures below that at which thermal fragmentation of the network occurs, must be viscous flow. This explains the reason why more compaction is locked in when the stress is non-uniform. There should also be a relation to temperature through the viscosity as a function of temperature; but it would be difficult to establish it with data currently available, because no measure of the non-uniformity of stress is available for these data. The process of locking in compaction by viscous flow is not unique to pressure compaction and other mechanically compacted states, such as the polishing compaction. The existence of the stress relaxation phenomena in the radiation compaction demonstrates that viscous flow also occurs there; it must contribute to the locking in. In the shock wave compaction, a very high thermal excitation sweeps the whole specimen; and it therefore seems likely that the dominating process is the recombination following network fragmentation, rather than viscous flow, despite the highly fluid state which must be present. The same must be true for the pressure compaction at high temperature. Other modes of compaction may now be conceived: e.g., hydrostatic pressure in the presence of ionization; but no such investigations for vitreous silica are known to this writer.

This realistic structural hypothesis is physically quite a different behavior from Primak's structural formalism presented above (see page 150). There can be no inward kinking of the network in the manner implied by his presentation and by Bridgman and Šimon's.[9] First, the movement of oxygen must be outward, not inward, hence void space would be displaced largely in neighboring loops of the network rather than the one being considered. Second, the change in bond angle can be only very small, hence large displacements of void space can occur only through the motility, a rotation of the Si–O tetrahedron about the Si–Si axis. A movement of this kind for a single Si–O tretahedron in the midst of the network can occur only by a readjustment or relaxation of the whole segment of which it is a part, each Si–O tetrahedron being affected only slightly. Such a relaxation should be locked in readily because of the complexity of the motions involved. The other possibility for a large displacement of void space would be the movement of a tetrahedron at a cleavage point in the network. Such compaction should be locked in less readily and thus may not show the exaggerated initial rate which might be anticipated for such events. The relative contributions of these several processes of compaction must be determined by kinetics and, therefore, must be influenced greatly by the local temperature and the extent of network cleavage or, using other terminology, the excitation and the segment length. Surely among these effects are to be sought the explanation for the variety of behavior encountered in radiation compaction by ions, electrons, and x-rays, and in the other modes of compaction.

IMPURITY

The role of impurities in vitreous silica is hardly known, but a hint of their possible importance is seen in Bridgman and Šimon's work[9] on the pressure compaction of glass, in the impurity expansion by ionization,[146] in the effect of OH on crystallization,[151] on the effect of impurity on viscosity.[138] It has been assumed here that impurities play a very important role in the structure of vitreous silica. A few studies of their effects on the properties are beginning to appear,[156,353] but how they affect the compaction and its behavior is largely an unexplored field. In the radiation effects, the influence of stored charge is not known. It has been assumed here that the concentration is low, 10^9–10^{11} per cm^3, in which case its effect may be overwhelmed by impurity effects; but no evidence on the subject exists.

LABILITY AND MOTILITY

Lability of the vitreous silica structure is evinced in all of these phenomena. The primary lability may be at the impurity sites, but there is also evidence of breaking of Si–O–Si links (particularly through the color center work), in the thermal release of compaction, and in the ionization release of compaction. It is also evident in the more severe processes, those involving radiation or high temperature. In addition to the lability, there is a motility which is seen in the viscous behavior, in the locking in of pressure compaction, in the radiation-induced stress relaxation by plastic flow, and in the time for thermal compaction. Motility is also indicated by the complex phenomena in the ionization release of compaction and in a less subtle way by the radiation homogenization (see page 124). Thus, the detailed structure of the network possesses a dynamic variability in addition to a variability from point to point and from specimen to specimen.

VARIABILITY OF STRUCTURE

There is no way of defining the state of compaction of vitreous silica in detail. However, reasonably consistent experimental results are obtained when a given product is led through the same sequence of operations. Ordinary vitreous silica is itself in an undefined state of compaction, and the definition of compaction used here, the negative dilatation with respect to this state is, of course, an inadequate definition of state. More serious is the fact that differently compacted vitreous silicas, or partially annealed vitreous silicas, or those prepared by some devious process, show quite different behavior when subjected to further compaction or to treatments which cause release of compaction. These vitreous silicas are quite different structurally, the compaction being locked in, in quite different ways. The compaction locked in by overlapping strain fields, as in the pressure compacted material, is particularly sensitive to release by ionization. The thermal annealing occurs in several stages and must therefore also distinguish different states of compaction. The different thermal annealing found by Primak and Kampwirth[146] for the ionization compaction shows there is also an impurity effect. These are virtually virgin fields for investigation. It will be shown below that the structural differences described here affect not only the behavior of vitreous silica, but can also be seen in the more sensitive properties.

FURTHER DEVELOPMENT OF THE THEORY

The theory developed here for the structure and behavior of vitreous silica is largely qualitative although a few quantities have been established; e.g., the network segment length, a radius of action, an explanation of the 3% effects, and the reduced power dependence for the ionization compaction. The greatest difficulty in developing the theory further is the dearth of data for well-defined material.

The difficulties encountered in attempting to utilize the literature are well illustrated by attempting to interpret the data given by Fraser.[156] He found that the dilatational velocity and modulus increase with compaction and are hardly affected by OH content. This would seem to be associated with an increase in anion repulsion and not with the kind of detail of interest here. He also found that the shear velocity and modulus decreased with thermal compaction and OH content. The latter would seem to be associated with network cleavage. If the shear velocity were associated with a transverse oxygen mode, it might be used to estimate the bond angle. However, such frequencies would be very high. In the ultrasonic range, studied by Fraser, it appears more likely that the effect involves much larger portions of the network, and therefore also shows effects of network cleavage. This is perfectly reasonable for the introduction of OH, but it raises very serious questions about the nature of the thermal compaction, for the velocity changes are hardly to be accounted for by the density changes, as shown in Table 12. They involve mainly a change in modulus. These decreases in shear modulus may be compared with Strakna et al.[355] who reported a 2% increase in shear modulus for the much larger compactions developed in neutron irradiation. It would thus seem that in Fraser's experiments, not only compaction was quenched, but also network cleavage; and thus, there arises immediately, the further question whether pressure compaction was quenched in because of thermal stresses accompanying quenching. The effects studied by Fraser seem to be largely impurity and network cleavage controlled. Possibly these questions could be resolved by studying the behavior under ionization. Again we have been frustrated in attempting to obtain fundamental quantitative information about the compaction, and more issues were raised than were settled.

Yet it must be pointed out that Fraser has made one of the most careful attempts of any in the literature to describe his materials.

Dealing with one of the coarser effects is Šimon's data (see Table 1), that neutron compaction caused a decrease of 4° in the mean bond angle for Si–O–Si corresponding to about a 3% compaction. It is unreasonable that such a rate of change could persist, for the change in mean bond angle for vitreous silica compacted to the density of quartz would then be unreasonable. It seems more likely that over the small range of bond angles which exist in vitreous silica, some were shifted over this region and the 4° is not be to be considered as a change in each bond angle. It would seem to be more desirable to utilize a physical property whose progressive change could be studied and interpreted rather than to utilize a direct structure determinations to determine the effect of compaction on bond angle. The work of Šimon[165] and others indicates the 9.09 μ infra-red absorption peak may be suitable for this purpose, but there is not enough data available yet to undertake such an analysis.

In attempting to interpret the anomalies, the difficulties encountered are similar to those just met in attempting to utilize Fraser's data. The number of impurity cleavages (including OH and Cl) in the network of a typical specimen of good vitreous silica may be 0.00035 per oxygen ion, and each would affect at least 2 tetrahedra and provide a population of free modes. These could contribute at least as much heat capacity as 0.002 cal/deg mol. For Suprasil, it would be 4 times as much. Nestrum's low temperature specific heat anomaly is about 0.004 cal/deg mol, and hence comparable. Thus, the possibility that the anomalies or part of them are related to network cleavage must be considered. However, at least some kinds of compaction reduce the magnitude of the anomalies in vitreous silica (see page 24). This is the case for the neutron compaction. It is not known whether the reduction in the anomalies in this case is caused by trapping charge (which may bind some of the free modes), by restricting the void space, by further cleavage (as suggested above, see page 127), or by other means. The portions of the structure contributing to the effects cannot be considered as identified.

The polarizability has been mentioned in several places above, but has been neglected in most of the presentation. It was pointed out above that when the void volume was altered, the volume of the oxygen ion was changed also. The effect is very apparent at ultra-high pressures. However, there should be a change in polarizability whenever the Si–O–Si bond angle is altered; and it should, therefore, occur in any compaction. It may be investigated by studying the refractive index and some of the secondary refractive properties. Fortunately, in the case of vitreous silica there is not a large dispersion of the refractive index changes, and thus the changes are largely to be associated with changes in polarizability of the oxygen ion rather than with the development or shifting of absorption bands of high oscillator strength. The effect of neutron compaction is mentioned by Primak[10] and by Primak and Post,[94] but there are no studies of the kind of details of interest here.

These illustrations are sufficient to show the problems in further developing the theory of the structure of vitreous silica. The primary problems are those of determining the bond angle, the void space, the network stress, polarizability, those quantities associated with the interatomic forces and modes. The secondary problems are those involving the impurities and other interruptions in the network, quantities which determine the free modes. The tools which are available for the investigation are the variation of physical properties with composition and with such treatments as heating, irradiation, and combinations of them. These simple means could identify the sources of most of the effects and provide a basis for evaluating them quantitatively.

Epilogue

WE HAVE seen that most of the work which has been done on vitreous silica is worthless for relating the properties and behavior to structure. Vitreous silica is a highly variable substance. It varies in impurity composition, by incomplete vitrification showing a residue of a crystalline starting material, by incipient devitrification as by annealing from a compacted state, by compaction associated with thermal, mechanical, or radiation history, by charge storage, by the presence of ionized atoms. Very few investigations have been made which have shown an appreciation for this variability of structure. The imperative for vitreous silica research now is to relate the behavior to the variability. The problem is quite different from that in research on crystalline material where, for most purposes, local behavior may be considered to occur in a sample of the typical environment. There is no typical environment in vitreous silica in this sense. The local environment is a sample of a spacially varying distribution of structure in a substance whose mean structure is usually undefined by most investigators. Thus, investigation of vitreous silica is in a primitive state, far behind the sophistication attained in other branches of solid state research.

Appendix I

On the Structure of Vitreous Silica

In the period preceding the writing of this monograph, Warren reconsidered x-ray diffraction by amorphous materials. An excellent account is now available.[356] Additionally, a new experimental determination for vitreous silica has appeared from his laboratory, Mozzi and Warren.[357] Basically, what was done was to use higher energy x-rays to obtain measurements to larger values of $\sin \theta/\lambda$. This was feasible primarily because the Compton scattered x-rays were greatly reduced by Warren and Mavel's method of fluorescence excitation,[358] and corrections for secondary scattering and for absorption were applied; and secondarily, by the application of more exact modes of computation involving pair functions and digital computer techniques, which became feasible with the acquisition of more precise experimental data. It is not necessary to discuss the techniques here because of Warren's own excellent evaluation.[356] Polished plates described as optical quality fused quartz under the trade name Amersil were employed. These are presumed here to have been equivalent to the grade Optosil, a material made by flame fusion from natural quartz and having a small content of OH and aluminum. The author inquired about the specimens hoping to have an opportunity to examine them, but they were no longer available.[359] The nature of the information obtained in Mozzi and Warren's investigation makes it unlikely that details of structure which have been of interest here would be revealed; yet a comparison of results for impure silicas, pure high OH silica, and pure low OH silica would be of interest. It was pointed out in the text that in Warren's earlier work there had been no determination of the Si–O–Si bond angle, and that those who tried to construe one from that work were being unjust. In this final study, a bond angle was construed and a distribution function for it is given. It is reproduced in Fig. 36. It is almost too much to hope that this result will not also be misconstrued despite Mozzi and Warren's careful qualifications about its interpretation. They say,

It should be emphasized that a measured pair function distribution curve such as that of Fig. 4 represents a structure which is averaged over the whole sample. If in a few small regions there is a higher degree of order such as that of the cristobalite and quartz structures, this could not be recognized as such, and the contributions of these regions would show up only as part of the general average.

162

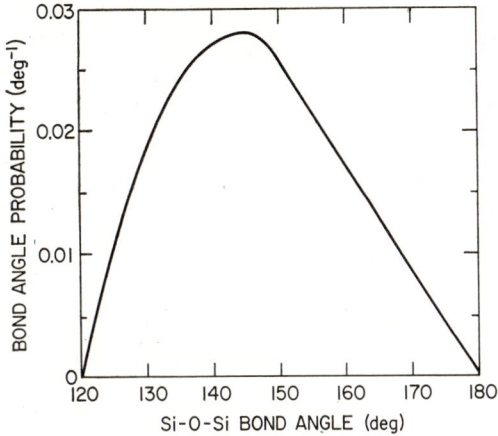

Figure 36. A trial distribution of Si–O–Si bond angles which fits Mozzi and Warren's x-ray data. (According to Mozzi and Warren[357]). Note that this distribution was not calculated from the data, that it is based on the assumption that all first Si–Si distances are associated with an Si–O–Si bond, and involves various approximations and corrections; e.g., for overlapping contributions to the Si–Si pair function, for termination, and for convergence. See the text for further comment.

The problems in deducing a bond angle from the x-ray data are many. The data do not give this angle; they yield only interatomic distances. In the text it was pointed out that the bond angle depends critically on the Si–Si distance. The distribution for this distance is not easily determined from the pair function because contributions from other pair functions are present in the region of the Si–Si pair function peak, and because this is the 3rd of the major peaks, and it is relatively small. The x-rays do not distinguish between Si–Si distances associated with Si–O–Si and Si–Si or Al–Si, etc. distances associated with other configurations such as network discontinuities and impurities; these may be much more serious than those associated with the inhomogeneities considered in the above quotation. Such perturbations would also affect all neighboring distances because of the high polarizability of the oxygen ion. Because of overlapping contributions to the pair functions, and because the data are otherwise not adequate for such a treatment, the pair functions could not be obtained by a deconvolution. They were therefore sought by examining various trial functions. Thus the finding that 144° is the most probable bond angle is significant, but the details of the distribution must be regarded as less certain. They also examined cristobalite and found the third peak to be much sharper than the one for vitreous silica. Thus the broadness is significant, but other evidence will have to be considered to

11*

understand the details of the distribution. In addition, they found that a histogram of distances measured for a model of randomly arranged tetrahedra was in reasonable accord with their pair function curves. This is a trivial result, but their statement (for which they give no detail) that other special orientations which suggested themselves gave poorer agreement does add support for the random network hypothesis.

Bell and his coworkers at the National Physical Laboratory concluded that generation of the random network of vitreous silica was much too difficult a task and therefore set about constructing several models, each of several hundred atoms, from polystyrene spheres and steel wire.[360] They then calculated a number of properties of these models. The Si–O–Si angle ranged from 120° to 160°. With a mean bond angle of 140°, the calculated density was 2.8 g/cm³ for Model I and 2.65 for Model II. The density was lower for larger mean bond angles. They anticipated a mean bond angle about 150° would give the correct density. It became more difficult to build a connected random network with mean bond angle greater than about 160°. A histogram of the radial distribution function when compensated for density and finite size of the model showed features found in the radial distribution function calculated from diffraction data for vitreous silica, Model I appearing somewhat better than Model II. Characteristically, for the models as compared to the diffraction data, the first peaks were sharper, the later peaks less distinct. In part this may be attributed to the finite size of the models, but from the viewpoint of this monograph, it is the expected result; because, in vitreous silica, the longer range order is attained by the molecular forces at the expense of forming bonds in the network, whereas Bell and Dean[360] purposely formed all bonds. This feature of vitreous silica is also to be found in Mozzi and Warren's[357] work. Although their distributions do not necessarily correspond to the distribution in their silica (having been trial distributions which accorded with the data rather than distributions which were derived from the data) they found large Si–Si distances which if used to calculate an Si–O–Si bond angle, would correspond to angles between 160 and 180°. Bell and Dean,[361] from their experience in building these models, were able to deduce the ways additional tetrahedra could be added to the system. This is in effect a calculation of the configurational entropy. Their result was 0.8 to 0.9 cal/deg mole and may be compared with experimental estimates between 0.67 and 1.08. This disposes of the argument that the structure of vitreous silica could not be a random network because such a network would possess too high a configurational entropy. The models were also used to calculate vibrational modes.[362] Three peaks were found corresponding closely to the 9.6, 13.7, and 24.4 μ bands. The 9.6 μ band appeared to be associated with a "bond stretching" mode, motion opposite to Si neighbors and parallel to the Si–Si direction; the 13.7 μ band to oxygens moving approximately per-pendicular to Si–Si directions in the Si–O–Si planes (the Si stretching mode described by Lippincott, *et al.*); and the 24.4 μ band to a bond rocking mode, perpendicular to the Si–O–Si plane. They also saw evidence for a nonbridg-ing oxygen vibration at 10.5–11 μ: the one found by Simon[165] in the neutron compacted material.

Gaskell[363] considered the thermal expansion of several phases of silica and reached conclusions about the thermal behavior of the Si–O–Si bond angle which are similar to those reached here. He[364] calculated the absorption band at 9.6 μ using Mozzi and Warren's[357] distribution of the Si–O–Si bond angle and obtained a band a little wider than the experimentally observed one. This supports the interpretation made here that Mozzi and Warren's distribution overemphasizes the largest bond angles.

(NOTE ADDED IN PROOF, 6/73:) It should be appreciated that the ionic radii and the polarizabilities which have been used in the arguments present-ed here, although generally accepted, are not experimental data. For the most part they have been deduced from a structural formalism. In some of the few cases where quantum mechanical calculations have been attempted or where electron density maps have been drawn from electron or x-ray diffraction data, the anionic radii have appeared smaller, the cationic radii larger, than generally accepted ones; cf. Lagowski, J. J., *Modern Inorganic Chemistry* (Marcel Dekker, New York, 1973), p. 67; Gilbert, T., *et al.*, Chemical Binding Effects in the Oxygen K-α X-Ray Emission Bands of Silica, *Phys. Rev.* (in press).

Appendix II

Miscellaneous Topics

Gaskell and Grove[365] studied the effect of thermal compaction on the 9, 12.5 and 21 μ infra-red absorption bands of vitreous silica and concluded that the shifts could not be explained by increases in density. They concluded that with increasing thermal compaction the Si–O distance increases and the Si–O–Si bond angle decreases.

The properties and structure of vitreous silica were reviewed by Brückner.[366] He mentions the types of silica glasses, optical properties, mechanical and thermal properties, transport phenomena, and action of radiation.

Evidence of the passage of energetic heavy particles through some solids can be seen in the electron microscope, and often these regions can be dissolved selectively. The affected regions are called tracks, and there is a large literature on them. Thus far, little of direct interest to the major subject of this monograph has developed. Fleischer, Price and Walker[367] studied a variety of materials and concluded that a critical rate of energy loss through ionization must occur before tracks can be seen. For silica they give ~ 15 MeV/mg cm^{-2}, and thus the lightest detectable particle would be about sulfur. Tracks often are not found at the end of the range where displacement is great. For these reasons and others, they hypothesized that the tracks were formed by ionization followed by an expulsion of positive ions from the track by mutual electrostatic repulsion,[368] a mechanism reminiscent of the Varley mechanism for the formation of F-centers. The hypothesis did not account for light ion tracks produced in plastics, and the subsidiary hypothesis of bond breaking by ionization was invoked for these substances. Of the work described in this monograph, only that involving argon and fission fragments may fall within the purvue of the track work; and perhaps not the former, because of the low energies employed. However, the damage mechanism suggested by them may be interpreted as an alternative to the mechanism presented here and therefore requires comment. Their hypothesis that the etchability of the tracks is caused by the strain field would hardly be satisfying to the chemist; the composition and constitution of the track and the physical chemistry of the dissolution process would have to be described.

The physical and chemical changes which constitute the tracks will surely be found to be different in different substances (a behavior typical of radiation damage) even as they had to conclude when considering the behavior of plastics. While they have established the possibility of the ion explosion process, a quantitative evaluation of this process and the subsequent history will have to be made and compared with quantitative evaluations of other processes involving displacement, thermal effects, phase changes, diffusion, etc. in the various substances of interest. Much of this they have mentioned themselves.

Revesz[369,370,371] has been interested in silica films. He considers that many of the property changes associated with imperfections in vitreous silica are related to changes in overlap of π-orbitals in the Si–O–Si bonding. These arguments are largely qualitative and based on calculations by Cruikshank[372] that the π-overlap is sensitive to the Si–O–Si bond angle.

The results and comments by Revesz and Zaininger, Gaskell, Mozzi and Warren, and this writer taken together raise some interesting questions for both theorizing and experimenting investigators. No simple relationship can be assumed between the Si–O–Si bond angle and the relative π- and σ-character of the Si–O bond if, accompanying a decreased bond angle, as at elevated temperature, there is an increased Si–O distance; under such circumstances the covalent character is probably decreased. The neighboring environment is also important as adjacent to a cleaved bond or other network irregularity covalency may be increased. Thus it would be of interest to learn about the particular conditions associated with the various Si–O–Si bond angles in vitreous silica.

A thesis[373] which reports a study of heavy ion tracks and heavy ion radiation damage in vitreous silica has appeared.

References

1. Sosman, R.B., *Properties of Silica*, The Chemical Catalogue Co., New York (1927).
2. *id.*, p. 305, Variation in density; p. 306, Density variation within a specimen; p. 308, Variation in isotopic composition.
3. *id.*, pp. 43, 44, Definition of vitreous silica.
4. *id.*, p. 116, Constancy of α–β-quartz inversion.
5. *id.*, pp. 122, 123, Speculations on the inversion range for α–β-quartz.
6. *id.*, p. 447, Modulus of rigidity of vitreous silica at high temperature.
7. *id.*, p. 137, Macroscopic inhomogeneity in vitreous silica.
8. Primak, W., and Edwards, E., "Radiation Induced Dilatations in Vitreous Silica", *Phys. Rev.* **128**, 2580 (1962).
9. Bridgman, P.W., and Šimon, I., "Effects of Very High Pressures on Glass", *J. Appl. Phys.* **24**, 405 (1953).
10. Primak, W., "Fast Neutron Induced Changes in Quartz and Vitreous Silica", *Phys. Rev.* **110**, 1240 (1958).
11. *id.*, p. 1248, Use of compaction.
12. *id.*, p. 1249, Refractivity of quartz.
13. Weyl, W.A., and Marboe, E.C., *The Constitution of Glasses*, Interscience, New York, Vol. I (1962); Vol. II, Part 1 (1964); Part 2 (1967).
14. *id.*, Vol. II, Part 2, pp. 1366–1367, Use of terms densification, compacting, densified, compacted form.
15. Sosman, R.B., *The Phases of Silica*, Rutgers Univ. Press, New Brunswick (1965).
16. *id.*, pp. 149–153, Phases of vitreous silica.
17. *id.*, pp. 148–150, Definition of vitreous silica.
18. *id.*, p. 93, Historical note on inversions of quartz.
19. *id.*, Chap. 5, The High-Low Inversions of Silica.
20. *id.*, p. 75, Characteristics of the high-low inversions.
21. *id.*, p. 79, Characteristics of α–β-quartz inversion.
22. *id.*, pp. 102–104, Variability of inversion temperatures in tridymite.
23. *id.*, p. 106, Each cristobalite crystal in an aggregate has its own inversion temperature.
24. *id.*, p. 65, Discovery of coesite and its properties.
25. Weyl, W.A., *Transition in Glass, Phase Transformation in Solids*, R. Smoluchowski, J.E. Mayer, W.A. Weyl, ed., John Wiley, New York (1951) p. 296.
26. *id.*, p. 311, Compacting used for increasing density on annealing chilled silicate glasses.
27. *id.*, p. 305, Changes in glass associated with heat treatment effects.
28. *id.*, p. 311, Chilled glass lower density, refractive index, greater thermal expansion.

29. *id.*, p. 325, Data on flint glass; also Prince Rupert drops.

30. Anderson, O.L., *The Kinetics of Structural Rearrangement in Glass under Pressure*, Traveaux du IVᵉ Congres International du Verre, Paris (July 2–7 1956) p. 310.

31. *id.*, p. 312, Compaction and densification definitions.

32. *id.*, p. 311, Uses "locked in".

33. Morey, G.W., *The Properties of Glass*, Reinhold Publishing Corp., New York (1938).

34. Anderson, O.L., and Dienes, G.J., *The Anomalous Properties of Vitreous Silica, Non-Crystalline Solids*, V.D.Frechette, ed., John Wiley, New York (1960).

35. Primak, W., "Review of the Gross Structural Effects of Energetic Atomic Particles on Vitreous and Crystalline Silica", *J. Phys. Chem. Solids* **13**, 279 (1960).

36. *id.*, p. 285, History of radiation effects in quartz and vitreous silica.

37. Lell, E., Kreidl, N.J., and Hensler, J.R., *Radiation Effects in Quartz, Silica, and Glasses, Progress in Ceramic Science*, J.E.Burke, ed., Vol. 4, Pergamon Press, Oxford (1966).

38. Traveaux du IVᵉ Congrès International du Verre, Commission Internationale du Verre, Paris (1956).

39. V. Internationaler Glaskongress, Glastechnische Berichte 32 K (1959), (Carl Retter, Wiesbaden).

40. American Ceramic Society (compiled by), *Advances in Glass Technology*, Plenum Press, New York (1962).

41. Mackenzie, J.D., ed., *Modern Aspects of the Vitreous State*, Vol. I. Butterworths, London (1960), Vol. II. Butterworths, Washington (1962), Vol. III. Butterworths, Washington (1964).

42. *The Structure of Glass*, Proceedings of a Series of Conferences on the Vitreous State, translated from Russian, Consultants Bureau, New York (1958–1966); Second All-Union Conf., Nov., 1953, Vol. I, E.B.Uvarov, trans., (1958); Third All-Union Conf., Nov., 1959, Vol. II, E.B.Uvarov and G. Del Re, trans., (1960); Pre-Conference Reports of the Fourth All-Union Conf., Dec., 1962, Vol. III, IV, V, E.B.Uvarov, trans. (1964–5); Fourth All-Union Conf., Mar., 1964, Vol. VI, VII, E.B.Uvarov, trans. (1966).

43. Zachariesen, W.H., "The Atomic Arrangement in Glass", *J. Am. Chem. Soc.* **54**, 3841 (1932).

44. Pauling, L., "The Principles Determining the Structure of Complex Ionic Crystals", *J. Am. Chem. Soc.* **51**, 1010 (1929).

45. Warren, B.E., "Summary of Work on Atomic Arrangement in Glass", *J. Am. Cer. Soc.* **24**, 256 (1941).

46. *id.*, p. 260, The borate anomaly.

47. Warren, B.E., "X-ray Diffraction of Vitreous Silica", *Z. Krist.* **86**, 349 (1933).

48. Warren, B.E., "X-ray Determination of the Structure of Glass", *J. Am. Cer. Soc.* **17**, 249 (1934).

49. Warren, B.E., "X-ray Determination of the Structure of Liquids and Glass", *J. Appl. Phys.* **8**, 645 (1937).

50. Warren, B. E., Krutter, H., and Morningstar, O., "Fourier Analysis of X-ray Patterns in Vitreous SiO_2 and B_2O_3", *J. Am. Cer. Soc.* **19**, 202 (1936).

51. Mackenzie, J.D., and White, J.L., "The Si–O–Si Angle and the Structure of Vitreous Silica", *J. Am. Cer. Soc.* **43**, 170 (1960).

52. Zarzycki, J., *Étude du Réseau Vitreux par Diffraction des Rayons X aux Températures Élevées*, Traveaux du IVᵉ Congrès International du Verre, Paris (1956).

53. Prins, J.A., *Non-Crystalline Solids*, V.D. Frechette, ed., John Wiley, New York (1960), Discussion, p. 139.

54. Porai-Koshits, E.A., *Crystal Chemical Aspects of the Structure of Inorganic Glasses the Structure of Glass*, Vol. 6, E.B. Uvarov, trans., Consultant Bureau, New York (1966) p. 6.

55. *id.*, p. 7, Heterogeneous structure, 55 Å pores in a borosilicate glass after heating at 750°C.

56. Paalman, H.H., and Pings, C.J., "Fourier Analysis of X-ray Diffraction Data from Liquids", *Rev. Mod. Phys.* **35**, 389 (1963).

57. Urnes, S., *X-ray Diffraction Studies of Glass, Modern Aspects of the Vitreous State*, J.D. Mackenzie, ed., Vol. 1, p. 10, Butterworths, London (1960).

58. Wyckoff, R.W.G., "The Crystal Structure of the High-Temperature Form of Cristobalite (SiO_2)", *Am. J. Sci.* **9**, 448 (1925); *Z. Krist.* **62**, 189 (1925) (German).

59. Barth, T.F.W., "The Cristobalite Structures, I. High-cristobalite", *Am. J. Sci.* V, **23**, 350 (1932).

60. Barth, T.F.W., "The Cristobalite Structures, II. Low-cristobalite", *Am. J. Sci.* V, **24**, 97 (1932).

61. Nieuwenkamp, W., "Die Kristallstruktur des Tief-Cristobalits SiO_2", *Z. Krist.* **92**, 82 (1935).

62. Nieuwenkamp, W., "Über die Struktur von Hoch-Cristobalit", *Z. Krist.* **96**, 454 (1937).

63. Bragg, W., and Gibbs, R.E., "The Structure of α and β Quartz", *Proc. Roy. Soc. Lond.* **109A**, 405 (1925).

64. *id.*, p. 412, About α–β-quartz inversion (quoted).

65. Gibbs, R.E., "The Structure of α-Quartz", *Proc. Roy. Soc. Lond.* **110A**, 443 (1926).

66. Wei, Pei-Hsiu, "The Structure of α-Quartz", *Z. Krist.* **92**, 355 (1935).

67. Machatschki, F., "Die Kristallstruktur von Tiefquartz SiO_2 und Aluminium-Orthoarsenat $AlAsO_4$", *Z. Krist.* **94**, 222 (1936).

68. Brill, R., Hermann, C., and Peters, C., "Röntgenographische Fouriersynthese von Quartz", *Am. d. Physik* **41**, 245 (1942).

69. Rice, O.K., *Electronic Structure and Chemical Binding*, McGraw-Hill, New York (1940) p. 270.

70. Pauling, L., *The Nature of the Chemical Bond*, Cornell University Press, Ithaca (1939) p. 326.

71. *id.*, p. 348, Tetrahedral correction.

72. *id.*, p. 222, Covalent structure.

73. Zwikker, C., *Physical Properties of Solid Materials*, Pergamon Press, London (1954), p. 235, Space filling factor for SiO_2.

74. *id.*, p. 26, Fig. 2.18.

75. Mueller, H., "The Theory of Photoelasticity", *J. Am. Cer. Soc.* **21**, 27 (1938).

76. *id.*, p. 29, Ratio of volumes of silicon to oxygen, 1/140.

77. Smyth, C.P., *Dielectric Constant and Molecular Structure*, The Chemical Catalogue Co., Inc., New York (1931) pp. 158, 159, Refraction of $O^=$ in SiO_2.

78. Evstropyev, K.S., *The Crystalline Theory of Glass Structure*, *The Structure of Glass*, E.B. Uvarov, trans., Consultants Bureau, New York (1958) Vol. I., p. 9.

79. Porai-Koshits, E.A., *Methods for Interpretation of X-ray Patterns of Glassy Substances and the Principle Hypotheses of Their Structure*, *The Structure of Glass*, E.B. Uvarov, trans., Consultants Bureau, New York (1958) Vol. II., p. 25.

80. Lukesh, J.S., "The Distribution of Metallic Atoms in Two-Component Glasses", *Proc. Natl. Acad. Sci.* **26**, 277 (1942).

81. Debye, P., and Bueche, A.M., "Scattering by an Inhomogeneous Solid", *J. Appl. Phys.* **20**, 518 (1949).

82. Brosset, C., *Some Aspects on the Structure of Glasses with High Silica Content*, VIII International Ceramic Congress, Copenhagen (1962) p. 62; "X-ray Investigations of the Distribution of Heavy Atoms in Glass", *Physics and Chemistry of Glasses*, Vol. 4 (3), pp. 99–102 (1963).

83. Robinson, H.A., "The Structure of Vitreous SiO_2, I. A New Pentagonal Dodecahedral Model", *J. Phys. Chem. Solids* **26**, 209 (1965): Priv. Comm. (Warren) Vit. Sil. Si–O 1.64, O–O 2.68, Si–Si 3.14 Å.

84. Prebus, A.F., and Michener, J.W., "Electron Microscopic Investigation of Glass", *Ind. Eng. Chem.* **46**, 147 (1954).

85. Warshaw, I., "Structural Implications of the Electron Microscopy of Glass Surfaces", *J. Am. Cer. Soc.* **43**, 4 (1960).

86. Zarzycki, J., and Mezard, R., "A Direct Electronic Microscopic Study of the Structure of Glass", *Physics and Chemistry of Glasses* **3**, 163 (1962).

87. Seward, T.P., III, Uhlmann, D.R., Turnbull, D., and Pierce, G.R., "Transmission Electron Microscopy of the Glass Samples", *J. Am. Cer. Soc.* **50**, 25 (1967).

88. Belov, N.V., "The Structure of Glass in the Light of the Crystal Chemistry of the Silicates", *The Structure of Glass*, Vol. 2, E.B. Uvarov and G. Del Re, trans., Consultants Bureau, New York (1960) p. 74.

89. *id.*, p. 77, Structure of glass determined by cation, not Si–O.

90. Vogel, W., "The Cellular Structure of Glass", *The Structure of Glass*, E.B. Uvarov and G. Del Re, trans., Consultants Bureau, New York (1960).

91. Winter, A., *Certain Aspects of Rayleigh Scattering in Glass*, Advances in Glass Technology, *VI International Congress on Glass*, Plenum Press, New York (1962), p. 115.

92. Eitel, W., *Silicate Science*, Academic Press, New York (1965) Vol. III. "The inversions."

93. Buerger, M.J., "The Silica Framework Crystals and Their Stability Fields", *Z. Krist.* **A90**, 186–192 (1935).

94. Primak, W., and Post, D., "Photoelastic Constants of Vitreous Silica and its Elastic Coefficient of Refractive Index", *J. Appl. Phys.* **30**, 779 (1959).

95. Tuttle, O.F., "The Variable Inversion Temperature of Quartz as a Possible Geologic Thermometer", *Am. Mineralogist* **34**, 723 (1949).

96. Keith, M.L., and Tuttle, O.F., "Significance of Variation in the High-Low Inversion of Quartz", *Am. J. Sci.*, Bowen Vol. 203–280 (1952).

97. Primak, W., Fuchs, L.H., and Day, P., "Effects of Nuclear Reactor Exposure on Some Properties of Vitreous Silica and Quartz", *J. Am. Cer. Soc.* **38**, 135 (1955).

98. Mayer, G., and Gigon, J., "Effects des Neutrons Rapide sur Quelques Constantes Physiques du Quartz Cristallin et de la Silice Vitreuse", *J. Phys. Radium* **18**, 109 (1956).

99. Mayer, G., Reported in a seminar at Argonne National Laboratory: *Difference of irradiated α–β-quartz transition.* (Nov. 20, 1957).

100. Zhdanov, G.S., Zubov, V.G., Kolontsova, E.V., Osipova, L.P., Telegina, I.V., "Radiation Effects in α-Quartz", *Soviet Physics-Cristallography* **8**, 154–158, English translation (1963).

101. Gibson, R.E., "A Note on the High-Low Inversion of Quartz and the Heat Capacity of Low Quartz at 573 °C", *J. Phys. Chem.* **32**, 1206–1210 (1928).

102. Yoder, H.S. Jr., "High-Low Quartz Inversion up to 10,000 Bars", *Trans. Am. Geophys. Union* **31**, 827–835 (1950).

103. Buerger, M.J., and Lukesh, J., "*Re-inversion of Tridymite*", Science **95**, 20–21 (1942).

104. Hill, V.G., and Roy, R., "Silica Structure Studies, Part VI. Tridymites", *Trans. Brit. Cer. Soc.* **57**, 496 (1958).

105. Wahl, F.M., Grim, K.E., and Graaff, R.B., "Phase Transformations in Silica as Examined by Continuous X-ray Diffraction", *Am. Mineralogist* **46**, 196 (1961).

106. Babcock, C.L., Barber, S.W., and Fajans, K., "Coexisting Structures of Vitreous Silica", Atti del III Congresso Internazionale del Vetro, Venezia (1953) International Commission on Glass, Rome (1954) pp. 195–207; *Ind. Eng. Chem.* **46**, (Jan.) 161 (1954).

107. Anderson, O.L., and Bommel, H.E., *J. Am. Cer. Soc.* **38**, 125 (1955).

108. Dienes, G.J., "The Temperature Dependence of the Elastic Moduli of Vitreous Silica", *J. Phys. Chem. Solids* **7**, 290 (1958).

109. Spinner, S., "Elastic Moduli of Glasses at Elevated Temperatures by a Dynamic Method", *J. Am. Cer. Soc.*, **39**, 113 (1956).

110. Marx, J.W., and Sivertson, J.M., "Temperature Dependence of Elastic Moduli and Internal Friction of Silica and Glass", *J. Appl. Phys.* **24**, 81 (1953).

111. Stevels, J.M., *Network Defects in Non-Crystalline Solids, Non-Crystalline Solids*, V.D.Frechette, ed., John Wiley, New York (1960) p. 412.

112. Turnbull, D., and Cohen, M.H., *Crystallization Kinetics and Glass Formation, Modern Aspects of the Vitreous State*, J.D.McKenzie, ed., Vol. I., p. 38, Butterworths, London (1960).

113. Reitzel, J., "Effect of Pressure on the Dielectric Constant of Vitreous Silica", *Nature* **178**, 940 (1956).

114. Bridgman, P.W., "The High Pressure Behavior of Miscellaneous Minerals", *Am. J. Sci.* 237, 7 (1939) p. 13.

115. Bridgman, P.W., "The Compression of 39 Substances to 100,000 kg/cm²", *Proc. Am. Acad. Arts Sci.* **76**, 55 (1948) pp. 67, 68.

116. Bridgman, P.W., "Rough Compressions of 177 Substances to 40,000 kg/cm²", *Proc. Am. Acad. Arts Sci.* **76**, 71 (1948).

117. Reitzel, J., Šimon, I., Walker, J.A., "Measuring Linear Compressibility of Solids", *Rev. Sci. Instr.* **28**, 828 (1957).

118. Adams, L.H., and Williamson, E.D., "On the Compressibility of Minerals and Rocks at High Pressures", *J. Frank. Inst.* **195**, 493 (1923).

119. Bridgman, P.W., "Compressibility of Several Artificial and Natural Glasses", *Am. J. Sci.* **10**, 359 (1925).

120. Birch, A.F., and Law, R.L., "Measurement of Compressibility at High Pressures and at High Temperatures", *Bull. Geol. Soc. Am.* **46**, 1219 (1935).

121. Birch, A.F., and Dow, R.B., "Compressibility of Rocks and Glasses at High Temperatures and Pressures, Seismological Applications", *Bull. Geol. Soc. Am.* **47**, 1235 (1936).

122. Primak, W., Edwards, E., Keiffer, D., and Szymanski, H., "Ionization Expansion of Compacted Silica and the Theory of the Radiation-Induced Dilatations in Vitreous Silica", *Phys. Rev.* **133**, A531 (1964).

123. The characteristics given by Primak, *et al.*[122] are between those for a spherical and for a cylindrical spike.

124. This formalism first appears as an order of magnitude calculation in W.Primak, *et al.*[122] It was later formalized in a series of articles with R. Kampwirth.[146,180,263,304]

125. Smyth, H.T., Londeree, J.W., Lorey, G.E., "Compressibility of Vitreous Silica", *J. Am. Cer. Soc.* **36**, 238 (1953).

126. Smyth, H.T., Skogen, H.S., and Hassell, W.B., "Thermal Capacity of Vitreous Silica", *J. Am. Cer. Soc.* **36**, 327 (1953).

127. Smyth, H.T., "Thermal Expansion of Vitreous Silica", *J. Am. Cer. Soc.* **38**, 140 (1955).

128. Warshavsky, M., and Robinson, H.A., "Internal Friction in Vibrating Granular Reeds and its Application to Vitreous Silica", *J. Appl. Phys.* **39**, 156 (1968).

129. Jack, K.H., and Hetherington, G., *Quarzglas and Quartzgut, Uhlmans Encyclopädie der technischen Chemie*, Urban & Schwarzenberg, München–Berlin, (1963) 3rd Ed., Vol. 14, p. 510.

130. Hetherington, G., "Vitreous Silica Terminology", *J. Brit. Cer. Soc.* **3**, 595 (1966).

131. Browell, T.P., and Hetherington, G., "Vitreous Silica for the Scientific Glassblower", *J. Brit. Soc. of Scientific Glassblowers* **2**, 1 (1966).

132. Hetherington, G., and Bell, L.W., "Analysis of High-Purity Synthetic Vitreous Silica", *Physics & Chemistry of Glasses* **8**, 206 (1967).

133. Stephenson, G.W., and Jack, K.H., *Trans. Brit. Cer. Soc.* **59**, 397 (1960): About H_2O and OH in vitreous silica.

134. Hetherington, G., and Jack, K.H., "Water in Vitreous Silica, Part 1. Influence of Water Content in the Properties of Vitreous Silica", *Physics & Chemistry of Glasses* **3**, 129 (1962).

135. Bell, T., Hetherington, G., and Jack, K.H., "Water in Vitreous Silica, Part 2. Some Aspects of Hydrogen Water-Silica Equilibria", *Physics & Chemistry of Glasses* **3**, 141 (1962).

136. Hetherington, G., Jack, K.H., and Ramsay, M.W., "The High-Temperature Electrolysis of Vitreous Silica, Part 1. Oxidation, Ultra-Violet Induced Fluorescence, and Irradiation Colour", *Physics & Chemistry of Glasses* **6**, 6 (1965).

137. Dunn, T., Hetherington, G., and Jack, K.H., "The High-Temperature Electrolysis of Vitreous Silica, Part 2. Active Electrodes and Anisotropic Electrolysis", *Physics & Chemistry of Glasses* **6**, 16 (1965).

138. Hetherington, G., Jack, K.H., and Kennedy, J.C., "The Viscosity of Vitreous Silica", *Physics & Chemistry of Glasses* **5**, 130 (1964).

139. Hetherington, G., and Jack, K.H., "The Oxidation of Vitreous Silica", *Physics & Chemistry of Glasses* **5**, 147 (1964).

140. Mohn, H., *The Optical Properties of Optical Quartz Glass*, Festschrift 100 Jahre Hereus Hanau, K. Ruthardt, ed., Brönners Druckerei, Frankfurt am Main (1951).

141. Primak, W., in *Ellipsometry in the Measurement of Surfaces and Their Films*, E. Passaglia, R. R. Stromberg, and J. Kruger, ed., National Bureau of Standards Misco Pub. 256, U.S. Government Printing Office, Washington D.C. (1964) p. 154.

142. Primak, W., (unpublished).

143. Primak, W., and Kampwirth, R., Priv. Comm., *Density of silica*, data, Jan. 28, 1965.

144. Weeks, R. A., and Lell, E., "Relation Between E' Centers and Hydroxyl Bonds in Silica", *J. Appl. Phys.* **35**, 1932 (1964).

145. *id.*, p. 1937, Analyses of vitreous silica. Weeks and Lell's units are ppm by weight, (private communication).

146. Primak, W., and Kampwirth, R., "Impurity Effect in the Ionization Dilatation of Vitreous Silica", *J. Appl. Phys.* **39**, 6010 (1968).

147. Dodd, D. M., and Frazer, D. B., "Optical Determinations of OH in Fused Silica", *J. Appl. Phys.* **37**, 3911 (1966).

148. Moulson, A. J., and Roberts, J. P., "Water in Silica Glass", *Trans. Farad. Soc.* **57**, 1208 (1961).

149. Douglas, R. W., and Isard, J. O., "Density Changes in Fused Silica", *J. Soc. Glass Technol.* **35**, 206 (1951).

150. Cohen, H. M., and Roy, Rustum, *Effects of High Pressure on Glass, Physics & Chemistry of High Pressures Symposium 1962*, Society of Chemical Industry, Gordon & Breach, New York, (1963) p. 133.

151. *id.*, p. 138, Traces of water not detectable by weighing cause devitrification to quartz or coesite in a few hours even at 20 kbar (temperature not stated), whereas crystallization of dry silica at temperatures over 700°C at 80 kbar is barely perceptible.

152. *id.*, p. 135, Molar refractivity for very dense silica 7.19 compared to 7.45 for vitreous silica and 7.19 for quartz.

153. *id.*, p. 135, Most of the birefringence in compacted vitreous silica is lost on crushing.

154. Uhlmann, D. R., Hays, J. F., and Turnbull, D., "The Effect of High Pressure on Crystallization Kinetics with Special Reference to Fused Silica", *Physics & Chemistry of Glasses* **7**, 159 (1966).

155. Blinov, V., and Roy, R., "Catalysis of Glass Crystallization under Extreme Pressure", *Bull. Am. Cer. Soc.* **41**, 253 (1962).

156. Fraser, D. B., "Factors Influencing the Acoustical Properties of Vitreous Silica", *J. Appl. Phys.* **39**, 5868 (1968).

157. Bridgman, P. W., "The Resistance of 72 Elements Alloys and Compounds to 100,000 kg/cm²", *Proc. Am. Acad. Arts Sci.* **81**, 167 (1952).

158. Šimon, I., (private communication), (Šimon to Primak, Dec. 4, 1967).

159. Christiansen, E. B., Kistler, S. S., Gogarty, W. B., "Irreversible Compressibility of Silica Glass as a Means of Determining the Distribution of Force in High Pressure Cells", *J. Am. Cer. Soc.* **45**, 172 (1962).

160. Mackenzie, J. D., "High Pressure Effects on Oxide Glasses, I. Densification in Rigid State", *J. Am. Cer. Soc.* **46**, 461 (1963).

161. Bridgman, P.W., "Miscellaneous Effects of Pressure in Miscellaneous Substances", *Proc. Am. Acad. Arts & Sci.* **84**, 111 (1955).
162. Primak, W., and Kampwirth, R., (unpublished).
163. Šimon, I., "Structure of Neutron Disordered Silica", *Phys. Rev.* **103**, 1587 (1956).
164. Šimon, I., "Structure of Neutron-Irradiated Quartz and Vitreous Silica", *J. Am. Cer. Soc.* **40**, 150 (1957).
165. Šimon, I., "Infrared Studies of Glass", *Modern Aspects of the Vitreous State*, J.D.Mackenzie, ed., Butterworth, London (1960), Vol. I., p. 120.
166. *id.*, p. 145.
167. Šimon, I., and McMahon, H.O., "Study of the Structure of Quartz, Cristobalite, and Vitreous Silica by Reflection in Infrared", *J. Chem. Phys.* **21**, 23 (1953).
168. Cohen, H.M., and Roy, Rustum, "Effects of Ultrahigh Pressures on Glass", *J. Am. Cer. Soc.* **44**, 523 (1961).
169. *id.*, p. 524, Kinetic experiments mentioned.
170. Roy, Rustum, and Cohen, H.M., "Effects of High Pressure on Glass A Possible Piezometer for the 100-Kilobar Region", *Nature* **190**, 798 (1961).
171. Dachille, F., and Roy, Rustum, "High-Pressure Region of the Silica Isotypes", *Z. Krist.* **111**, 451 (1959).
172. Mackenzie, J.D., "High-Pressure Effects on Oxide Glasses, II. Subsequent Heat Treatment", *J. Am. Cer. Soc.* **46**, 470 (1963).
173. Mackenzie, J.D., "High-Pressure Effects on Oxide Glasses, III. Densification in Non-rigid State", *J. Am. Cer. Soc.* **47**, 76 (1964).
174. Cohen, H.M., and Roy, Rustum, "Densification of Glass at Very High Pressure", *Physics & Chemistry of Glasses* **6**, 149 (1965).
175. *id.*, p. 153, Rate of densification.
176. *id.*, p. 159, Packing of tetrahedra.
177. Cohen, H.M., and Roy, Rustum, Reply to Comments on "Effects of Ultrahigh Pressure on Glass", *J. Am. Cer. Soc.* **45**, 398 (1962).
178. Weir, C.E., and Spinner, S., Comments on "Effects of Ultrahigh Pressure on Glass", *J. Am. Cer. Soc.* **45**, 196 (1962).
179. Weir, C., Spinner, S., Malitson, I., and Rodney, W., "Optical and Volume Relaxation Effects in Glass Following Removal of High Hydrostatic Pressure", *J. Res. National Bureau of Standards* (U.S.) **58**, 189 (1957).
180. Primak, W., and Kampwirth, R., "Ionization Expansion of Pressure-Compacted Vitreous Silica", *J. Appl. Phys.* **40**, 685 (1969).
181. *id.*, p. 686, Peripheral compaction.
182. Keiffer, D., (unpublished); Roaldi, A., and Szymanski, H., (unpublished); Kuczkowski, R.L., Thesis, Canisius College (1960) (unpublished).
183. Primak, W., and Szymanski, H., "Radiation Damage in Vitreous Silica, Annealing of the Density Changes", *Phys. Rev.* **101**, 1268 (1956).
184. Primak, W., "Large Temperature Range Annealing", *J. Appl. Phys.* **31**, 1524 (1960).
185. Primak, W., Szymanski, H., and Keiffer, D., "Frequency Factors for Annealing Fast-Neutron Induced Density Changes in Vitreous Silica", *J. Appl. Phys.* **32**, 660 (1961).
186. Brückner, R., "Das Thermische Ausdehnungsverhalten von Kieselglas als Funktion der Thermischen Vorgeschichte", *Naturwissenschaft* **49**, 150 (1962).

187. Fraser, D.B., Orally at IEEE Ultrasonics Symposium, Cleveland (1966).
188. Fraser, D.B., (private communication), Density of various grades of silica quenched from various temperatures.
189. Joffe, H., *IEEE Ultrasonic Symposium*, (Oct. 12–14, 1966).
190. Cornish, D.C., "The Mechanism of Glass Polishing", British Instrument Research Association, Chislehurst, Kent, *BSIRA Res. Rep.* **R267** (1961).
191. id., p. 3, Beilby's experiments.
192. Pinsker, F.G., *Electron Diffraction*, Butterworths, London (1953) p. 378.
193. Primak, W., and Luthra, J., "Radiation-Induced Expansion and Increase in Refractive Index of Magnesium Oxide; Evidence for the F-Center", *Phys. Rev.* **150**, 551 (1966).
194. id., p. 552, Increased refractive index.
195. Primak, W., and Luthra, J., (unpublished); Electron diffraction pattern of MgO vanished on rubbing on an abrasive.
196. Twyman, F., *Prism and Lens Making*, Hilger and Watts Ltd., 2 Ed., London (1952), Chapter 3, "The Nature of Grinding and Polishing".
197. id., p. 318, The Twyman effect.
198. id., p. 130, Delayed fracture caused by atmospheric attack.
199. Rayleigh, Lord, "The Surface Layer of Polished Silica and Glass with Further Studies on Optical Contact", *Proc. Roy. Soc.* **A160**, 507 (1937).
200. Rabinowicz, E., "Polishing", *Sci. Am.* **218** (June), 91 (1968).
201. Hillig, W.B., "Sources of Weakness and the Ultimate Strength of Brittle Amorphous Solids", *Modern Aspects of the Vitreous State*, Vol. II, J. D. Mackenzie, ed., Butterworths, Washington, D.C. (1962) p. 152.
202. id., pp. 186–190, Ultimate strength of glass.
203. Yokota, H., Kinosita, K., and Sakata, H., "Ellipsometric Study of Polished Glass Surfaces", *Japan. J. Appl. Phys.* **3**, 805 (1964).
204. Sissingh, R., and Groosmuller, J.T., "Optische Bestimmung der Dicke einer Oberflächenschicht auf Glas aus Reflexionsbetrachtungen", *Phys. Z.* **27**, 518 (1926).
205. Vasicek, A., "Künstlich hergestellte Oberflächenschichten auf Glas", *Kolloid Z.* **86**, 288 (1936).
206. Primak, W., (unpublished).
207. Primak, W., "Dispersed Depolarization by Altered Surface Layers", *J. Opt. Soc. Am.* **57**, 430 (1967).
208. Osterburg, H., and Smith, L.W.., "Transmission of Optical Energy along Surfaces", *J. Opt. Soc. Am.* **54**, 1073, 1078 (1964).
209. Primak, W., "Determination of Small Dilatations and Surface Stress by Birefringence Measurements", *Surface Science* **16**, 398 (1969).
210. Wackerle, J., "Shock-Wave Compression of Quartz", *J. Appl. Phys.* **33**, 922 (1962).
211. DeCarli, P.S., and Jamieson, J.C., "Formation of an Amorphous Form of Quartz under Shock Conditions", *J. Chem. Phys.* **31**, 1675 (1959).
212. Wackerle, J.D., (private communication) (Mar. 26, 1968).
213. Fowles, G.R., *Shock Wave Compression of Quartz*, Poulter Laboratories Technical Report 003-61 Stanford Res. Inst., Menlo Park, Calif., (Oct. 1961).
214. Fowles, R., "Dynamic Compression of Quartz", *J. Geophys. Res.* **72**, 5729 (1967).

215. Seeger, R.J., "Fluid Mechanics", *Handbook of Physics*, E.V. Condon and H.Odishaw, ed., McGraw-Hill Book Co., New York (1958) pp. 3–24, Rankine-Hugoniot relations.

216. Fowles, G.R., "Shock Wave Compression of Quartz, CA 57:11,868^e", *Thesis-Univ. Microfilms Order* $\neq$62-2332 67 pp, Dissertation Abstract **22**, 4384-5 (1962).

217. Ahrens, T.J., and Duvall, G.E., "Stress Relaxation behind Elastic Shock Waves in Rocks", *J. Geophys. Res.* **71**, 4349 (1966).

218. Chao, E.C.T., Shoemaker, E.M., and Madsen, B.M., "First Natural Occurrence of Coesite", *Science* **132**, 220 (1960).

219. Coes, L. Jr., "A New Dense Crystalline Silica", *Science* **118**, 131 (1953).

220. Stishov, S.M., and Papova, S.V., "New Dense Modification of Silica", *Geokhimiya* **837**, (1961), CA **57**, 5393 (1962).

221. Chao, E.C.T., Fahey, J.J., Littler, J., and Milton, D.J., "Stishovite SiO_2, A Very High Pressure New Mineral from Meteor Crater, Arizona", *J. Geophys. Res.* **67**, 419 (1962).

222. Chao, E.C.T., Fahey, J.J., and Littler, J., "Coesite from Wabar Crater near Al Hadida, Arabia", *Science* **133**, 882 (1961).

223. Chao, E.C.T., (private communication) May 2, 1968, "I have observed dense glasses from crater ejecta and am currently studying annealing characteristics of dense feldspar glasses."

224. Stishov, S.M., "Equilibrium Between Coesite and Stishovite", *Dokl. Akad. Nauk SSSR* **148**, 1186 (1963), CA (1963) **58**, 13617f.

225. Ostrovskii, I.A., "Experimental Determination Curve of Phase Equilibrium Coesite-Stishovite", *Chem. Abst.* **64**, 1837^e (1966); *Izv. Akad. Nauk SSSR, Ser. Geol.* **30** (10), 132 (1965) (Russian).

226. Bell, P.M., "Solid-Solid Phase Equilibria Found at High Pressure and Temperature", *U.S. Dept. Tech. Services* AD418,014 (1963), CA **60**, 15201f.

227. Preisinger, A., "Structure of Stishovite, High Pressure Form of SiO_2", *Naturwissenschaft* **49**, 345 (1962).

228. Sclar, C.B., Corrison, L.C., and Cocks, G.G., "Stishovite, Thermal Dependence of the Crystal Habit", *Science* **144**, 833 (1964).

229. Dachille, F., Zeto, R.J., and Roy, Rustum, "Coesite and Stishovite: Stepwise Reversal Transformations", *Science* **140**, 991 (1963).

230. Skinner, B.J., and Fahey, J.J., "Observations on the Inversion of Stishovite to Silica Glass", *J. Geophys. Res.* **68**, 5595 (1963).

231. Fahey, J.J., "Recovery of Coesite and Stishovite from Coconino Sandstone of Meteor Crater, Arizona", *Am. Mineralogist* **49**, 1643 (1964).

232. Mason, B., *Meteorites*, John Wiley, New York (1962), p. 18.

233. Heide, F., *Meteorites*, Trans. E.Anders and E.R.DuFresne, Univ. Chicago Press, Chicago (1964) p. 34.

234. Kirk-Othmer, *Encyclopedia of Chemical Technology*, 2nd Ed., Vol. 8, Interscience, New York (1965) p. 633.

235. Hughes, B.C., *Technical Director's Summary Report*, Report PNE-507, U.S. Army Engineer Nuclear Cratering Group, Livermore (Oct. 1966), pp. 34, 35.

236. Videon, F., *Crater Measurements*, Report PNE-713f, U.S. Army Corps of Engineers, Livermore, Calif., (Oct. 1965), pp. 8, 9.

237. Benfer, R.H., *Apparent Crater Studies*, Report PNE-508, U.S. Army Engineer Nuclear Cratering Group, Livermore, Calif., (May 1967), pp. 8–10, p. 28.

238. Ballard, R.F., Jr., *Structure Instrumentation* (Project Pu-Gondola I), PNE-1106, U.S. Army Engineer Nuclear Cratering Group, Livermore, Calif., (Aug. 1967).

239. McQueen, R.G., Fritz, J.N., and Marsh, S.P., "On the Equation of State of Stishovite", *J. Geophys. Res.* **68**, 2319 (1963).

240. Ahrens, T.J., and Gregson, V.G., Jr., "Shock Wave Compression of Crustal Rocks", *J. Geophys. Res.* **69**, 4839 (1964).

241. Primak, W., Fuchs, L.H., and Day, P., "Radiation Damage in Insulators", *Phys. Rev.* **92**, 1064 (1953).

242. Fuchs, L., and Primak, W., *Optical Properties of Irradiated Quartz and Silica*, Argonne National Laboratory Report, ANL 4797 (July 1952), p. 31.

243. Day, P., and Primak, W., *The Density of Irradiated Silica*, Argonne National Laboratory Report, ANL 4833 (Jan, 1953), p. 22.

244. O.C.Simpson was then Associate Director of the Chemistry Division at the Argonne National Laboratory. This was part of the usual route of transmitting information in the period when Radiation Effects was a classified subject.

245. Berman, R., Klemens, P.G., Simon, F.E., and Fry, T.M., "Effect of Neutron Irradiation on the Thermal Conductivity of Quartz Crystal at Low Temperatures", *Nature* **166**, 864 (1950).

246. Wittels, M.H., "Lattice Expansion of Quartz due to Fast Neutron Bombardment", *Phys. Rev.* **89**, 656 (1953).

247. Lukesh, J.S., "Neutron Damage to the Structure of Vitreous Silica", *Phys. Rev.* **97**, 345 (1955).

248. Sowman, H.W., and Lukesh, J.S., *An Exploratory Investigation of Glasses Exposed to Intense Neutron Radiations*, Knolls Atomic Power Laboratory Report, KAPL 1242 (Nov. 1954).

249. Lukesh, J.S., *An X-ray Diffraction Study of the Effects of Intense Neutron Irradiation on the Structure of Some Glasses*, Knolls Atomic Power Laboratory Report, KAPL 1307 (March 1955).

250. Šimon, I., "Note on Thermal Expansion of Neutron-Irradiated Silica", *J. Am. Cer. Soc.* **41**, 116 (1958).

251. Curie, P., and Curie, M., "The Chemical Effects Produced by Becquerel Rays", *Compt. Rend.* **129**, 823 (1899).

252. Twyman, F., and Brech, F., "X-irradiation of Fused Silica", *Nature* **134**, 180 (1934).

253. Koch, J., "Reduction of Optical Reflectivity of Glass Surfaces Resulting from Ion-Bombardment", *Nature* (London) **164**, 19 (1949).

254. Hines, R.L., "Radiation Effect of Positive Ion Bombardment on Glass", *J. Appl. Phys.* **28**, 587 (1957).

255. Hines, R.L., and Arndt, R., "Radiation Effects of Bombardment of Quartz and Vitreous Silica by 7.5-kev to 59-kev Positive Ions", *Phys. Rev.* **119**, 623 (1960).

256. Hines, R.L., and Wallor, R., "Sputtering of Vitreous Silica by 20–60 kev Xe$^+$ Ions", *J. Appl. Phys.* **32**, 202 (1961).

257. Stewart, R.W., "A Method for the Determination of the Index of Refraction of Thin Transparent Films", *Can. J. Res.* **A26**, 230 (1948).

258. Primak, W., *Summary and Bibliography of Some Research on Radiation Damage in Ceramic Materials Performed at the Argonne National Laboratory*, Argonne National Laboratory Report, ANL 4952 (June 1958).

259. Starodubtsev, S.V., and Azizov, S., *Change in Linear Dimensions of Fused Quartz During Gamma Irradiation*, Proceedings of the Tashkent Conference AEC-tr 6398, Vol. I, p. 283.

260. Lell, E., "Radiation Effects in Doped Fused Silica", *Physics & Chemistry of Glasses* **3**, 84 (1962).

261. Primak, W., and Bohmann, M., "Radiation Damage", *Progress in Ceramic Science*, Vol. 2, J.E.Burke, ed., Pergamon Press, Oxford (1961).

262. Primak, W., "Fast Neutron Damaging in Nuclear Reactors. III. The Radiation Damage Dosage", *Nucl. Sci. Eng.* **2**, 320 (1957).

263. Primak, W., and Kampwirth, R., "The Radiation Compaction of Vitreous Silica", *J. Appl. Phys.* **39**, 565 (1968).

264. Primak, W., "Gamma-Ray Dosage in Inhomogeneous Nuclear Reactors", *J. Appl. Phys.* **27**, 54 (1956).

265. Wittels, M., and Sherrill, F.A., "Radiation Damage in SiO_2 Structures", *Phys. Rev.* **93**, 1117 (1954).

266. Primak, W., "Experimental Evidence for Thermal Spikes in Radiation Damage", *Phys. Rev.* **98**, 1854 (1955).

267. Brooks, H., *The Thermal Spike Picture of Radiation Damage*, Knolls Atomic Power Laboratory Report, KAPL 360, (Aug. 1950).

268. The question of a thermal spike had been considered by Seitz (private communication) at the Metallurgical Laboratory prior to 1945; and, therefore, presumably had been at least a subject of discussion by others there. The only written reference to this work encountered by This Author is F.Seitz, *Physics Today*, **5**, (6), 6 (June 1952) where a typographical error was uncorrected: the 104 deg should have been 10^4 deg.

269. Seitz, F., "On the Disordering of Solids by Action of Fast Massive Particles", *Discussions Faraday Soc.* **5**, 271 (1949).

270. Seitz, F., and Koehler, J.S., *Displacement of Atoms During Irradiation, Solid State Physics*, F.Seitz and D.Turnbull, eds., Vol. 2, Academic Press, New York (1956), p. 307.

271. Primak, W., and Kampwirth, R., "Cause of the Radiation Compaction of Vitreous Silica", *Bull. Am. Phys. Soc.* **14**, 327 (1969); (Formal paper in preparation).

272. *id.*, This was presented as paper BE 11 at the meeting of the American Physical Society, Philadelphia, (March 24, 1969). The abstract[271] describes an earlier aspect of the work.

273. Lindhard, J., Nielsen, V., and Scharff, M., "Approximation Method in Classical Scattering by Coulomb Fields", *Mat. Fys. Medd. Dan. Vid. Selsk.*, **36** No. 10 (1968).

274. Lindhard, J., Scharff, M., and Schiott, H.E., "Range Concepts and Heavy Ion Ranges", *Mat. Fys. Medd. Dan. Vid. Selsk.*, Vol. 33, No. 14 (1963).

275. Lindhard, J., Nielsen, V., Scharff, M., and Thomsen, P.V., "Integral Equations Governing Radiation Effects", *Mat. Fys. Medd. Dan. Vid. Selsk.*, Vol. 33, No. 10, (1963).

276. Primak, W., (unpublished).

277. Mayer, G., *Effet des Neutrons Rapides sur le Graphite et sur le Quartz, Action des Rayonements de Grande Energie sur les Solids*, Y.Cauchois, ed., Gauthier-Villers, Paris, (1956), p. 107.

278. Mayer, G. and Lecomte, M., "Effect of Fast Neutrons on Crystalline Quartz and Vitreous Silica", *J. Phys. Radium* **21**, 846 (1960), p. 852; (NSA **15**, 14816).

279. Kolontsova, E.V., "The Nature of the Residual Defects in Monocrystals after Neutron Irradiation and Deformation", *At. Engerg. (U.S.S.R.)* **10**, 227 (1962).

280. Lungu, S., "Point Defects in Neutron-Damaged Silica Glass", *Phys. Stat. Sol.* **23**, 147 (1967).

281. Private communication, Lungu to Primak, Jan. 30, 1968, $3 \times 3 \times 50$ mm silica glass bar irradiated in sealed aluminum tube, 8 mm diam $\times$ 1 mm wall, in a 40 mm channel of the reactor.

282. Primak, W., Delbecq, C.J., and Yuster, P., "Photoelastic Observations of the Expansion of Alkali Halides on Irradiation", *Phys. Rev.* **98**, 1708 (1955); **102**, 1688 (1956).

283. Arnold, T.W., and Compton, W.D., "Radiation Effects in Silica at Low Temperatures", *Phys. Rev.* **116**, 802 (1959).

284. Compton, W.D., and Arnold, G.W., "Radiation Effects in Fused Silica and α-Al_2O_3", *Discussions Faraday Soc.* **31**, 130 (1961).

285. Mitchell, E.W.J., and Page, E.G.S., "On the Formation of Color Centers in Quartz", *Proc. Phys. Soc.*, London **B67**, 262 (1954).

286. Mitchell, E.W.J., and Page, E.G.S., "The Anisotropic Absorption of the Visible Bands in Irradiated α-Quartz", *Phil. Mag.* **46**, 1353 (1955).

287. Mitchell, E.W.J., and Page, E.G.S., "Optical Effects on Radiation-Induced Atomic Damage in Quartz", *Phil. Mag.* **1**, 1085 (1956).

288. Bambauer, H.V., "Trace Element Content and γ-Color Centers in Quartzes from Fissure Deposits in the Swiss Alps", *Schweiz. Minerol. u. Petrogra. Mitteil.* **41**, 335 (1961).

289. Bambauer, H.V., Brunner, G.O., and Laves, F., "Beobachtungen über Lamellenbau an Bergkristallen", *Z. Krist.* **116**, 173 (1961).

290. Shockley, W., *Problems Related to p–n Junctions in Silicon*, Proceedings of the International Conference on Semiconductor Physics, Prague, 1960, Academic Press, New York (1961), p. 13.

291. Carter, G., and Grant, W.A., "The Ion Bombardment of Glass", *Physics & Chemistry of Glasses* **7**, 94 (1966).

292. Doremus, R.H., *Diffusion in Non-crystalline Silicates, Modern Aspects of the Vitreous State*, J.D. Mackenzie, ed., Butterworths, Washington (1962) Vol. II, p. 1.

293. Primak, W., "Radiation Induced Stress Relaxation in Quartz and Vitreous Silica", *J. Appl. Phys.* **35**, 1342 (1964).

294. Smith, W.J., Leivo, W.J., and Smoluchowski, R., "Surface Studies of X-ray Irradiated Potassium Chloride Crystals", *Phys. Rev.* **101**, 37 (1956).

295. Yokota, H., Sakata, H., Nishibori, M., Kinosita, K., "Ellipsometric Study of Polished Glass Surfaces", *Surface Science* **16**, 265 (1969).

296. King, R.J., and Downs, M.J., "Ellipsometry Applied to Fibres on Dielectric Substrates", *Surface Science* **16**, 288 (1969), p. 295.

297. Schroeder, J.B., and Dieselman, H.D., "Ellipsometric Analysis of Radiation Damage in Dielectrics", *J. Appl. Phys.* **40**, 2559 (1969).

298. Primak, W., "Radiation-Induced Changes in Dimensions, Index of Refraction, and Dispersion of Lithium Fluoride", *Phys. Rev.* **112**, 1075 (1958).

299. *id.*, p. 1082, Relation of radiation induced changes in dimensions to F- and 450-centers.

300. Schineller, E.R., Flam, R.P., and Wilmot, D.W., "Optical Waveguides by Proton Irradiation of Fused Silica", *J. Opt. Soc. Am.* **58**, 1171 (1968).

301. James, H.M., *Neutron Damage in Graphite*, Oak Ridge National Laboratory Report ORNL 307, (March 1949).

302. In part, James followed an approach taken by F.W.Brown, North American Aviation Report NAA-SR-4, (Feb. 1948) who utilized experimental ranges for calculating effects by accelerated ions.

303. Primak, W., (unpublished).

304. Primak, W., and Kampwirth, R., "Ionization Expansion of Pile-Exposed Vitreous Silica", *J. Appl. Phys.* **40**, 2565 (1969).

305. Primak, W., (unpublished).

306. Primak, W., and Kampwirth, R., "Automatic Photoelastimeter for Determining Very Small Induced Dilatations", *J. Opt. Soc. Am.* **59**, 1542 (1969), (Abstract).

307. Levy, P.W., "Reactor and Gamma Ray Induced Coloring of Corning Fused Silica", *Physics & Chemistry Solids* **13**, 287 (1960).

308. Staff article, *Bonding with Electrostatic Force, Assembly Engineering*, Hitchcock Publishing Co., Wheaton, Illinois, (March 1969), p. 34.

309. Gross, B., *Charge Storage in Solid Dielectrics*, Elsevier Publishing Co., Amsterdam (1964).

310. Fowler, J.F., "Radiation-Induced Conductivity in the Solid State and Some Applications", *Phys. in Med. Biol.* **3**, 395 (1959).

311. Proctor, T.M., "X-ray Induced Electrical Polarization in Glass", *Phys. Rev.* **116**, 1436 (1959).

312. Hardtke, F.C., and Ferguson, K.R., *The Fracture by Electrical Discharge of Gamma Irradiated Shielded Window Glass*, 11th Hot Lab Proceedings ANS, (Nov. 1963).

313. Gross, B., "Irradiation Effects in Borosilicate Glass", *Phys. Rev.* **107**, 368 (1957).

314. Gross, B., and Murphy, P.V., "Electrical Irradiation Effects in Solid Dielectrics", *Nukleonik (Germany)* **2**, 279 (1960).

315. Culler, V., *Gamma Ray Induced Electrical Discharge in a Radiation Shielding Window*, Proceedings 7th Hot Laboratories and Equipment Conference, ASME, Engineers Joint Council, New York, (1959), p. 120.

316. Gross, B., "The Compton Current", *Z. Physik* **155**, 479 (1959).

317. Murphy, P.V., and Gross, B., "Polarization of Dielectrics by Nuclear Radiation. II. Gamma-Ray-Induced Polarization", *J. Appl. Phys.* **35**, 171 (1964).

318. Gross, B., "Thermovoltaic Effect in Gamma-Irradiated Borosilicate Glass", *Phys. Rev.* **110**, 337 (1958).

319. Hardtke, F.C., "Thermoelectricity in Irradiated Glass", *Phys. Rev. Letters* **9**, 339 (1962).

320. Hardtke, F.C., "Thermoelectricity in Irradiated Dielectrics", *J. Chem. Phys.* **42**, 3000 (1965).

321. Billington, D.S., and Crawford, J.H., Jr., *Radiation Damage in Solids*, Princeton Univ. Press, Princeton (1961).

322. *id.*, pp. 244–246, About ordering and compaction.

323. *id.*, p. 225, Thin walled capillaries used by Wittels and Sherrill for their annealing experiments.

324. *id.*, pp. 225–6, Evidence of thermal conductivity and heat capacity measurements for order in irradiated vitreous silica.

325. Roy, Rustum, and Busmer, C.P., "Influence of Neutron Irradiation on 1st Order Displacive Reactions in Quartz and Cristobalite", *J. Appl. Phys.* **36**, 331 (1965).

326. Crawford, J.H., Jr., and Wittels, M.C., *A Review of Investigations of Radiation Effects in Covalent and Ionic Crystals*, Proc. First Internat. Conf. on Peaceful Uses of Atomic Energy, Geneva, (1955), Vol. 7, p. 654, United Nations, New York, (1956).

327. Weissmann, S., and Nakajima, K., "Defect Structure and Density Decrease in Neutron-Irradiated Quartz", *J. Appl. Phys.* **34**, 611 (1963).

328. Weissmann, S., and Nakajima, K., "Crystallinity in Fused Silica Induced by Fast Neutron Irradiation", *J. Appl. Phys.* **34**, 3152 (1963).

329. Gossick, B.R., "Correlation Between Certain Extinction Bands of Solids and Plasma Resonance", *J. Appl. Phys.* **31**, 650 (1960).

330. Guinier, A., (private communication), Letter, Guinier to Primak, April 20, 1969.

331. Roy, Rustum, and Busmer, P., "Effect of Neutron Bombardment on the Kinetics of Some Reconstructive Phase Transformations", *Am. Mineralogist* **50**, 1473 (1965).

332. Westrum, E.F., Jr., *The Low Temperature Heat Capacity of Neutron Irradiated Quartz,* Traveaux IV^c-Congrès International du Verre, Paris, (1956), p. 396.

333. Strakna, R.E., "Investigation of Low-Temperature Ultrasonic Absorption in Fast-Neutron Irradiated SiO_2 Glass", *Phys. Rev.* **123**, 2026 (1961).

334. Clark, A.E., and Strakna, R.E., "The Low Temperature Excess Specific Heat of SiO_2 Glass", *Physics & Chemistry of Glasses* **3**, 121 (1962).

335. White, G.K., and Birch, J.A., Thermal Properties of Silica at Low Temperatures, *Physics & Chemistry of Glasses* **6**, 85 (1965).

336. Flubacher, P., Leadbetter, A.J., Morrison, J.A., and Stoicheff, B.P., "The Low-Temperature Heat Capacity and the Raman and Brillouin Spectra of Vitreous Silica", *J. Phys. Chem. Solids* **12**, 53 (1959).

337. Schroeder, J.B., Bashkin, S., and Nester, J.F., "Ionic Polishing of Optical Surfaces", *Appl. Opt.* **5**, 1031 (1966).

338. Narodny, L.H., and Tarasevich, M., "Paraboloid Figured by Ion Bombardment", *Appl. Opt.* **6**, 2010 (1967).

339. Malitson, I.H., Dodge, M.J., and Gonshery, M.E., "Radiation-Induced Instability of Some Optical Glasses", *J. Opt. Soc. Am.* **55**, 1583 (1965).

340. Dodge, M.J., Malitson, I.H., and Gonshery, M.E., "Space-Radiation Affects Refractive Index of Optical Glass", *J. Opt. Soc. Am.* **56**, 1432 (1966).

341. Vand, V., "A Theory of the Irreversible Electrical Resistance Changes of Metallic Films Evaporated in Vacuum", *Proc. Phys. Soc. (London)* **A55**, 222 (1943).

342. Neubert, T.J., *Thermal Annealing of Neutron-Induced Discomposition in Artificial Graphite, I. Rate of Heating Experiments*, Argonne National Laboratory Report, ANL 4369 (1949); *II. Asymptotic Annealing Experiments*, Argonne National Laboratory Report, ANL 4477 (1950).

343. Neubert, R.J., and Lees, R.B., "Stored Energy in Neutron Bombarded Graphite", *Nucl. Sci. & Eng.* **2**, 748 (1957).

344. Primak, W., "Kinetics of Processes Distributed in Activation Energy", *Phys. Rev.* **100**, 1677 (1955).

345. Lanczos, C., *Applied Analysis*, Prentice Hall, Englewood Cliffs, (1956), p. 272.

346. Keiffer, D., *Electron Spin Resonance and Optical Absorption in Compacted Vitreous Silica*, Final Report No. ORO-3303-2, Contract No. AT-(40-1)-3303, (Dec. 15, 1966).

347. Haindel, B., and Keiffer, D.G., "Spin-Lattice Relaxation in Compacted Vitreous Silica", *Bull. Am. Phys. Soc.* **13**, 255 (1968).

348. Keiffer, D.G., and Haindel, B., "EPR Studies in Irradiated Compacted Vitreous Silica", *Bull. Am. Phys. Soc.* **13**, 255 (1968).

349. Lungu, S., Rîbco, L., and Beleută, L., "Radiation Induced Volume Changes and Annealing in SiO_2-UO_2 Vitroceramics", *Rev. Roum. Phys.* **12**, 353 (1967).

350. Anderson, O.L., "Lattice Dynamics of Glass", *The Structure of Glass*, E.A.Porai-Koshits, ed., E.B.Uvarov, trans., Consultants Bureau, New York (1966) Vol. 6, p. 25; *Physics of Non-Crystalline Solids*, J.A.Prins, ed., North Holland Publishing Co., Amsterdam (1965). (These are virtually the same article.)

351. Eitel, W., *The Physical Chemistry of the Silicates*, Univ. Chicago Press, Chicago (1954) p. 291, Ref. 108, § 281, p. 294.

352. Salmang, H., and Stoesser, K. von, "Effect of Heat Treatment of Glasses upon Their Density and Chemical Stability", *Glastechnische Berichte* **8**, 463–82 (1930).

353. Brückner, R., "Der Einfluß des Hydroxylgehaltes auf die Dichte und auf den Diffusionsmechanismus in Kieselgläsern", *Glastechnische Berichte* **38**, 153 (1965).

354. Brückner, R., *Zur Struktur der Glasfasern insbesondere der Kieselglasfasern*, Proc. 7th International Congress; International Comm. on Glass, Brussels (1965) 2 Vols., 1.3.2/**38**.

355. Strakna, R.E., Clark, A.E., Bradley, D.L., and Slie, W.M., "Effect of Fast-Neutron Irradiation on the Pressure and Temperature Dependence of the Elastic Moduli of SiO_2 Glass", *J. Appl. Phys.* **34**, 1439 (1963).

356. Warren, B.E., *X-Ray Diffraction*, Addison-Wesley, Reading, (1969), Chap. 10.

357. Mozzi, R.L., and Warren, B.E., "The Structure of Vitreous Silica", *J. Appl. Cryst.* **2**, 164 (1969).

358. Warren, B.E., and Mavel, G., "Elimination of the Compton Component in Amorphous Scattering", *Review of Scientific Instruments* **36**, 196 (1965).

359. Warren, B.E., to Primak, W., (private communication, 11/1/71).

360. Bell, R.J., and Dean, P., "Properties of Vitreous Silica: Analysis of Random Network Models", *Nature* **212**, 1354 (1966).

361. Bell, R.J., and Dean, P., "The Configurational Entropy of Vitreous Silica in the Random Network Theory", *Physics & Chemistry of Glasses* **9**, 125 (1968).

362. Bell, R.J., Bird, N.F., and Dean, P., "The Vibrational Spectra of Vitreous Silica, Germania, and Beryllium Fluoride", *J. Phys. C. (Proc. Phys. Soc.)* II-**1**, 299 (1968).

363. Gaskell, P.H., "Thermal Properties of Silica. Part 2. Thermal Expansion Coefficient of Vitreous Silica", *Trans. Farad. Soc.* **62**, 1505 (1966).

364. Gaskell, P.H., "Vibrational Spectra of Simple Silicate Glasses", *Disc. Farad. Soc.* (1970) **50**, 82.

365. Gaskell, P.H., and Grove, F.J., *The Effect of Fictive Temperature on the Optical Vibrations of Silica*, Proc. 7th International Congress; International Comm. on. Glass, Brussels (1965) 2 Vols., Paper 363.

366. Brückner, R., "Properties and Structure of Vitreous Silica", *J. of Noncrystalline Solids*, Part I **5**, 123 (1970), Part II **5**, 177 (1971).

367. Fleischer, R.L., Price, P.B., and Walker, R.M., "Solid State Track Detectors: Applications to Nuclear Science and Geophysics", *Annual Review of Nuclear Science*, Vol. 15; Annual Reviews, Inc., Palo Alto (1965).

368. Fleischer, R.L., Price, P.B., and Walker, R.M., "Ion Explosion Mechanism for Formation of Charged-Particle Tracks in Solids", *J. Appl. Phys.* **36**, 3645 (1965).

369. Revesz, A.G., and Zaininger, K.H., "Si–SiO$_2$ Solid-Solid Interface", *R.C.A. Review* **29**, 22 (1968).

370. Revesz, A.G., "Noncrystalline Structure and Electronic Conduction of Silicon Dioxide Films", *Phys. Stat. Sol.* **24**, 115 (1967).

371. Revesz, A.G., "A New Model for Defects in Noncrystalline Silicon Dioxide", *J. of Noncrystalline Solids* **4**, 347 (1970).

372. Cruickshank, D.W.J., "The Role of 3d-Orbitals in π-Bonds between (a) Silicon, Phosphorous, Sulfur, or Chlorine Atoms and (b) Oxygen", *J. Chem. Soc.* (London) 1961, 5486.

373. Krätschmer, W., *Die anätzbaren Spuren künstlich beschleunigter schwerer Ionen in Quartzglas*, Doctoral Dissertation to Ruprecht–Karl Universität, Heidelberg; published by W.Krätschmer, Berlin (1971).

374. Goldsmith, A., Waterman, T.E., and Hirschborn, H.J., *Handbook of Thermophysical Properties of Solid Materials*, Pergamon Press, New York (1951) Vol. III, Ceramics.

375. Kawada, K., "Studies of the Thermal State of the Earth. 15: Variation of Thermal Conductivity of Rocks", *Bull. Earthquake Res. Inst. (Japan)*, Part 1. **42**, 631 (1964); *Part 2.* **44**, 1071 (1966).

376. Kanamori, H., Mizutani, H., and Fujii, N., "Method of Thermal Diffusivity Measurement", *J. Phys. Earth (Japan)* **17**, 43 (1969).

377. Romashin, A.G., "Thermal Conductivity of Transparent Materials", *High Temperature* (a translation of *Teplofizika Vysokikh Temperatur*) **7**, 604 (1969).